MODERNIZE
Your Executive Job Search
Get Noticed ... Get Hired

MASTER RESUME WRITERS
**Louise Kursmark &
Jan Melnik**

Modernize Your Executive Job Search
Get Noticed ... Get Hired

Copyright © 2021 by Louise Kursmark and Jan Melnik

ISBN 978-0-9966803-5-6

Publisher: Emerald Career Publishing
               www.emeraldcareerpublishing.com

Cover & Interior Design: Deb Tremper, Six Penny Graphics
http://sixpennygraphics.com

Distributor: Cardinal Publishers Group
www.cardinalpub.com

Printed in the United States of America

CONTENTS

Introduction v

CHAPTER 1
High-ROI Search Strategies 1

      Strategy #1: Targeted Search
      Strategy #2: Networking
      Strategy #3: Executive Recruiters and the VC/PE World
      Strategy #4: Posted Opportunities
      Strategy #5: Interviewing Techniques
      4-Week Accelerated Executive Job Search Plan

CHAPTER 2
ROI Content for Your Career Marketing Documents and Messages 29

      Exercise #1: Articulate Your Target and Capture Signature Strengths
      Exercise #2: Write Your CAR Stories
      Sample CAR Stories and Ways to Use on Resume and LinkedIn

CHAPTER 3
Your Executive Resume 47

      Resume FAQs | Draft Your Resume | Special Situations | Design Your Resume

CHAPTER 4
Your LinkedIn Profile 73

      LinkedIn FAQs | Draft Your LinkedIn Profile

CHAPTER 5
Additional ROI Documents 83

      Cover Letters | Email Messages | Networking Cards | "Elevator" Pitches | LinkedIn
      Messages | Networking Scripts | Executive Leadership Briefs | One-Page Executive
      Resumes | Board Resumes | Professional Biographies | Detailed "Mulligan" Thank-You
      Letters | 30-60-90-Day Plans

CHAPTER 6
Transition Stories and Portfolios 119

Thanks and Dedication

We appreciate the opportunities to have assisted so many talented clients in navigating their executive journeys. And we're grateful to our talented, top-tier colleagues for sharing their exceptional materials in this book.

Thanks also to our husbands, Bob Kursmark and Ron Melnik, who served as sounding boards and provided in-the-trenches executive perspectives. Most of all, we dedicate this book to our children, Meredith, Matt, Dan, Wes, and Stephen, who already inspire us with the accomplishments of their diverse and upward-moving careers.

Introduction

Return on investment is the theme that drives executive decisions around the globe. To make a compelling business case for any action, payback *must* exceed cost. From the executive's perspective, this is as true for personal career decisions as it is for corporate actions.

Modernize Your Executive Job Search is designed to provide you with maximum ROI—a large return on the investment of time, effort, and a few dollars that you expend to acquire this book and apply its proven strategies to advance your career.

With a game plan designed specifically for executives, we tell you exactly what you need to know and do to maximize the results from your resume, LinkedIn profile, and job-search efforts—whether you favor traditional headhunter searches, the latest digital networking tools, a highly targeted person-to-person campaign, or—most likely—a combination of those approaches and more.

From our years of experience working with executives in career transition, we have chosen the activities and career investments that are likely to produce the highest ROI. We also provide additional ideas that typically offer lower dividends but may be worthwhile for you, depending on your unique circumstances. Because we specify ROI and the bottom line, you will be able to quickly assess the value of each strategy, follow the easy-to-implement steps, and immediately position yourself for the most advantageous results.

Fundamental to any executive search campaign is an exceptional resume that clearly conveys the value you will bring to your next challenge. Equally important today is a LinkedIn profile that carries the same message of value while providing additional insights into who you are, what you do, and how you do it. *Modernize Your Executive Job Search* provides a wealth of samples and structured exercises that will guide you in capturing career details, drafting your documents, and telling your story powerfully and authentically.

We—authors Louise Kursmark and Jan Melnik—have a combined *50+ years of experience* working with executive job seekers. In our private practices, we have each consulted with thousands of C-suite and upper- and middle-tier executives across a wide range of disciplines and industries.

Our approaches are highly individualized yet consistently client-centric, always focusing on the ROI: Will this strategy produce the desired results in the most time- and cost-effective means possible? Will this technique help the candidate gain traction within a target organization? Does this solution provide a competitive edge?

In writing this book, we asked these same pragmatic, results-focused questions to create a comprehensive program that will deliver results for you, just as it has for our clients. You will literally learn from the masters (we were the first two people in the world to earn the prestigious Master Resume Writer credential and are two of only about two dozen MRWs globally today). To help you successfully manage your own career, we give you the tools you need—leading-edge documents and time-proven strategies that work at the highest corporate levels.

> **PRO TIP: Because there's always more to talk about when it comes to executive job search, we've created a 6-part audio podcast series** that complements and supplements the strategies in this book. Through interactive presentation and dynamic conversation, we share our favorite tips, new ideas, problem-solving scenarios, and additional recommendations. For details about the podcasts, email jan@janmelnik.com or louise@louisekursmark.com.

What *Modernize Your Executive Job Search* provides to propel your search:

- A four-week accelerated job-search plan comprising concrete, actionable steps with ROI-rated recommendations—readily transferable strategies you can implement immediately to accelerate your job search.

- Proven solutions to actual problems—scenarios focusing on issues unique to senior executives and explaining *what* to do, *how* to do it, and *why* it works.

- Exercises and examples to help you uncover distinctive career success stories and use them effectively in all of your career marketing messages.

- Guidelines for creating career marketing materials for *today's* job search—explanations for issues that impact the content, format, and design of every document you write.

- Portfolios of complementary resumes, LinkedIn profiles, executive bios, cover letters, and more—all focusing on executive ROI and demonstrating candidate value in a variety of interesting formats.

- Quick-read FAQs that give you immediate answers to your most pressing resume-related questions.

- Pro tips in every chapter—our insider advice based on decades of experience helping senior executives make successful career moves.

Here's an abbreviated chapter-by-chapter rundown of what you can expect in return for your investment of time:

Chapter 1, High-ROI Search Strategies, explores a variety of executive-level search methods and provides a clear statement of the anticipated ROI for each. We cover today's best practices for structuring a targeted search, networking, pursuing VC/PE, working with recruiters, handling posted opportunities, optimizing the interview process, and using online services. And we pull all of the pieces together into an easy-to-follow four-week job-search plan that will help you accelerate your start and maintain momentum.

Chapter 2, ROI Content for Your Career Marketing Documents and Messages, leads off with the essential steps to help you define your differentiators (your all-important value proposition) and mine the content you'll need for telling the right story.

This is where you'll find the heart and soul of this book: How to translate what you've achieved into salient content that spells solution and success to a prospective employer. We share easy-to-implement strategies for developing material for your own branded resume and LinkedIn profile. You'll find liberal doses of thought-provoking exercises designed to get at the root of your own success stories. Included is a formula for creating CAR (challenge–action–result) stories to outline your top contributions/accomplishments in each of your positions. Finally, we provide easy-to-follow tools for capturing this important content.

With well-developed outlines, you'll find the pointers in **Chapter 3, Your Executive Resume,** helpful as you polish your raw material into this critical career marketing document. We address how to emphasize or downplay specific information, share tactics for addressing issues of concern (age, underemployment, lack of degree, and so forth), and provide practical strategies for developing content and refining appearance. In an easy-to-reference "Special Situations" section, we discuss a number of dilemmas common to many executives—and answer each with expert advice and 1-2-3 solutions.

Today, having a robust and distinctive LinkedIn profile is no longer an option—it is essential, even for very senior executives. In **Chapter 4, Your LinkedIn Profile,** we take you step-by-step through the sections of the profile and provide examples and recommendations for building an online presence that goes far beyond your resume to express your personality and your unique value.

Moving on to **Chapter 5, Additional ROI Documents,** you'll find materials that can add tremendous value to your transition process. These resources include scripting for elevator pitches, high-impact cover letters and email messages, executive leadership briefs, one-page executive resumes, board resumes, and other documents that may prove instrumental to your successful search.

Chapter 6, Transition Stories and Portfolios, provides inspiration, motivation, and know-how through concise vignettes and accompanying documents. You'll read how actual executives—perhaps with circumstances like your own—addressed specific challenges in their job search and successfully navigated the waters to their next big opportunity.

* * * * *

So, what's the bottom line? Whether you are a seasoned and successful executive with a multi-decades track record or an aspiring executive on an accelerated career track, you will gain exceptional value—and results—from the strategies we share in *Modernize Your Executive Job Search.* Let's get started!

CHAPTER 1
High-ROI Search Strategies

Just as investors seek the best return and hiring authorities choose the candidates who can deliver the greatest value, we want you to select the search strategies designed to give you the highest return on your expenditure of time, money, energy, and other assets at your disposal.

Not only that, we want you to have a clear understanding of how the strategies fit together, how you should structure them into your week, and how you can move smoothly from one step to the next toward your ultimate goal.

This chapter details a fast-start, efficient, highly effective four-week plan of initiatives that should help you build your prospect pipeline, generate a flow of opportunities, and put you well on the way to your next job.

To begin, we'll give you a big-picture overview of five key strategies for modern executive job search and then provide specific action steps to help you execute these strategies quickly, easily, and with a clear understanding of the process, path, and expected results.

With each strategy, you'll find our recommendations with ROI value presented on the following scale:

★ ★ ★ ★	= maximum value
★ ★ ★	= reasonable value
★ ★	= limited value
★	= marginal value

Our primary focus is on the actions that are most effective—as proven by our thousands of clients over the years and by any number of surveys taken to determine how people actually find jobs.

All too often, even savvy executives who are normally decisive and action-oriented find themselves feeling overwhelmed at the start of the complex—and sometimes all-new—endeavor of a job search. So we help you kick your search into high gear right from the get-go with a week-by-week plan of action that incorporates all of the strategies.

Our plan gives you the structure and control you need to jump confidently into action—even if you've navigated years or even decades of career advancement without a formal plan…even if you're unfamiliar with today's best practices in career documents and job search…even if you're uncertain how to use today's tools and technologies to boost job-search success.

Finally, sprinkled throughout the text in this and every chapter you'll find **Pro Tips,** our insider secrets gleaned from hundreds of clients over many years and designed to accelerate your results and give you an advantage over the competition.

Five Key Strategies for Modern Executive Job Search

#1 Targeted Search
#2 Networking
#3 Executive Recruiters and the VC/PE World
#4 Posted Opportunities
#5 Interviewing Techniques

STRATEGY #1: Targeted Search

ROI Value: ★ ★ ★

What do we mean by targeted search? Simply, you research, identify, and pursue *specific target companies* that are a good fit for your expertise and interests. As will be explained in Chapter 2, for best results—a swift and successful search—you must first articulate your target and sharply define your "selling points" that will appeal to your prime audience (the decision-makers at your target companies).

Done correctly, the exercises we outline in Chapter 2 will paint a complete picture of the type and size of company where you want to work. You'll have identified specific industries and geographic regions and given some thought to the culture that is most appealing to you. Now it's time to match these criteria with the companies that represent your prime targets.

Targeted search activities go hand-in-hand with networking activities, described in Strategy #2 (page 5). The better you can define to your networking contacts what you are seeking—industries, organizational size, and even specific company names—the better they'll be able to help you. Combined, these two key strategies—networking and targeted search—should consume at least 75% of your time, energy, and other resources.

For very busy senior-level executives, it can be a challenge carving out time for consistent effort with respect to job search. But our clients' success stories reflect the value of building momentum through consistent, diligent effort. Even if you can devote just 10 or even five hours a week, try to sustain the same level of activity on a regular basis. This helps to build traction and is far more effective than taking a week off, expending 50+ hours of energy on your search, then having no time in the following three weeks to devote to follow-up calls and emails.

> **PRO TIP: Maintain a tight focus for best results.** On first thought, you might assume that narrowing your search to selected targets will harm rather than help. After all, isn't it better to be open to what's available, and aren't you qualified to work at a variety of functions and in multiple industries?
>
> In fact, the tighter your focus, the easier it is for contacts to understand what you want and refer you appropriately. A sharp focus allows your contacts to maintain a clear mental image of "who you are" and how they can best help you.
>
> Not only that, but by clearly articulating a precise target, you portray yourself as decisive, visionary, and results-focused—exactly the qualities companies are looking for in their executives.

When you have completed your prep work of defining your ideal next position (again, this process is outlined in Chapter 2), you can begin to match the target to specific companies. Start out with a large list and follow the action items to narrow down all of the possibilities to a manageable number of good-fit organizations.

Targeted Search Tactical Action Plan

Action Item: Identify target companies.

☐ 1) Start with competitors to your current/most recent employer and other past employers, where your direct experience and competitive information will be of value (of course respecting terms of non-disclosure and non-compete agreements).

☐ 2) Consider your employers' vendors and alliance partners, who will value your industry knowledge and ability to lead them to new channels or new markets.

☐ 3) One of your best sources will be LinkedIn—from researching where each of your first-degree contacts works presently and worked previously to researching that same level of detail for each of *their* first-degree contacts. Using modest numbers—a typical senior executive will generally have at least 250 first-degree contacts; that number *times* each of *their* 250 first-degree contacts yields more than 60,000 possibilities. In Strategy #2, Networking (beginning on page 5), we provide detailed instructions for mining your LinkedIn contacts.

☐ 4) Read the business section of your daily newspaper and your city's or region's business journal. Look for companies that have good ideas, new market opportunities, or aggressive growth plans and where your expertise can help them achieve their goals.

☐ 5) Expand your search beyond your local area to national and international business news articles. We strongly suggest using a news aggregator or RSS reader to make this task easier, faster, and more efficient. You can find a list of recommended aggregators at http://blogspace.com/rss/readers and explore such websites as Google News, Feedly, Alltop, Panda, Flipboard, News360, Techmeme, Pocket, and Inoreader.

❑ 6) Explore other online resources, such as:
- www.fortune.com for information on present and past members of the Fortune 500
- www.bloomberg.com and www.reuters.com for financial data and trends, names of top executives, descriptive company snapshots, and links to recent news
- www.glassdoor.com for general job listings—most ideal for background about culture, albeit from contributions of sometimes disgruntled ex-employees
- www.dnb.com (Dun&Bradstreet, of which Hoover's is a subsidiary) for extensive business data, including lists of companies sorted by NAICS industry code
- www.google.com and www.linkedin.com for information on specific individuals at your target companies
- other sites and resources that you may find through search engines or through links

Some of these in-depth resources require fee-paid membership. You may be able to tap into them for free via your college or university career center, generally available to alumni as well as current students, or through your local public library.

❑ 7) Visit the reference librarian at your public library. (The downtown/main library may offer more comprehensive search services than a small branch library.) A reference librarian is a treasure-trove of knowledge and can help you find directories, news articles, annual reports, financial information, and other resources that will help you identify and ultimately pare down target companies.

Action Item: Thin your list.

❑ 1) Collect information on your "possible" companies and measure it against your target. You can use all of the sources listed immediately above and also visit each company's website. Any or all of these criteria—and more—might come into play:

- Geographic location (headquarters, international locations, production sites, branches, and so forth)
- Size of company
- Growth plans
- Reputation of CEO and top executives
- Legal and/or financial difficulties
- Products (current and projected)
- Markets (current and projected)
- Recent history such as changes in leadership, acquisition, divestiture, IPO status, etc.
- Company mission and values
- Industry outlook (contracting or expanding?)
- Opportunities in the market; threats or challenges to achieving desired results

❑ 2) Be particularly alert to opportunities that would benefit from your specific skills, experience, knowledge, and track record. When approaching the company, it is vital to connect what you offer with the needs you've uncovered, to convey that you understand the challenges and can help them achieve their goals.

❑   3)   Create a short list of companies that are your prime targets. Keep all of your notes, however, even for companies that don't make the cut; you will revisit, fine-tune, and expand your target list throughout your search as you learn more about your target companies and their culture, people, and potential.

❑   4)   Be 100 percent sure that your objective is achievable and your targets are a good fit *before* you launch an aggressive targeted search. Ask your closest contacts to give you feedback on your targets. Share with them your ideal position information and ask whether it's realistic. Solicit their input into your decision-making as you narrow the list.

Action Item: Incorporate your target list into your networking strategy. Your goal in every networking interaction is to gain a lead or connection to a person at a target company or in a target industry. To do this, you need to educate your contacts about your targets.

❑   1)   When possible, ask for a specific resource: "I'd love to get an introduction to Chris Anderson, CFO at Acme Holdings." Use a combination of all the resources noted in the action items above to identify the right contacts. LinkedIn can prove especially valuable.

❑   2)   Use examples: "I'm looking for a company *like* Worldwide Widgets." This is more meaningful to most people than "a company with $300 million in sales in a traditional manufacturing industry."

❑   3)   Consider creating a one-page networking resume that includes a brief summary of your qualifications along with your top target companies. You can hand this out at networking meetings or forward it to your circle of contacts, so they'll better understand what you are looking for and how they can best help you. You can see an example in Chapter 5.

❑   4)   Ensure you have a well-developed letter of introduction (a version of your cover letter) so that your contacts who make referrals on your behalf have a tool to augment your resume and properly (and briefly!) tell your story. Don't make your networked connections have to spend time figuring out the message to use when passing your name along. You'll find a sample in Chapter 5.

STRATEGY #2: Networking

ROI Value: ★ ★ ★ ★

Networking includes both online networking (easier and more effective than ever because of technology) and offline, person-to-person networking (phone, meet-ups, coffee, etc.). Different surveys provide slightly different numbers, but in every survey we've ever seen networking has consistently emerged as the #1 strategy for finding a new job. What this means, simply, is that most people—from 60% to 85%, depending on the survey—find their jobs through people they know or people they are referred to.

PRO TIP: Your contacts want to help you. Don't buy into the stereotype of networking as "begging people for favors." Rather, think of it as an opportunity for your friends to offer their advice (people love to give advice) and assistance. If they genuinely know of someone or something that can help you, they are sure to mention it.

Even for the new contacts you'll be making, as long as you approach them in the spirit of a business dialogue to which you both bring value, the "ask" will not be seen as "begging for a favor" but, rather, exchanging business information. Think about how you can help them, as well.

Statistics consistently show that nearly *100% of referred candidates who are qualified for a specific opportunity will be contacted*—at least for a conversation, and likely for an interview. Think about the implications to your job search. If you identify an opportunity with a particular company AND you have a networked connection who can make an introduction, there is an almost 100% likelihood you will be contacted *if you present the right story and are qualified.*

Yes, that's a lot of caveats, but this scenario is hugely important, as we'll discuss below. Acting on the strength of a trusted relationship, those who recommend you wield tremendous power in what we might call "getting to the dance."

You know your value proposition and your story (more about that in chapters to come). You can tell it better than anyone. Given an entrée to the right decision-maker, you are in the door and doing what you do best: Drawing a connection between what an employer needs and the value you can deliver…illustrating the solutions you can provide to the points of pain or turnaround challenges or new opportunities a company is struggling with.

The bottom line with respect to networking: It is to your definite advantage to tap into your existing web of contacts and build new connections so that those who know you, trust you, and like you can point you to your next job opportunity.

PRO TIP: Prepare before you connect. Personal contacts—those you have now and those you'll develop during your search—are an incredibly valuable resource. Before you reach out, be sure that you're ready to deliver the right message. Use the exercises in Chapter 2 to prepare an introduction that is clear, concise, and value-focused.

Don't ask your contacts for a job; it's rare that they'll know of a perfect-fit opportunity. Instead, ask for their help, advice, specific information, ideas, or referrals. The better you can articulate who you are and the value you offer, and the more specifically you can ask for what you need, the more they'll be able to help you.

Networking Tactical Action Plan

Action Item: Identify and organize your network.

NOTE: If you are an active LinkedIn user already (and not just someone who has said "yes" to many invitations to connect), start with the second Action Item on page 8, then backfill additional contacts from this Action Item. If you are not fully using LinkedIn, begin here.

☐   1)   Create a database of at least 120 networking contacts, capturing as much contact information (email address, phone numbers, physical address) as you can. To identify your network, consider the following categories, listed in the order that is typically *most valuable* for executives in transition:

- Closest friends and colleagues
- Past and present work colleagues, employers, managers
- People who will serve as your professional references
- Other business contacts (vendors/suppliers, fellow board members)
- Association contacts
- Alumni connections
- Professionals (CPA, attorney, financial planner, banker, dentist, doctors, etc.)
- Neighbors
- Relatives
- Acquaintances (through kids, schools, church/temple, clubs)

Possibly you keep your current contacts stored in your smartphone. But you might also have a pre-technology data storage system—a Rolodex, Day-Timer, Filofax, or address book—that contains contacts from some of your earliest career days. You'll likely be able to find up-to-date contact information for many of them on LinkedIn. Be sure to consider all of your contacts, both current and blasts from the past, as you are developing your job-search database.

☐   2)   Prioritize your contacts into four groups, your A (optimal), B, C, and D (least likely) prospects; include 30 contacts per group. If you have significantly more than 120 contacts, add more groups or increase each group to 50 people.

☐   3)   Create an organizational system that will enable you to record and track your contacts, all of their leads and referrals, and your follow-up activities. Circling back to early contacts will show that you valued and acted on their suggestions—and give you another opportunity to connect for more ideas.

- An Excel spreadsheet can provide a flexible way to build out and track your job-search activities.
- Comprising a spreadsheet and much more, this networking tracking system devised by our colleague Barbara Safani is an elegant, highly useful tool: careersolvers.com/job-search-networking-tracking-system.
- Another resource that we like is JibberJobber.com, a relationship management tool designed specifically for career management.
- A fourth option is a notebook with sections and chronologically arranged material.

Whatever organizational system you choose, be sure to record the source of each opportunity or connection—and which version of your resume you send. You'll be reading in Chapter 3 about the importance of tweaking your resume for specific opportunities. Weeks into the search—as you are balancing *many* contacts and calls—you don't want to be caught off-guard before returning a call about "Which company was that? Who told me about the lead? Which resume and letter did I use?"

Action Item: Activate your LinkedIn network. Without question, your LinkedIn network should figure prominently in your career-search efforts.

Founded in 2003 and now with more than 165 million users in the US and 675 million globally, LinkedIn (www.linkedin.com) offers a robust platform and exceptional opportunities to connect to its member base of high-level professionals—provided you can link to them through people you know.

> **PRO TIP: Like any technology platform, LinkedIn evolves as new features are added and others retired.** All of the advice and instructions below are valid as we go to press, but it's possible that some things may have changed by the time you are reading this book. However, we expect that most will still be valid, and as you increase your familiarity with LinkedIn and its interface and resources, you should be able to navigate easily to find the tool or capability that you're seeking.

☐ 1) If you aren't yet on LinkedIn, get there ASAP. In Chapter 4, we provide detailed how-tos for building your profile. Now, before we network, some housekeeping tips:

- Have just one LinkedIn account. This may seem obvious, but back when LinkedIn first came on the scene, many executives created an account while in a specific job, promptly forgot about it, and then created one or more additional accounts with subsequent professional moves. From LinkedIn's home page, follow instructions (from the "Me" icon, go to "Help") to merge your accounts.
- Customize your LinkedIn URL—ideally, use just your first/last name, middle initial if necessary—rather than defaulting to the standard alpha-numeric appendage LI applies. From the "Me" icon, go to "Help" and enter "customizing your public profile URL."
- Upgrade to a premium LinkedIn account—at least through the duration of your executive job search.

☐ 2) Follow best practices for creating and managing your LinkedIn account. You'll find lots of content strategies in Chapters 2 and 4, but here are a few standout things to keep in mind.

- Do include a professional-looking headshot photo—engaging, accessible, and smiling (garners 75% more views than not smiling).
- Do add a customized background image that complements your overall brand and creates instant visual distinction.
- Don't upload your resume to LinkedIn (even though "encouraged" by LI to do so); you want people to reach out and take the conversation offline as quickly as possible.
- Don't use the default headline—your current job title. It's important that your headline absolutely differentiate you. Use our tips in Chapter 4 to craft a compelling headline.

- Do write your all-important About and Experience sections in first person using the word "I," and strive for a conversational tone to engage your readers right from the start.

Back to our LinkedIn networking approaches. After refining your LinkedIn profile, using checkpoints above and content guidelines from Chapters 2 and 4, it's time to delve into your own first-degree connections.

As described in the "Targeted Search" section earlier in this chapter, your first-degree contacts represent the ideal place to start. They give you access to tens of thousands, even hundreds of thousands of additional contacts. In job search, it is often those second- and third-degree contacts that are the direct source of a prime lead or referral. It is definitely worth your while to spend some serious, productive time mining leads and introductions. So here we go!

❑   3)   Start by sorting your own contact list into priority order. First, from your own profile, go into your "Settings" and select "Privacy." Click on "How LinkedIn uses your data," then select "Getting a copy of your data."

            Check off the "Connections" box and you'll be told how long the download will take (based on the number of connections you have). Select the blue button, "Request archive." You will be asked to enter your LI password to continue and authorize the download. An email will be sent when the download is ready. Once you've opened the file, you'll be able to manipulate the data, alphabetize, and organize it in a way to methodically track your outreach. An alphabetical sort by last name is probably the easiest way to structure the data.

❑   4)   We suggest using three highlighters to go through this list to organize contacts similar to those in step #1 in this networking section. Take your favorite color and highlight every contact A-Z that you would instinctively want to reach out to first in a stealth job search.

❑   5)   Then do a second pass—different color—of people who may not be as close in your network but are associated with great companies and/or likely to have solid connections. Repeat a third time, using a third color. The final group—the names not highlighted—are probably people you do not know well or have any kind of real connection to.

Action Item: Strategically connect to existing contacts through LinkedIn—and expand your network.

❑   1)   Start with your highest LI contacts (the first group highlighted). Cherry-pick your top candidates—those who are your very first go-to contacts. Begin with them and then work your way alphabetically through the balance. What are you doing, exactly? Two things:

❑   a)   Using the message feature, extend a short message to anyone with whom you haven't already been in contact—informing them of your confidential quest, providing a brief update, and (depending on the contact) asking for a short phone call or meet-up, introduction, or other action.

❑   b)   This second strategy takes time (and you'll see why it is important to keep track of your progress methodically, as it's easy to get off track or forget where you left off), *but it can yield exceptional results.*

- For each of your highest-value, first-degree contacts highlighted in your top color, look at *their first-degree connections* (these, of course, are second-degree connections to you).
- To do this, go to the profile of each of your top, highlighted first-degree connections.
- Right beside their location in the top portion of the profile, click on their "number" of connections.
- You'll readily see the number of results—and who, in their network, is a first-degree connection of yours (you ignore those at this time)—and you'll focus on those labeled "2nd"—these are the *first-degree connections of your first-degree connections.*
- Carefully (again, methodically!) look through each of these contacts, capturing information in whatever way is easiest for you—on a pad of paper, in a Word document or spreadsheet, etc. You are looking to identify (1) people you may have heard of who could prove instrumental in your quest, (2) people you don't know but who work at companies that are on your target list, or (3) people who spark a note of interest for you.
- You'll see in Chapter 5 various ways of messaging that can bring the greatest value to these connections—whether it's a direct message/invitation to connect or (usually best) seeking an introduction from your first-degree connection. Particularly when your first-degree connection is linked to someone not in your network who is affiliated with a target company, you can get the inside scoop and an introduction through your connection.

☐ 2) After that thorough reach-out to everyone in your first group of contacts and mining all of the valuable first-degree connections among your top contacts, you'll then move on to the second, third, and fourth (if necessary) groups of contacts in your highlighted colors.

☐ 3) Expand your LinkedIn network organically through invitations. Here's what LinkedIn says about invitations: "Invitations are an essential tool to help you grow your professional network and make meaningful connections. Reach out to people you know or those you want to meet with the help of LinkedIn's suggestion feature, People You May Know. You can quickly and easily connect with people in your community."

While that is true, when it comes to extending an invitation to someone you've identified, we *strongly recommend against* using LinkedIn's suggestion of connecting with "people you may know" by hitting a button with the word "Connect" in blue. Why? The invitation gets sent immediately without any personalization—the equivalent (almost) of spam.

Instead, here is the best way to send an invitation: Be strategic. If the suggestion is of a person you do know professionally—or would like to know—click on the person's name to go directly to their LinkedIn site and select the "Connect" button there. This will allow you to "customize the invitation" and, as LinkedIn notes there, "LinkedIn members are more likely to accept invitations that include a personal note"—and they are! You'll find examples of what to say in Chapter 5.

Action Item: Mine alumni and employer/former employee contacts through LinkedIn.

❑   1)   As noted in the very first step under networking, fellow alumni can be powerful connections in your job search. LinkedIn is one of the best ways to optimize these contacts, especially if you've kept up with only a few classmates.

In the search bar at the top (next to the LI logo and magnifying glass), type in the name of your university(ies). When the school site opens, scroll down the left to "Alumni." With a premium subscription (recommended when in active search), you'll have the ability to parse the data in many different ways—for instance, selecting where they work, where they live, any keywords of particular interest, and from/to years.

Start small, then build out. For example, depending on the size of your school, pick your year of graduation. It can then be useful to expand to the three years before you and the three years after (producing names you are most likely to recognize).

See who is working where—any companies that are on your target list? Go to the classmate's LinkedIn profile to see what they are doing—could they prove instrumental in making an introduction?

After exhausting the many possibilities this exercise typically yields, expand the search to include years and decades before or after your own attendance. While you might not know these alumni personally, you can use your university connection as an entrée when reaching out.

❑   2)   The same process for seeking out alumni (undergrad and graduate) works equally well for contacts from former employment. Experiment with entering different company names as well as former employee names. For larger companies, often you will find alumni groups that can be a rich source of possible contacts to add to your network. LinkedIn highlights those members who are already among your first-degree connections, of course; be sure to check *their* first-degree connections.

Action Item: Make use of LinkedIn's jobs feature.

❑   1)   While senior executive opportunities are certainly less prevalent than mid-tier professional roles on LinkedIn, *should* you find an opportunity of particular interest, do not use the "easy apply" button that LinkedIn makes so readily available (white text on a blue button). Instead, you'll want to strategically explore the opportunity. See if the recruiter handling the opportunity is identified (internal or retained/contingent). Explore who in your network is closely aligned to or may be able to make an introduction to the hiring manager/C-suite.

This is unlikely to be a high-ROI activity, but as you explore jobs, be aware of a few key things:

- You may surface companies (smaller, emerging, tech start-ups, etc.) you don't already know about. You can then do your own research and determine if there is a viable target play.
- If you do find something worth pursuing, pay attention to timing. A premium subscription to LinkedIn will provide you with good data—from how long ago the position was posted to the number of applicants who've applied through LinkedIn.

- You'll gain insider details about the company, the job, the number of employees, and even the caliber of applicants, once a measurable pool of people have applied for the job. You'll see how competitive candidate background compares to yours—from the percentage who hold advanced degrees and what schools they represent to the number of top skills you have as compared to your competition.
- All of this information can be very helpful as you structure your search. While an executive search process typically takes more than just a few weeks, do be mindful of not wasting time on a search started months ago without first ascertaining current status.

Action Item: Strengthen your LinkedIn Recommendations.

☐   1)   We don't suggest that you immediately rush to populate the "Recommendations" section of your profile. Ideally, this is an activity you should do regularly and over time, so that the recommendations show a range of dates and are there when you need them.

       However, if you haven't paid attention to Recommendations, start the process of capturing a few meaningful endorsements from a variety of professionals who can speak to your abilities and your value.

       How many recommendations should you have? Generally, a half dozen to a dozen is about the right number. You don't need 50 or hundreds. Be selective—and consider those in the best position to reflect on your breadth of management expertise and results, thought leadership, and key attributes that have fueled your professional success.

☐   2)   The ideal time to further strengthen your Recommendations section is after you land your next position. Your professional references and others who played a role in helping you capture that opportunity will be delighted to hear the news and probably quite willing to post a LinkedIn recommendation for you.

Action Item: Maximize your LinkedIn membership.

☐   1)   In Chapter 5 we provide a variety of scripts and language for messaging, texting, LinkedIn, and emails so that you don't need to reinvent the wheel—just customize to make it uniquely your message.

☐   2)   Join strategic groups on LinkedIn where you can add thought leadership. Additionally, share regular professional articles, posts, and infographics relevant to your expertise.

☐   3)   Periodically tweak and refine your LinkedIn profile, maintaining strong positioning for the role you want now as well as for future career advances.

☐   4)   Once you've landed your next gig, update your profile and keep the connections on LinkedIn going—and not necessarily in preparation for your *next* career move. You want to be sought for potential board positions, speaking gigs, foundation work, and other opportunities.

Action Item: Tap into additional online networks. Blogs, chat rooms, online databases, and other exchanges can create a virtual community and be a good source of leads and referrals. As with in-person networking, you will need to find the forums that are most appropriate for you and most helpful in advancing your career.

☐   1)   Research online networks. Some good starting places:

- ExecuNet (www.execunet.com): Membership is required to join interactive online networking groups.
- Online networking organizations for your profession: Good examples are the Financial Executives Networking Group (www.thefeng.org) and the American Marketing Association's Executive Marketer Group (www.ama.org/ama-executive-marketer/—formerly Marketing Executives Networking Group, mengonline.org).
- Professional associations related to your profession or industry.
- Blogs that are read by decision-makers in your industry.

☐   2)   Schedule time weekly to visit your preferred sites. For blogs/chat rooms, ask questions, post advice and suggestions, and establish a visible, credible identity. As appropriate, follow up directly with individuals to explore areas of mutual interest and possible job opportunities. With online networking sites, you can be more direct and ask for specific help, such as a connection to a company or an individual related to your job search. It is always a good idea to lurk before you jump in—get a feel for those sites that are active with robust thought leadership. Weigh whether being more visible in a small but vital network can yield deeper connections than being a "small fish in a big sea."

Action Item: Connect with and build your network.

☐   1)   Create a script and practice your introduction. (See Chapters 2 and 5 for guidelines and ideas.) Be sure you are providing enough specific information so that your contacts will know how they can help you; your targeted research (described in Strategy #1 above) will provide critical information.

☐   2)   Initiate contact with your first group of 30. For best results and greatest efficiency, we recommend the **call–send–call strategy,** first contacting (or attempting to contact) each person by phone, then immediately following up by sending your resume with a short note, preferably by email but by snail-mail if necessary. In your second call, a few days later, answer questions and glean ideas and recommendations from that contact.

☐   3)   Be sure to ask your contacts who they know…in your industry, at your target companies, or simply people who are well connected. In this way, you will steadily expand your network from your own circle of acquaintances to a broad and deep web of contacts.

☐   4)   Track all ideas, leads, and referrals and schedule your follow-up action.

☐   5)   Keep the ball in your court to stimulate the most and the fastest activity—whether it's a return phone call or contact with a new referral. Remember, your job search is the #1 priority for you, but not for most of the people in your network!

❑   6)   As you receive referral names, add them to your contact database and schedule them into your call-send-call activity chain.

❑   7)   Each week, launch a new call-send-call campaign to your next group of 30; in this way, you'll reach all 120 contacts in just four weeks.

Action Item: Participate in structured networking events. Designed specifically for job seekers, these events can help you tap into a large network in your local area. It's important to attend the right events—those that include a good number of executive-level participants and emphasize productive activities for a swift transition. Avoid those that seem to be a "poor me" club of dispirited job seekers.

❑   1)   Identify events in your area—here are some places to find them:

- The "business events" section of your daily paper.
- Your local business journal.
- ExecuNet (www.execunet.com): In-person networking meetings, moderated by a career professional and often featuring a guest speaker, recruiter panel, or other helpful presentation, are offered in a few cities around the nation. Look on the ExecuNet website under "Live Networking Events" to find events near you. Membership is not required, but in some cases a steeper meeting fee is charged to non-members.
- GetFive (www.getfive.com): Formerly the Five O'Clock Club, this organization offers tools, resources, and events for job seekers.
- Gray Hair Management (www.grayhairmanagement.com): Virtual networking events are held regularly; membership is not required.
- Large churches in your area that sponsor job clubs or support groups for people in transition. Some of these programs are large, vibrant, and well worth attending; others are too small or do not include enough executive-level participants to be truly valuable. However, as with many options, "you can't win if you don't play"—these can be excellent opportunities to meet others who can prove useful in your quest and expand your network, especially in your local area.
- Programs for job seekers held frequently at many community libraries. These are free of charge to attendees, and while the content of presentations may not skew to the C-suite executive, you may have opportunities to network with other attendees, likely including a few senior-level professionals. They may be in a position to make introductions to target companies or to their own contacts.

❑   2)   Try out several of the more promising meetings. Be prepared with your clear, concise, ROI-packed message and specific ways that the network can help you. Offer as many referrals and as much advice and support as you can. In networking, when you focus on giving it's amazing how much you receive!

❑   3)   Select one or more groups to attend on a regular basis—typically once a week or once a month. Don't expect to necessarily have results after just one meeting; make a reasonable commitment and attend at least three or four meetings to assimilate and assess value.

❑   4)   Use the group's database or participant list as an additional source for new contacts. Your participation in the group gives you an "in" that will warm up a cold call.

❑   5) Take advantage of these workshops and networking events to perfect your elevator pitch and practice telling your story—in a variety of customized ways—to different audiences. You'll learn more about crafting your pitch from content in Chapters 2 and 5.

> **PRO TIP: Create a support and accountability team.** As a key part of your networking strategy, we recommend that you recruit a small team of people to give you feedback and support for the duration of your search. Your team might include your spouse/partner, close friends or business colleagues, financial advisor, fellow board members, or other professionals. You might even wish to hire a professional career advisor or coach for objective, expert guidance. (You can find contact details for all of this book's contributors at the beginning of Chapter 6.)
>
> Your team members should possess a positive attitude and genuinely care about you and your success. However, they should not be "yes people," agreeing to everything you suggest; you are relying on them for honest opinions and fresh perspectives.
>
> To keep your team motivated and engaged, ask them to keep you accountable for performing your action items and doing what you say you are going to do. Knowing that you have to report in at your weekly coffee meeting or Monday-morning check-in will give you the task orientation that is so critical to persevering in your job search, which can be repetitious, tiring, and even dispiriting (hearing all those "no's" before you get to one "yes"). But sustained momentum is critical in job search—it fuels traction and quicker success.

STRATEGY #3: Executive Recruiters and the VC/PE World

ROI Value: ★ ★

Recruiters, also known as "headhunters," can be an excellent resource during your executive job search. After all, they specialize in placing mid- to senior-level executives in jobs at companies of all sizes and in most industries, and it stands to reason that they are always looking for good candidates just like you to fill those positions.

We've rated this strategy with just two stars—but *if* you are the perfect candidate and connect with the right executive recruiter at the right time and land an ideal opportunity you wouldn't have found otherwise, it can easily represent a four-star approach for you!

We have found, though, that misconceptions abound regarding the role and value of executive recruiters. When considering this strategy, keep these facts in mind:

- **Recruiters work for their client (the employer), not for you.** This means that the commonly held belief that recruiters will "find a job for you" is false. This can be a rude awakening to high-performing executives who assume they will be a hot property for recruiters.

- **Recruiters work to fill tightly specified openings.** Thus, it's fruitless to think you can convince a recruiter that you can do the job if you don't have the precise background specified for a particular search. When hired to find candidates with "a-b-c" credentials, that's precisely what a recruiter must deliver.

- **You will be most attractive to recruiters if you are a passive candidate, presently employed, and looking for the same type of job you've held previously, in the same industry.** Again, recruiters need to fill specs. If the spec says a "financial executive with 10 years' experience in manufacturing, preferably automotive," your 10 years in technology services will not be seen as a good fit. Most often, recruiters seek individuals with a strong background in a specific industry.

- **Perversely, available and unemployed (but highly qualified) candidates are typically not as desirable to recruiters.** This can be particularly disheartening for those executives caught in post-M&A fallout or pyramid-pruning following corporate consolidation.

Regardless of the rigid nature of most recruiter assignments, there are some things you can do to make this strategy an effective part of your search. Just be sure you are not over-relying on recruiters. And recognize, too, that after reaching out to the executive recruiters already in your network, your best method is likely to do a very targeted but broad-sweeping campaign to all high-level recruiters specializing in searches for candidates with your background and in your target industries. The greater the numbers, the more likely you'll find one or two current searches that could be a fit.

It stands to reason that you'll also be more attractive as a candidate if you are completely open to relocation (obviously, for the right opportunity).

Related to a recruiter strategy, we have worked with many executives who are interested in aligning with **venture capital** and **private equity** firms—either to join the team that identifies and invests in companies or to serve as an executive with a portfolio company. Because many of these firms tap into their inner circle when searching for executive talent, the best approach is to use the networking strategy we've just outlined to gain a referral into the company. Action Item #2 below can also be an effective tactic—although, just as with recruiters, this audience may not be receptive to your cold outreach.

Executive Recruiters and the VC/PE World Tactical Action Plan

Action Item: Reconnect with personal recruiter contacts. Chances are, you've had contact with recruiters in the past. Maybe you hired them to find executives for your company. Perhaps you were called on a semi-regular basis by recruiters in your industry or were even recruited for one or more of your past positions. Now is the time to tap into those contacts.

❑   1)   Using the same call-send-call strategy we recommend for your networking contacts, reach out to recruiters you know and ask if they have any suggestions—perhaps they can consider you for an open position or refer you to another recruiter who is a better fit for your background.

❑   2)   Periodically update your recruiter contacts with the progress of your search, updates to your resume, or details that will help them fit you to opportunities they have or know about.

Action Item: Identify and contact the right recruiters and/or VC/PE firms. While we don't suggest that you blast your resume to every recruiter or VC/PE firm under the sun, we do recommend for many executive candidates that you get your resume into the databases of the *right* firms. This means VC/PE firms that specialize in your expertise and recruiters who place people with your background, at your level, in your target industries.

Evaluate mass-distribution services to find which one gives you the options that are best for you. For example, can you pinpoint specific industries? Select retained-only recruiters? Send to VC/PE firms in addition to, or instead of, recruiting firms? Include your resume as a Word or PDF attachment? Looking at several services will give you the data you need to make an informed decision.

Based on our experience executing this strategy for many senior-level executives, we suggest you work with a career strategist to implement a plan. Consult the beginning of Chapter 6 for recommendations.

Action Item: Post your resume. For executive job seekers, we *don't recommend* posting your resume on Monster, CareerBuilder, or other mass-market sites. And, as we noted earlier, do not upload your resume on LinkedIn—instead, share strategically with others after making initial contact. Posting your resume on the Internet is just not an effective strategy for drawing the right kind of contacts.

However, as part of your recruiter strategy, you might wish to post your resume in the databases of top recruiters and, as appropriate, on the websites of professional associations for your field. This passive strategy can put your documents in the right place at the right time. Just keep in mind, the odds are low that you'll find a job this way, so don't rely on a posting as your *only* or even *primary* strategy.

❑   1)   Identify the sites and firms that are right for you and carefully follow instructions for posting your resume and profile to their database. In addition to the following top firms, review websites of your professional associations to see if a resume-posting service is available.

- Heidrick and Struggles (www.heidrick.com)
- Russell Reynolds Associates (www.russellreynolds.com)
- Korn/Ferry International (www.kornferry.com)
- Spencer Stuart (www.spencerstuart.com)
- Egon Zehnder (www.egonzehnder.com)

> **PRO TIP: Build recruiter relationships when you're not looking for a job.** While this strategy may not help you *now*, make note of it for your future career management. When you are employed and not looking for a job, look for opportunities to build relationships with recruiters. You can do this best by being a resource to them—referring them to good candidates when they have a specific need. In other words, take those headhunter calls, even if it is not for an opportunity that's a fit for you.
>
> You might also be in the position to retain a recruiter to conduct a search for your company. You hold the power in that engagement and can build the relationship for your long-term advantage. When you are again in a job search, the recruiters who are already part of your network will be much more helpful to you than those you don't know.

STRATEGY #4: Posted Opportunities

ROI Value: ★

Whether posted online or published in a newspaper, business journal, or professional association website or magazine, published leads represent an obvious avenue for you to pursue during your job search. Your application can give you an entrée into your target companies, or others you haven't yet identified, and can put your resume into the databanks of executive recruiters.

The upside to published leads is that they're easy to find and easy to respond to. The downside is that everyone else knows about them, too; thus your chances of gaining an interview—even when you match the stated requirements to a "T"—are quite slim. After all, the employer has dozens or hundreds of resumes to review and needs to quickly weed out candidates to keep the search to a manageable size. Any excuse to eliminate you from contention helps in this scaling-down process.

Given this scenario, we recommend that you respond to published ads in a manner that's quick, efficient, and leaves most of your time for networking and targeted search activities. Here's how to do it.

Posted Opportunities Tactical Action Plan

Action Item: Identify best sources for published and posted ads.

❑   1)   At the start of your search, spend some time reviewing various sites for executive job postings and see which have the greatest number of appropriate listings. Bookmark these sites and return periodically to review and respond to postings. (In addition to your own research, see our suggestions for executive sites on page 22. Some require fee-paid membership.)

❑   2)   Identify publications that list appropriate openings. In addition to professional journals and business journals, you may wish to regularly review online editions of major papers in geographic areas you'd include in your search. Although the days of huge sections of employment want ads are long gone, there will occasionally be opportunities of interest. Online subscriptions (many of which allow for Sunday-only) may be useful for some.

Action Item: Create an efficient process for ad responses.

❑   1)   Once per week, dedicate time to review all of your identified sources, select appropriate postings, and quickly respond.

❑   2)   Write a template cover letter that you can rapidly adapt for individual ads (you will find some good ideas in Chapter 5). Spending hours composing custom-crafted letters for this purpose is not a wise investment of your time, given the relatively low rate of response you can expect.

❑   3)   Quickly review the job posting and highlight keywords that will be used by resume scanners (and eventually by humans) to find a match. If your resume includes most or all of these keywords, you're all set. If not, take a few minutes to edit your resume content so that it more faithfully reflects the words and phrases you've highlighted. Again, don't invest a lot of time.

❑   4)   Create an easy-to-manage process for storing the ads with a note as to when you responded and perhaps a copy of your cover letter.

❑   5)   If an ad appears for one of your target companies, in addition to responding through formal channels, redouble your efforts to connect with someone at that company—preferably the hiring manager or other senior executive. The very best way to make yourself a prime candidate is through a personal introduction or referral.

STRATEGY #5: Interviewing Techniques

ROI Value: ★ ★ ★

How, you might be wondering, do interviewing techniques fit into your upfront job-search activities as a strategy? After all, you have much to do before landing an interview.

However, it is critical that you be fully prepared for every conversation and ultimately every interview during your search. Some of those conversations will begin with your first networking calls, so it is of prime importance that you prepare yourself at this early stage in the process.

Interviewing Techniques Tactical Action Plan

Action Item: Prepare for the expected and the unexpected.

❑ 1) Never take for granted that your executive presence and ability to "wing it" will serve you during job interviews. Devote adequate time for preparation before every interview—whether a prescreening phone call, a Skype or Zoom video interview, or an in-person meeting with top executives or board members.

❑ 2) If you've been provided with a job description, deconstruct it line-by-line and prepare for every item detailed. Take notes about the specific talking points that address each aspect of the job description. Know your CAR stories (see Chapter 2) and be prepared to recount them in a clear, concise, logical storytelling flow.

❑ 3) Be fully prepared for "typical" interview questions—those you can be fairly certain will be asked during the course of every interview. Role-play aloud to identify the questions you have trouble answering and to smooth out your responses. Typical questions might include:

- Tell me about yourself.
- What interests you about this role or our company?
- How do those you've managed describe your leadership style?
- What is the most difficult management decision you've had to make?
- What are your signature strengths?
- What scares you most about this opportunity?
- How do you measure your own success?
- Why should we hire you?
- …and, of course, many others you've asked in conducting interviews yourself and in being a candidate repeatedly over the lifetime of your career.

❑ 4) Role-play aloud and/or with a partner, and consider recording your responses so you can evaluate your presentation and know what questions typically are more challenging for you to answer. Redouble your preparation for those questions.

❑ 5) For video or other remote interviews, verify the technology that will be used. Prepare your interview ensemble just as you would for an in-person interview. Experiment with lighting that presents you at your best. Test your appearance as viewed from your computer monitor.

We like to use a stack of books to elevate the camera so that it's at a perfect, flattering level. Nothing is worse than a camera angled to capture the not-so-attractive lower chin/jowls/neck!

For the interview itself, equip yourself with a glass of water and strategic notes (taped to the perimeter of a screen can work well). Secure any household pets, silence all electronic devices, and close all applications to ensure no sound from emails or notifications. Post a note outside your meeting space so that others know not to disturb you.

❑ 6) For in-person interviews not requiring travel, be absolutely certain of the meeting location; it's not too paranoid to test-drive if there's any uncertainty. Often office parks lack clear directions to particular buildings or suites, so if you don't test-drive, be extremely early and spend extra time in a quiet location revisiting key CAR stories before announcing yourself in reception about ten minutes ahead of your scheduled appointment.

Action Item: Check your appearance.

Before you launch into meetings and interviews, whether virtual/video or in-person, make sure that your physical appearance is as top-notch as every other aspect of your job search and executive career. Appearance matters and is particularly important if you are concerned that you may be perceived as "too old"—but it's essential that candidates of all ages make their best impression.

❑ 1) Both men and women should ensure an up-to-date professional wardrobe with multiple options for subsequent rounds of interviews. Pay attention to the details—is your tie the right width and length? Are your eyeglass frames up to date? Does your outfit flatter you while reflecting current trends?

❑ 2) Hair (on your face and on your head) should be neat and well cared for. Our executive clients often ask us, to dye or not to dye? That is a personal choice. Choose the style that puts you at your most confident—whether that means bald, graying, silver, fully dyed, or any other permutation.

❑ 3) For in-person meetings and interviews, if you wish to carry a briefcase, tote, or purse, make sure it is in impeccable condition.

❑ 4) Bring a professional-looking portfolio and a high-quality pen for note-taking. This is not the time to quickly grab a Bic from the car.

Action Item: Put preparation into action.

❑ 1) Be ready with your practiced (NOT memorized), concise responses to "tell me about yourself" and other to-be-expected interview questions.

❑ 2) Arm yourself with the thought, "this is a business discussion." An interview is not a grilling; it is an opportunity to explore mutual fit and culture.

❑ 3) Don't hesitate to ask for clarification of a convoluted or multipart question. Restating a question can be helpful to both you and the interviewer. And when you need a few extra seconds to consider a reply, it's fine to say, once or twice, "That's an excellent question. Let me think for a moment…"

❑ 4) Pausing is good. Don't feel you need to immediately jump in with a quick-trigger reply to every question.

❑ 5) Vary your responses—go deeper on areas where you can tell good (succinct) stories that align with points of pain.

❑ 6) Prepare exceptional questions to ask at the end of the meeting. At a minimum, always ask about the next steps in the candidate selection process, what the anticipated timing is, if there is an opportunity to speak with current team members, and similar queries that will keep you in the know and in the flow of the selection process.

Action Item: Debrief strategically.

❑ 1) Whether in your home office immediately after a phone/Skype/Zoom interview or in your car or a coffee shop right after an in-person interview, attempt to capture in writing everything you recall as soon as possible.

❑ 2) While the interview is fresh, write down everything you can remember about pain points, opportunities for expansion/new direction, anything at all about the role and the company/division that could prove useful to the pitch for your candidacy.

❑ 3) Capture anything that prompted you to say to yourself afterward, "how did I manage to forget a-b-c when they probed me about x-y-z…".

❑ 4) Record precisely what the next steps are based on your ending questions in the interview (prelim candidate selection the next week or two, likely next-stage interviews the middle of next month, goal of bringing on the selected candidate early in Q4).

Action Item: Take a mulligan.

❑ 1) Golfers know the strategy—a mulligan is essentially a "do-over" for a muffed shot. In job search, you have the chance to take a mulligan in the thank-you letter you'll be sending to everyone who participated in any of your interviews every step of the way leading up to an offer.

❑ 2) We recommend sending your letter by email the same day or within 24 hours of all interviews. It is not too over-anxious in appearance to send within a half hour of the close of an interview. In particular for phone/Zoom, if you have multiple interviews over the course of a day, try to compose, carefully edit, and send each email if time allows between interviews. Your content will be more focused and easier to remember than waiting until later that night to write many emails. Decisions are often made regarding next-stage candidates at the close of a day of interviews—hence the recommendation to be extremely prompt with your emails.

❑   3)   Beyond the normal courtesies expressed in a typical thank-you letter, you can reiterate key points, clarify things you said, or introduce entirely new material to respond to items uncovered and notes you captured during your debriefing. As appropriate, use as many mulligans as necessary (typically just a few) and keep to perhaps two or three lines each (bulleted points) in your email thank-you letter. You can see examples of mulligan content in Chapter 5.

❑   4)   Your follow-up letter should clearly express enthusiasm and restate your value proposition—aligned with what you have learned through due diligence, research, and takeaways from the interview itself.

❑   5)   For a highly coveted position where you are a semi-finalist to finalist, consider the value of following up with a customized and strategic 30-60-90-day business plan. See Chapter 5 for tips.

> **PRO TIP: For best results, implement all five of our recommended strategies simultaneously, as outlined in the four-week plan below.** Multiple vigorous efforts will yield the best results and help you avoid mistakes that derail or prolong many executive job searches, such as:
> - Reliance on just one method.
> - Over-dependence on less-effective search methods such as posting your resume or responding to online postings or want ads.
> - Belief that a recruiter will find a job for you; all you have to do is send your resume to a few headhunters and wait for the opportunities to roll in.
> - Abandonment of all other activities when you are pursuing a "hot" prospect or when a job offer appears imminent.
> - Assumption that some people in your network can't or won't help you.

An executive job search typically is not a quick, slam-dunk process and, as with many things in life, it's important not to put all your eggs in one basket. Over the course of a number of months, repeating activities, revisiting approaches, and applying steady diligence to many methods will help to bring around a positive result more quickly than jumping from one action to another and not handling multiple steps concurrently.

Additional Approaches: Internet Job Sites and Services for Executives

The five strategies detailed above are, without doubt, the most effective methods for finding your next executive opportunity. But here are a few additional resources to consider. Depending on your individual circumstances, some of these can be home runs while others will yield little to no direct benefit to the typical senior executive job seeker.

The Internet abounds with fee-based sites and services targeted to senior executives. Many of these services are excellent, and you may want to consider joining one or several as part of your integrated job search.

In addition to job postings, on these sites you might find such services as resume posting, virtual networking, teleclasses and webinars, complimentary review of your resume, newsletters and other publications, and any number of additional benefits to help you become more knowledgeable about and proficient in the skill of executive job search.

Two cautions: Don't rely on this as your only strategy, and thoroughly investigate fees and services before joining.

Action Item: Investigate and consider joining one or more appropriate executive career sites.

❑   1)   Start with our list of recommended sites, presented here in alphabetical order, and see which one seems to offer the best package of services to fit your needs.

- BlueSteps (www.bluesteps.com)—a membership site, founded in 2000, affiliated with the Association of Executive Search and Leadership Consultants.
- ExecuNet (www.execunet.com)—one of the longest-established executive career services, founded in 1988 and going strong.
- Gray Hair Management (www.grayhairmanagement.com)—nationwide network of senior executives.
- The Ladders $100K+ Club (www.theladders.com)—multi-site source for $100K jobs, both general and in specific functional areas.
- RiteSite (www.ritesite.com)—founded by John Lucht, author of *Rites of Passage at $100,000+*.

❑   2)   Join the organization and maximize your ROI by investigating and taking advantage of the full range of services.

❑   3)   One of your primary activities on these sites will be to search for and respond to job postings, as discussed in detail in Strategy #4.

Four-week Accelerated Executive Job Search Plan

Hit the ground running with our four-week plan to create a strong foundation and energetic momentum for what is likely to be a three- to nine-month search. Our methodical approach will train you in all of the critical aspects of searching for a new executive position, and you'll be able to redeploy them as needed for the remainder of your search.

Week 1	• *ROI Message:* Develop ROI material, resume, LinkedIn, and addendum materials, template cover letters, 30-second introduction ("elevator pitch")
	• *Targeted Search:* Define your target market—industry, company size and type, and specific companies
	• *Physical Preparation:* Review and refresh your appearance and wardrobe for both business-casual meetings and formal interviews
	• *Networking:* Develop your A contacts from your own database
	• *Networking:* Dig into LinkedIn and define those top prospects that will comprise your LinkedIn A contacts
	• *Activity Tracking:* Develop/maintain spreadsheet/notebook/other tool for capturing all job-search activities
Week 2	• *Networking:* Reach out to A contacts (call–send–call)
	• *Networking:* Pursue follow-up activities with leads generated through A group
	• *Networking:* Begin strategic outreach to your LinkedIn A contacts
	• *Networking:* Pursue follow-up activities with leads generated through LinkedIn A group
	• *Targeted Search:* Continue to refine your target market, adding and deleting companies through information you develop via research and your personal contacts
	• *ROI Message:* Practice telephone-screen interview replies and your top CAR stories
	• *Networking:* Research structured networking events in your area and schedule or attend as appropriate
	• *Recruiters:* Connect with personal recruiter contacts
	• *Recruiters and VC/PE firms:* Execute mass emailing
	• *Published Leads:* Once per week, review all of your sources and respond with a quickly edited cover letter and your resume
	• *Activity Tracking:* Continue maintaining spreadsheet/notebook/other tool for capturing all job-search activities

Week 3	• *Networking:* Reach out to B contacts (call–send–call)
	• *Networking:* Pursue follow-up activities with leads generated through A and B groups
	• *Networking:* Continue strategic outreach to your LinkedIn A contacts and *their* first-degree connections
	• *Networking:* Pursue follow-up activities with leads generated through LinkedIn A group/their contacts
	• *Targeted Search:* Continue to refine your target market
	• *ROI Message:* Practice interview skills and manage timely follow-up thank-you correspondence for leads, informational/"talk-shop" meetings, and interviews
	• *Published Leads:* Respond with a quick cover letter and resume
	• *Activity Tracking:* Continue maintaining spreadsheet/notebook/other tool for capturing all job-search activities
Week 4	• *Networking:* Reach out to C contacts (call–send–call)
	• *Networking:* Pursue follow-up activities with leads generated through A, B, and C groups
	• *Networking:* Continue strategic outreach to your LinkedIn A contacts and *their* first-degree connections
	• *Networking:* Conduct strategic outreach to your LinkedIn B contacts and *their* first-degree connections
	• *Networking:* Pursue follow-up activities with leads generated through LinkedIn A and B groups/their contacts
	• *Targeted Search:* Continue to refine your target market
	• *ROI Message:* Critically evaluate your interview performance and spend some time on preparation/improvement as needed
	• *ROI Message:* Research companies and prepare for second (more in-depth) interviews as appropriate—factoring in what you've learned about the company during your research activities
	• *Published Leads:* Review sources and respond with a quick cover letter and resume
	• *Activity Tracking:* Continue maintaining spreadsheet/notebook/other tool for capturing all job-search activities

Identify and Remove Roadblocks

The four-week point is a good time to step back, review what you've done, and reflect on how well you're progressing. By this point, you should be scheduling both formal interviews and informal networking discussions/"talk-shop" sessions at least three to ten times per week. You should have a broad and deep web of contacts, have penetrated several of your target companies, and be adept at communicating your ROI messages in networking situations and interviews.

Now, keep that momentum going by repeating the appropriate steps in this four-week plan until you convert those meetings to interviews and interviews to offers.

Always be careful of time thieves, those activities that spiral into hours of unproductive activity.

If, on the other hand, your progress has stalled or has never gotten off the ground, it's time to take a critical look at what you are doing, what you are saying, and how you are being perceived by your many audiences. We believe in taking a problem-solution tack, evaluating precisely where the sticking point occurs and fixing the problem at that point.

Incidentally, if you have been in active job search for any amount of time prior to reading our recommendations, approach everything from a fresh perspective, including contacts to those you reached out to initially. "John, I'm reinvigorating my job search and wanted to provide you with my most up-to-date resume and value proposition. Would love just five minutes of your time to explore a few ideas." (Those "ideas" can be asking—in light of the new focus—if any new leads have come up or if speaking with others in his network could be useful.)

Here are some of the typical problems we see, along with our recommended solutions.

Problem #1...Not generating enough leads, referrals, and meetings.

Solutions:
- Step up your networking activities…make more calls, attend more meetings, reach out to more people.

- Sharpen your focus and hone your ROI message so that your network understands who you are and how to help you.

- Double-check that all of your communications and career marketing materials (resume, LinkedIn profile, bio, cover letter, etc.) are absolutely top-notch.

- Put in the time. If you are spending just an hour or two a week on your job search, it's tough to generate substantial activity. If you are unemployed at this point, you should be devoting 40+ hours each week, every week, to your search.

- Review all of the recommended strategies in this chapter and see where you could be more diligent. Most often, we find that job seekers are focusing on the easy-but-ineffective strategies (responding to published leads) and skimping on the more challenging but indisputably more effective activities (networking and targeted search).

Problem #2...Getting meetings, but no interviews.

Solutions...
- Be more assertive in your meetings. If you sense there might be a need for your services, say, "I think there is a fit here for me. Who do you suggest I speak with to get to the next step?"

- Be more direct in your networking. Don't be afraid to ask, "What companies do you know that are expanding? Who do you know at Worldwide Widgets?"

- Sharpen your focus and polish your ROI message so that your contacts can relate your value to an identified need and can easily describe/recommend you to others.

Problem #3...You are in limbo, constantly waiting for responses that are slow to arrive...if they arrive at all.

Solutions...
- As we recommended earlier, keep control over the networking process by offering to make connections directly rather than waiting for your contact to do it.

- At the end of each interview, be sure you are clear about the next steps, when you can expect to be contacted, and what to do if you don't hear by that date.

- Always capture each step of the process and your anticipated follow-ups in your calendar system.

Problem #4...Not advancing beyond the first or second interview.

Solutions...
- Review, refine, and practice your ROI messages; be sure every interview response communicates how you can solve business challenges.

- Be sure your follow-up thank-yous to all meetings and interviews are immediate, packed with value, and express your interest and enthusiasm.

- Get feedback from your "accountability team" with regard to your interview answers.

- Ask a trusted friend or department-store personal shopper to review your appearance and be sure you are conveying a tip-top executive presence.

- Sharpen your focus to avoid interviewing for jobs that are not a good fit for your skills, expertise, and passions.

Problem #5...Reaching finalist status, but never earning the offer.

Solutions...
- Review all of the solutions immediately above.

- Relax! If you are getting everything but the offer, you are doing many things right, and it is just a matter of luck and timing till the right job rolls around.

Problem #6...Not succeeding despite months of hard work in a focused search.

Solutions...

- For executives who are action-oriented and solution-focused, the lack of clear direction in job search can be frustrating. You know, in general, what you have to do, but the ROI from each activity is not always clear. To help your mindset, establish aggressive and definable goals each week—number of calls, number of networking meetings, number of interviews—and check them off as you complete them. You'll derive a small feeling of satisfaction while, in the larger picture, propelling your search.

- Remember that steady, constant activity fuels the greatest likelihood of momentum and traction to the desired result.

- Again, relax. (We know it's easier to say than to do.) Job search *always* takes longer than people expect. As long as you are executing a dynamic search, consistently generating leads and interviews, and presenting yourself well during the interview process, you can be confident your search is on the right track.

PRO TIP: Consider hiring a coach or career agent. As we've detailed in this chapter, it's entirely practical to execute your job search on your own. The steps can be learned and the processes managed. But you may be able to accelerate your search and outsource some of the "grunt work" by hiring a career coach, executive resume writer, interview coach, executive coach, career agent, targeted search expert, virtual assistant, or another professional service provider who has expertise in executive career transitions.

We especially recommend professional assistance when:

- you are dealing with a difficult or unusual termination situation
- you are trying to cross over to a new industry or new function
- you are not confident that your written materials are top-notch
- you are working full time at a demanding job and have limited time to conduct your search
- you feel less than confident about your presentation/interviewing skills
- you are uncomfortable at the prospect of networking
- you are a senior executive accustomed to handing over the detail work to an assistant
- you haven't searched for a new position in years (or decades)
- your search has gone on with limited productivity for more than two months.

When discussing your needs with potential coaches, be clear about what you want and make sure you thoroughly understand what they provide and what their fees are. Acknowledge that you must play a part in every process (in reality, a coach can't handle the entire job search for you), and be sure each prospective coach has experience working with executives.

CHAPTER 2
ROI Content for Your Career Marketing Documents and Messages

In Chapter 1, you learned recommended job-search strategies, specific tactical action plans, and a four-week program of activities to create fast-moving momentum for your executive transition. Examining a variety of tools and projected return on investment for each, we repeatedly recommended that you pack your resume, LinkedIn, cover letters, networking interactions, and interviews with ROI content that will convey your value.

In this chapter we give you the detailed how-to techniques for translating what you have achieved into that powerful content for use in your career marketing documents and messages, to demonstrate your value proposition to a prospective employer or recruiter. Think of it this way: You are developing robust content that provides proof of performance.

You'll also learn how to employ the CAR formula to develop critical stories for use in your resume and related documents as well as during interviews. Following our step-by-step guidelines, you'll actually develop three to five CAR stories that succinctly tell the **C**hallenge, **A**ction, and **R**esult. This approach extracts the maximum value from each of your key accomplishments and creates substantiated sound-bites for you to share with decision-makers. Using this foundation, you can go on to develop additional CAR stories for all of your significant career accomplishments.

Getting Started

In our private practices, we like to lead off client consultations with critical questions that get at what drives our clients. Consider these three topics:

1. **Describe your ideal next position:**
   - What title would that job have?
   - In what industry would it be?
   - What type and size of company would be desirable?
   - What challenges or opportunities might exist?
   - Are you relocatable?
   - What expectations do you have relative to compensation?

2. **What do you want to do?** Sounds pretty basic, doesn't it? But to best respond to this question, think of those skills you absolutely must use to derive greatest satisfaction from your next job. At the same time, it is useful to consider what skills you *don't wish to continue using* (however well developed they may be).
   - Are you happiest when you are hands-on?
   - Do you enjoy managing multiple sites remotely?
   - Do you want an organization that is nimble, adaptive, and ready to rally to the new vision you instill?
   - Do you love global travel?
   - Or have you played road warrior far too long in your most recent career moves and seek a little less travel/more stability for yourself and your family?
   - Can you look back on your career and see that where you were happiest is when you were faced with seemingly insurmountable challenges—and successfully turned things around?
   - Do you get bored easily?
   - If you join a well-run organization that simply turns over the reins to you and doesn't support new initiatives, will you be stir-crazy in 18 months?

3. **What are your signature strengths?**
   - For what areas of strength are you best known?
   - For what "hard" skills have you been consistently recognized over the course of your career?
   - What are those "signature capabilities" that you're really good at?
   - And what about the "soft" skills that help to shape your leadership style? Consider your EQ (emotional intelligence) when thinking about your responses.
   - What are the distinctions in your background and skill set that you think will prove most interesting (i.e., transferable or desired) by subsequent employers?
   - What are some of the reasons you've been recruited or hired in the past?
   - What capabilities have led to your greatest business successes?
   - This is the time to retrieve results of any testing you've had—from Myers Briggs (https://www.myersbriggs.org) to DISC (https://www.everythingdisc.com/Home.aspx). In addition to these, among the many options, we also recommend 360Reach (https://www.reachcc.com), VIA Strengths Assessment (http://www.viacharacter.org), and Gallup/CliftonStrengths 34 (https://www.gallup.com/cliftonstrengths). Results from these assessment tools help to validate perceptions, soft skills, and strengths. Details can also provide fodder that you can use as part of your deep dive into articulating your value proposition and branding.

Caveat…This question is *not* meant to elicit your attributes (i.e., hardworking, organized, self-motivated, and so on). What you want to define are those skills you possess that are critical to performance in your target position. Some examples to prompt you:

- leading teams
- identifying profitable new markets for existing products or services
- improving manufacturing yield and team productivity while cutting costs
- assimilating organizations post-M&A
- driving business-to-business sales of complex services

Here's how this exercise might look for a CEO.

#1 Describe your ideal next position. *"I'm targeting a role as CEO or President of a multisite manufacturing company with revenues >$750M. The company would ideally have a strong and growing global presence, but I'd also consider a national firm with a well-established presence in the US. I'd want an opportunity for spearheading further expansion–either through organic growth or strategic acquisitions."*

#2 What do you want to do? *"Champion growth. Lead turnaround if required (company-wide or within specific divisions or silos). Institute continuous process improvements. Lead new initiatives that demonstrate corporate responsibility. Create avenues for development and advancement among talent at all levels. Build strategic partnerships across all divisions of the company and heighten visibility of our brands in the industry through enhanced social media and thought leadership."*

#3 What are your signature strengths? *"I'm known for bringing exceptional leadership and coaching skills cross-organizationally in every role I've held. My track record is superb with respect to promoting direct and indirect reports. Probably drawing from my early career talent in sales, I'm a connector—someone who easily builds and sustains highly productive relationships with people at every level. And while every top organizational leader must be highly driven and results-oriented, I'm all about giving people the tools and the runway to deliver outstanding results."*

Here's a second example of how responses to this exercise might look for a Senior-level Marketing Director.

#1 Describe your ideal next position. *"Depending on the organization's size, I'd want to be at either a director level or be the vice president of marketing. If it's a larger company, this could be divisional. I'd want to be challenged by the opportunity to grow the company (or division) to the next level—whether this means turning around an underperforming organization or continuing to advance an already successful operation or effectively launching a new business unit or division."*

#2 What do you want to do? *"I need to be in a role where I can really shape the organization—to create greater value, produce higher returns. I'm especially energized by opportunities to do more. If revenues of a product line have stagnated at a 25% market share for several years (or, worse, continually eroded on, say, a heritage brand), I want to turn the line upside down, always retaining the signature strengths, and architect ways to boost this to 40% or 50%."*

#3 What are your signature strengths? *"I'm a true visionary. Overused term, I know, but it defines at all levels what I bring to the table. I'm a creator—I see opportunities where others have long since moved on to something else. Perhaps even more importantly, I <u>create</u> opportunities of significant impact to the company, and to the bottom line. I'm recognized for consistently combining these things—<u>I have creative vision</u>—and implementing initiatives that have far-reaching strategic importance. I'm equally comfortable leveraging an organization's strengths both for the short-term and long-term."*

*   *   *   *   *

The purpose of Exercise #1 is to assess, extract, and capture your signature strengths. For some people, it is one of the most difficult exercises in the career transition process. However, virtually everything else that you'll be doing stems from this critical information.

Thus it doesn't make sense to start your search until you can define—precisely and uniquely—**who you are, what you want to do, and the skills and performance traits that distinguish you. Now it's your turn.**

> **PRO TIP: If you do nothing else, *be authentic*** when you capture your own responses to these seemingly-simple-on-the-surface questions. Think critically (positively!) about yourself and your contributions. Be as expansive as you wish—but keep coming back to the three critical questions and try to get down on paper what really drives you.

EXERCISE #1: Articulate Your Target and Capture Signature Strengths

#1 Describe your ideal next position. This is the easiest of the three questions for most executives to answer. In addition to the ideas suggested earlier, consider the following in crafting your reply:

- Organizational size.
- Span of control.
- Geography (both for the company/division/operation and where you want to live).
- Scope—local? regional? national? global?
- Do you want multi-divisional and/or multi-plant responsibility?
- Single or multiple sites?
- Exactly how important is title to you? (Be honest.)
- Will you consider—or even prefer—the challenge of a startup? If so, translate this desire to the underlying issues and challenges to give yourself more options.
- What kind of environment and culture do you prefer?
- What are your compensation expectations?

All of these factors point toward what an individual <u>really wants</u> to do next.

#1 Describe your ideal next position.

_____

_____

_____

_____

_____

_____

_____

_____

_____

_____

#2 *What do you want to do?* If you are targeting a new CEO opportunity or even a presidential or divisional GM level, do you still want to be able to touch customers, be involved in specific client interactions, keep your "finger on the pulse" of exactly what's going on within the sales and marketing organization, for instance? In a smaller, more entrepreneurial organization, this is likely to be very possible. In a large, multi-conglomerate corporation, you may find yourself missing that ready ability to make a difference and feel a surge of excitement from occasionally being out there on the front lines.

In instances where we've worked with executives who've grown out of the engineering ranks, it's sometimes difficult to leave totally behind an involvement with R&D and the opportunity to add value in the design and launch of a new product. That may resonate with you—and be something important to identify as a skill area that you want to be able to use in your next position.

A good way to get started on this question is to think in reverse: If you weren't able to do certain things in your next position (or perhaps even currently), would you be unhappy/unfulfilled? What are those skills?

Perhaps cultivating strategic alliances is a real strength—and something that creates energy for you and the organization. Remember, you must be authentic. Your "what do you want to do" statement should reflect those activities that are most important to you, not those that you *think* will be most prominent in the job or the level to which you aspire.

The key is to identify what really separates you from anyone else at this level…what you *know* to be true about yourself. Some executives find it useful to consider how others have described them—in letters of commendation, LinkedIn recommendations, and performance reviews and evaluations. What truly distinguishes you and your leadership/management style? What really defines you from the standpoint of the value you have added?

#2 What do you want to do?

_____

_____

_____

_____

_____

_____

_____

_____

_____

#3 *What are your signature strengths?* Possible ideas include:
- Leadership
- Ability to identify, cultivate, and retain talent
- Communication skills
- Ability to develop people
- Team building
- Networking skills
- Ability to spot emerging opportunities

Do these qualities describe you?
- Highly focused
- Results driven
- Inspirational

Or, looking at yourself in another way, do you see yourself as a…
- Rainmaker
- Leader by example
- Consensus builder
- Motivator
- Creator
- Mentor
- Champion
- Advocate
- Deal broker
- Turnaround expert
- Innovator
- Idea generator
- Master at leveraging organizational strengths

#3 What are your signature strengths?

_____

_____

_____

_____

_____

_____

_____

_____

_____

_____

The time and effort you devote to answering these three "target/signature strength" questions will pay large dividends later in the process of writing your resume and LinkedIn profile—and, in fact, in every stage of your career transition.

For the resume, your responses will come into play when identifying keywords, target titles, and specific components of your qualifications profile.

On LinkedIn, they'll support the personality-driven branding that tells your story in a compelling manner. They'll also prove useful in developing the content of your letters of introduction and traditional-but-innovative cover letters. And you'll find them essential in crafting your introductions to network contacts and potential employers.

> **PRO TIP: To help inspire you in this process of identifying your career target,** what you'd like to do, and signature strengths, consider sleuthing on the Internet to locate several possible job targets (even if all the criteria do not fit). It's not essential that these be positions you'd actually consider; rather, such listings may provide helpful information for focusing your resume and cross-checking qualifications.

Moving on to the task of creating your unique ROI content, we'll set aside the results of the three exercises you completed above. Now we want to go to what's truly the heart and soul of your resume: What you've achieved, what you've produced, and forward-thinking examples that predict what value you'll bring in a subsequent position. These are your predictors of success.

After all, you can talk all you like about what you want, what you're good at, and how others perceive you, but to be credible you'll need to offer proof of performance—what you've accomplished in the past using your signature skills and tackling the challenges that delight you and showcase your talents.

Shape Your Success Stories

The art of writing an executive resume is often likened to storytelling with a purpose. Your goal? To select and present examples that give a snapshot overview of the influence you've wielded, the quantified results you've produced, and the know-how behind your most significant initiatives.

To maximize the impact of everything you're writing, we recommend that you consciously put any examples you are considering using through the lens of *What are my signature strengths?* (You may refer to the target/signature strength exercises from earlier in this chapter.) *Does this story support that strength and illuminate for the reader exactly what challenge I faced, what the context was at the time, what initiatives I planned, what actions I took, and what outcome I delivered?*

This is the CAR (Challenge-Action-Result) approach to career storytelling. Start with what you consider to be your top two or three "career-defining" achievements. Consider how you would prepare for a scheduled 15-minute prescreening call with an executive recruiter: What are the best takeaways and examples of leadership success you'd want to be certain to share?

For this stage, we recommend you tell your story in narrative fashion. Don't worry about the resume or try to use "resume language." The stories you select should be relevant to your current goals and reflect your signature skills and leadership strengths. Be certain they are not too dated; it's okay to go back in time for one or more stories, but do bring the timeline forward and include others that are more recent in nature—ideally with a focus on career highlights over the past five to 10 years as opposed to those 20 or more years ago.

In the pages following this exercise, you will find five completed examples of CAR stories for executives in a variety of fields. But first, here is the three-step process to use in crafting your own CAR stories.

EXERCISE #2: Write Your CAR Stories

#1...Challenge. What is the challenge you faced? What was the opportunity presented? What was the context? What was going on at the time? It doesn't necessarily have to be a negative—a problem; it could be an opportunity that you perceived or was presented to you, such as an under-optimized sales avenue or unexplored distribution channel…maybe a product launch in a new vertical market, country, or continent.

At this stage in the exercise, provide as much detail as possible in **quantifying** the challenge or opportunity and describing the situation. The emphasis on *quantify* is deliberate: When you use numbers to identify the size or scope of a challenge, you immediately create context for your achievements. Rather than saying you "inherited a division that was substantially underperforming," use the exact numbers: "a division whose growth was perenially 5% below projections and had the lowest profitability in the company."

Your goal is to put your readers or listeners "in the picture" so that they thoroughly understand the context before you start talking about what you did.

_____

_____

_____

_____

_____

_____

_____

_____

_____

#2...Action. This is usually easy to describe. What did you actually do? Give your readers and listeners insight into how you solve problems. How do you attack a situation? What resources do you bring to bear? What kind of planning process do you find most effective when facing a challenge or opportunity? Describe what you did in this particular instance to position yourself for a positive outcome.

Use precise action verbs to describe your actions: Led...Spearheaded...Quarterbacked...Orchestrated... Drove...Championed...Turned around...Managed...Implemented...Directed...Overhauled...Reengineered...and so on.

And while it's important to provide enough detail to fully describe your activity, don't get bogged down in the minutia of a project or include too many tactical steps.

_____

_____

_____

_____

_____

_____

_____

_____

_____

#3...Result. Here's the bottom line: What happened? What were the results of your actions in response to the challenge? What success was realized? What foundation was established going forward? Did you achieve any awards (internal to organization or industry-wide), formal recognition, or commendation? Here, again, it's essential that you quantify your results wherever possible, in percentages or absolutes; without these hard numbers, your stories will lack credibility.

Select the best way to showcase your achievements numerically. It could be that an absolute number best achieves this or, possibly, a percentage of growth might tell the story more favorably—especially if your role at the time was with a smaller division or organization where the absolute ending number might not seem significant, but the percentage of change was double-digit.

Think broadly about both specific measurable outcomes and any less-definable but no less important results. And, whenever possible, look long-range toward the strategic impact of your actions. For example, perhaps you can demonstrate that you were instrumental in positioning your company for long-term success or avoiding a significant problem that plagued your industry.

_____

Additional CAR Story Blank *(copy as many as you need into a Word document)*

#1...Challenge.

_____

#2...Action.

_____

_____

_____

_____

_____

_____

_____

_____

#3...Result.

_____

_____

_____

_____

_____

_____

_____

_____

_____

Sample CAR Stories and Ways to Use on Resume and LinkedIn

Below you'll meet five senior-level executives—each telling a CAR story in their own words reflecting one significant accomplishment each. Just as we recommend for you, they will ultimately have three to five CAR stories, maybe more, for each of their past positions, and they will select highlights from their stories for their resume and LinkedIn profile as well as other career documents, for networking, and for interviewing. (You'll read more about other tools in Chapter 5 and see full portfolios in Chapter 6.)

As you will see, any one of these CAR stories makes for great reading and storytelling—in a biography or even in an in-depth interview. But it's clearly impractical to present nearly a full page of narrative for just one key success story as part of a resume or LinkedIn. That's where careful writing and judicious editing are needed.

Following each case below, you will see an example that transforms the CAR story into a powerful bullet point on the resume and a mention on LinkedIn, either in the summary section or in the experience category.

It's important to note that a single CAR story might result in several different bullet points and even sub-bullet points reflecting various key strengths. For example, one CAR story might demonstrate both fiscal leadership and talent management strengths and results.

Generally speaking, you'll want to draw out more CAR stories from your more recent years of experience. For instance, you will probably have at least four or five CAR stories for your current role, but a position that appears on page 2 of your resume from 15 years ago might have just one or two high-impact CAR stories.

As you are reading these examples, we hope you'll be inspired and consider your unique background and the many key stories you can tell about your achievements.

Case #1: Glynnis Davenport

Background: Glynnis is a 42-year-old senior hospital administrator managing the emergency department of a large Southeastern hospital. She's been in the field for more than 15 years, working her way up from assistant director to director to AVP to, now, Vice President, recruited to a new facility with each promotion. She's been brought on board as VP to standardize emergency medical care, synthesize procedures, and develop a plan of action that assures quality and profitability.

#1...Challenge

Southeast Medical Center has more than doubled its physical size in the past few years and nearly tripled its professional and administrative staff. I was hired to evaluate overall operations and instill new policies to boost poor patient satisfaction metrics, address a continued lack of profitability despite increases in outpatient procedures, and turn around faltering staff morale. Patient surveys conducted over the past two years revealed scores in the 1.5 to 2.25 range (1 being the lowest rating, 5 being the highest). The Emergency Department, while increasing in utilization commensurate with the increase in overall facility size, had suffered decreases in overall margin the last three years to the point of hitting an all-time low the year before I was hired. Staff morale was considered poor, absenteeism was up significantly (30% over the previous year), and there was a higher rate of turnover.

#2...Action

A review of Southeast Medical Center's mission statement revealed nothing about community; I recognized this focus could prove key in turning around patient perception of the facility as a whole. It was also apparent that the institution's expansion had been undertaken without a truly cohesive plan—no one was paying attention to overall allocation of resources and fiscal accountability.

I pulled together the Director of Emergency Nursing (a veteran with a real understanding of what was needed in terms of clinical care), several physicians, and key representatives of both nonprofessional and clerical staff to brainstorm and identify an optimal way to deliver patient care in a relatively new state-of-the-art facility. They were initially given no parameters and charged with creating the best plan possible to assure quality and service objectives. All factors were taken into account—from risk management and community image to improved utilization of Emergency Department services. Equal attention was paid to processes for ensuring effective coding and documentation to capture the highest reimbursement possible. Especially throughout the idea-generation process, I encouraged people to take risks in their problem-solving approach—no idea would be discarded without careful consideration.

#3...Result

With key input from every representative of the Emergency Department team, I spearheaded design of a facility and policies that everyone could embrace. Six months post-implementation, patient survey responses were at an all-time high (4.75 average), reimbursement rates climbed to their highest levels ever (in excess of 80%, compared to rates for the previous five years between 57% and 68%), staff morale has turned around 180 degrees (absenteeism is well within normal limits, staff is happier, and people are not "posting" to leave the department), and service utilization has nearly doubled—for the FY just ended, average monthly patient visits had grown from 1,250 one year earlier to nearly 2,500.

Sample CAR Statement for Resume:

- In one year improved department utilization 100% while simultaneously increasing patient satisfaction from 1.83 to 4.75 (on a 5-point scale) through implementation of standards of care, improved community outreach, and consistent focus on staff performance and development.

Use of CAR Story on LinkedIn:

Brought on board to optimize overall operations, I recognized an opportunity to deepen community engagement, improve the public's view of our Medical Center, and turn around flagging employee morale. I created a task force with key stakeholders at every level, and we achieved the following in under a year:

- 100% increase in department utilization.
- Gains in patient satisfaction—from an average 1.83 to 4.75.
- Newly implemented standards of care, improved community outreach, and consistent focus on staff performance and development.

Case #2: Dom Billings

Background: Dom is the new 61-year-old GM of a $30 million aerospace manufacturing company. Maxim Aerospace had been in existence for more than 35 years and was facing an industry-wide erosion in its customer base (it had shrunk by more than 20% over the past three–four years) and overall profitability (steady declines were posted over the preceding five years). Dom was recruited for his 20+ years of successful background turning around other small manufacturers in the aerospace sector and for his vision for Maxim.

#1...Challenge

From as early as the first interview to the point of my first few weeks on the job, I quickly realized that while Maxim had been able to stay slightly ahead of the curve and generate a consistent profit to its owners (privately held), it was in danger of rapidly losing ground in this competitive industry. My diagnosis? A failure to stay ahead of the game, an absence of lean manufacturing methods, and no plan for implementing same.

#2...Action

I was fortunate to have a willing team ready to jump on the bandwagon of the magnitude of change I was proposing. I initially identified strategic targets for immediate attention: reduce outsourcing of tooling (instead, optimize existing resources), improve quality assurance to save on extensive backend costs and ongoing customer service issues, implement MRP, and aggressively attack a longstanding backlog.

I worked with our engineers, QA folks, procurement staff, and expediters to develop pinpoint plans to address each area of deficit. I simultaneously put in place an acquisition process for the capital equipment necessary to optimize internal processes. I also held weekly strategy planning and checkpoint meetings. Amazingly, the staff had never met regularly before except when there was a major problem. This served the dual purpose of ensuring benchmarks were attained and morale stayed high. I instituted measures on the shop floor to provide a visual checkpoint on progress. With engineering's help, we reorganized the production control group and put in place a build-to-stock plan.

#3...Result

In the first few months, remarkable gains were achieved across nearly every measure. By the end of 9 months, the outstanding backlog had been reduced by 70%, tooling costs were shaved more than 50%, and measurable gains in quality were realized, leading to an overall 50% cost reduction. Newly acquired equipment and MRP set the stage for future gains and I began phase 2 of my master plan— working directly with the Sales VP to penetrate new markets for Maxim.

Sample CAR Statement for Resume:

- Reduced overdue backlog by 70% in 9 months through multiple initiatives: Restructured production control organization, deployed build-to-stock plans, introduced visual metrics on shop floor, and conducted daily management walkarounds.

Use of CAR Story on LinkedIn:

In my first 9 months, I rallied a dedicated group of managers to champion aggressive, productivity-driving initiatives that reduced overdue backlog by 70%. We achieved this by restructuring the production control organization, deploying build-to-stock plans, and introducing visual metrics on the shop floor.

I also started the tradition of conducting daily management walkarounds to create a stronger connection with the workforce and keep my hands "dirty" in the production process.

Case #3: Eduardo Ruiz

Background: Eduardo is a 54-year-old CFO hired 12 months ago by a multimillion-dollar, multisite manufacturer in the semiconductor industry, Premium Alloy, Inc. He is specifically tasked with reining in the finance-and-admin organization, eliminating duplication of resources, and establishing a smooth-running team.

#1...Challenge

Following costly acquisition of a larger competitor (immediately before I was hired), Premium was cash-poor, key customers were complaining about improperly applied credits and inaccurate invoicing, there was excessive overhead in the finance and administration departments, and organizations were working at cross-purposes with no integration between Premium's former finance organization and the "new" group. The company president was employing a hands-off approach to assimilation.

#2...Action

My first step was to assemble a team comprising the comptrollers of the original company and the acquired company, my best IT resource, and several of the top accounting and admin resources within both groups to analyze and discern the optimal systems from both organizations. I developed a vision and ensured everyone was clear on the desired outcome. Everyone also understood that in the new landscape, only the best talent and resources would remain.

The team then mapped out a strategy, determined the technology necessary to implement a complete assimilation, and developed a timeline for execution. I drove the process with specific success milestones and recalibration as necessary.

#3...Result

Within 6 months, I established a singular finance-and-admin team that supports all of the company's operations efficiently. I effectively preserved relationships with strategic customers by aligning finance staff with key accounts and implementing new Ts and Cs that benefit customers and Premium Alloy alike. I pared close to $.5 million in overhead costs by creating one team; some resources were hired in other company departments, some took advantage of favorable early retirement offers, and under-performing staff were released to seek work elsewhere. The new finance team is focused on a forward direction to support a turnaround in the company's financial direction.

Sample CAR Statement for Resume:

- Cut $500K in overhead by streamlining finance and administration and eliminating duplication of resources following merger.

Use of CAR Story on LinkedIn:

One of my top accomplishments was generating more than $.5M in overhead savings. This was achieved by synthesizing the finance and administration department of 2 organizations post-merger. I spearheaded measures that streamlined operations and improved overall efficiency by putting in place key controls that eliminated the duplication of resources.

Case #4: Jayne Beaumier

Background: Jayne is the new 38-year-old Director of Marketing with a major consumer goods manufacturer, Long+Thompson. Specifically handling personal care products, she has inherited marketing ownership of a heritage line of products that has begun to falter over the past few years for the first time in the company's 85-year history. Revenues were down more than $22M and market share had slipped by enough points to put the company in the #3 spot after years of being #1.

#1...Challenge

With constant competitive influx and new distribution channels continually eroding Long+Thompson's product base, I knew my greatest challenge would be directing all resources toward innovating not

52 of 256

only L+T's heritage products, but ensuring that new product launches would be on target, capture the desired audiences, and put this division of the company back on a trend-setting track.

#2...Action

I was fortunate to have a background rich in creative, hands-on brand leadership and product development. I could bring to this role experience with a variety of boutique advertising agencies. I also had a solid creative team at my disposal internally. My first plan was to develop a twofold approach designed to (a) overhaul and rejuvenate the heritage line to capitalize on key brand attributes while addressing new market opportunities (new formularies plus new packaging will be inherent to success) and (b) institute demographically dictated lifestyle product tiers linked to progressive stages of life to solidify long-time customer loyalty in new products.

I have always been considered to be a high-energy performer. Taking a cue from past successes, I established near-daily product innovation mini-conferences with my design team, brand managers, promotions assistants, and product engineers to mastermind brand rejuvenation strategies. I brought in not only focus group feedback, but in-the-field research culled from hands-on participation and analysis and that of key company staff nationwide. Top boutique talent acting in a consultative manner joined my team for creative sessions to spin new thought-leader campaigns. I divided groups into teams—my brand-overhaul "a" team and the new lifestyle product development "b" team. Creative incentives were put into place in a spirit of collaborative-yet-focused competition.

#3...Result

Long+Thompson's heritage brand was transformed back to #1 in its category with a 64% increase in revenues over 18 months. Brand penetration was increased significantly. Further, I can take credit for leading L+T's most successful launch ever with an innovative product introduction featuring tiered lifestyle skincare products; the campaign produced $125M in new revenues in just over 1 year.

Sample CAR Statement for Resume:

- Executed the company's most succesful product-line launch in 85 years with revenues of $125M in year 1 and projections in excess of $400M by year 3.

Use of CAR Story on LinkedIn:

One of the things I'm most proud of is turning around a well-respected L+T heritage product line that had fallen from #1 to #3 in its category. I pulled together a great team to overhaul the brand image and develop new line extensions—including the most successful product-line launch in company history!

In 18 months, we restored the brand to #1 in its category and generated more than $100M in new revenue from new products.

Case #5: Michael Goldstein

Background: Michael is a 59-year-old senior investment manager recently promoted within a premier Wall Street brokerage. In addition to ensuring SEC compliance, Michael has been challenged to take over custody operations and put in place systems and architecture to efficiently handle transfers and reorganization.

#1...Challenge

While not out of compliance, I could see that Evensong Mutual Funds would be facing many risks for lack of enforced policies and other regulatory concerns. Systems were not clearly in place for the movement or accounting of securities. Staff had not been cross-trained. There appeared to be little focus on professional development and virtually no written development plans or performance evaluations.

#2...Action

I initially assessed that there was a "people problem" to fix first—I wanted to understand core competencies, goals, and unfulfilled needs. At almost the same time, I could see a need for getting a real handle on the workflows of the operation.

Working with my most senior associate (JoAnn), I mapped out a strategy for JoAnn to develop optimal workflows that adhere to all regulatory requirements and assure the proper handling of securities. I then tackled the inventorying of all staff—assessing skill level, training completed, licenses held, etc.—and determining through one-on-one meetings the best alignment of talent with task. Melding the necessary workflows with staffing capabilities, JoAnn and I created a master plan that could be immediately implemented. Ongoing performance checks with collaborative written performance assessments every six months would help keep everyone on the same page. At the same point, regulatory compliance would be verified on a biweekly basis to assure no unanticipated outages.

#3...Result

In less than six months following my promotion to the head of custody operations, Evensong Mutual Funds had a sustainable game plan in place that assures compliance, productivity, and staffing levels. With newfound gains in productivity and a systematized workflow, the organization is poised to efficiently address significant growth and expansion of operations.

Sample CAR Statement for Resume:

- Led design and launch of new staffing structure featuring enhanced service interactions, cross-training, and alignment of competencies with business needs. Results:
    - —Greater job satisfaction (75% reduction in staff turnover)
    - —Improved operational efficiency (cut cycle times in half) in high-volume environment

Use of CAR Story on LinkedIn:

I championed key human capital initiatives that combined a new staff structure launch with cross-training and alignment of team competencies with business needs. The result? We were able to boost job satisfaction (slashing staff turnover by 75%) and improve operational efficiencies (cutting cycle times in this high-volume environment by half).

* * * * *

Putting it All Together to Create Your Own ROI Resume and LinkedIn Profile

You've done it! You have just finished creating the cornerstones to your resume, your LinkedIn profile, and your entire career marketing strategy. Your signature strengths and high-impact CAR stories are the most important strands of a tightly woven, compelling, and branded resume and accomplishment-rich LinkedIn profile. The exercise of crafting your top career achievements into CAR statements also prepares you to effectively network, interview, and tell your story.

Chapter 3 will give you step-by-step strategies to weave all of these threads together to create a resume that will uniquely position you for the targets you have established.

You'll find approaches in Chapter 4 for translating your CAR stories into compelling LinkedIn content. And, in Chapter 6, you'll see fully developed LinkedIn profiles and resumes that illustrate multiple CAR stories and strategies.

CHAPTER 3
Your Executive Resume

In Chapters 1 and 2, you created a game plan for your search and compelling CAR stories to serve as the raw material for your career marketing messages. Now you are ready to craft your resume—the fundamental document you'll need for your search and the basis for all of the additional materials we describe in Chapters 4 and 5.

Let's quickly review the key elements of an executive resume. Keep in mind that you might not have information in every category (for instance, military or civic/community).

1) Contact Information
2) Executive Profile/Summary
3) Professional Experience
4) Education and Professional Development
5) Affiliations and Professional Memberships
6) Military Experience
7) Civic and Community Background
8) Presentations and/or Publications

Below you will find discussion, recommendations, and examples for every one of these eight elements. But before we plunge in, it's important to address a few perennial questions, dispel a few myths, and give you some insights—based on our 50+ years of combined experience writing executive resumes—that will help you create a resume that is powerful, effective, and authentic to you and your career.

Resume FAQs

How long should my resume be?
You may have heard this anecdote about Abraham Lincoln. When asked "How long do you think a man's legs should be?," he responded, "Long enough to reach the ground."

You can apply this wisdom to your resume. It should be long enough to convey your expertise, distinguish you from other candidates, and give readers a solid sense for what you've done in your career. For most executives, these goals can be accomplished with two pages of carefully written and well-formatted text. Occasionally, as you'll see in Chapter 6, three pages are needed to convey all of the essential information. And a one-page resume, although rare for executives, might be exactly what *you* need.

Bottom line: Don't fall into the trap of assuming your resume "must" be three pages, or one page, or two pages. It "must" be long enough to tell your story. Follow our guidelines, use our samples as inspiration, and write a resume that works for you.

Should my resume be functional or chronological?
In nearly every case, we strongly recommend a chronological format for executive resumes. It's actually *reverse*-chronological—leading with most recent experience and working backward.

A *functional* resume, unlike the chronological format that we recommend, puts all of your achievements and activities into a single section, separated from the career chronology. This structure can be useful for hiding gaps in experience, widely disparate background, and frequent job jumps. Precisely *because* of that fact, recruiters and hiring authorities are inclined to suspiciously scan a functional resume to determine what the candidate is hiding. That's certainly not the reaction you want to evoke.

The chronological format is preferred almost universally by recruiters and hiring authorities alike—and that is reason enough for you to use it. It creates a logical flow and clearly explains *where* you did *what* you did and *when*.

Of course, not everyone has a picture-perfect career with stair-step progression and unbroken employment. If you're struggling with some of the issues that the functional format disguises so well, be sure to review the section later in this chapter, **Special Situations** (page 64), for strategies and examples that will help you address your particular challenge and, ideally, create an effective resume in the preferred chronological format.

What is "resume language"?
Like any specialty document, resumes are written in a specific way:

- **First person/subject understood.** The subject, in most cases, is yourself. When writing your resume, omit the word "I" from the beginning of your sentences and you'll have the correct structure and tense. For example:
  — [I] Increased sales 17%.
  — [I] Manage a team of 47 advisors serving clients in 8 offices statewide.
  An error that we see quite often is the use of third person when writing in the present tense—that is, when writing about things that are happening *now*. It just feels odd to some people to write "*Direct* all operations across Northeast" rather than "*Directs* all operations." You can check your work by mentally inserting the word "I" in front of your verbs to be sure that you've done it correctly.

- **Telegraphic writing style.** You can omit articles (such as a, an, the) and otherwise tighten your writing to include only the essential information. This is not a hard-and-fast rule, however. Sometimes it just sounds better to include the articles, and that's fine. But the telegraphic style can be a great help in keeping your resume to a manageable length, so don't be afraid to omit and truncate—so long as you are still clearly conveying the essential information.

- **Abbreviations and other shortcuts.** As you will see from the sample resumes in this book, it's fine to use a few techniques that will shorten individual lines and overall length of your resume. For example, many resume writers use digits for all numbers, including one through ten that are normally spelled out in text. We like the brevity of digits, and we like that those all-important numbers stand out on the page! You can use abbreviations (Dep't.), acronyms (VP), and other length-shortening techniques ($5M). Just be consistent, and make certain that everything is clear to your readers.

Do I have to list everything I've ever done on my resume? If I omit something, doesn't that raise a red flag with employers?
Think of it this way: Your resume is only a couple of pages long. It's impossible to include everything you've ever done in your career. Therefore, you must make strategic decisions about what to detail and what to omit.

Choose information that positions you for your current goal and supports your executive brand. Omit details that are less relevant and that will obscure the larger picture.

Yes, you might choose to leave off earliest career experiences. Just be ready to discuss and describe those experiences when you are meeting with recruiters and potential employers. You don't want to appear deceptive. Rather, communicate that you've chosen the most important information for your resume but are happy to share further details.

Yes, you can omit dates from your education and early career history. Read the specific sections below, and the **Special Situations** advice at the end of the chapter, for considerations and options for handling dates.

And, as we recommend throughout this chapter, first create a record of everything—all jobs and education, all dates—and then, as you refine your first-draft resume, selectively omit details that are less important given your current career situation and goals. The two most important considerations are (1) consistency in your written materials and (2) transparency when asked about any of these items.

How can I be sure that my resume will pass the automated scanners (often referred to as ATS—Applicant Tracking Systems) that are the first barrier when I apply for a job?
The good news is that scanning software is getting smarter and more sophisticated all the time. Formatting issues that plagued earlier systems are no longer a problem. For example, it's fine to use color, lines, borders, and graphics in your resume. You can list your title first, or your company name first—either is fine. You can list months/years of employment or simply years. And you are no longer restricted to specific machine-readable fonts.

Assuming that you're creating a chronological resume (functional resumes don't fare well when scanned, because activities and achievements are separated from when and where they took place), there are only a few issues that you need to think about with regard to scannability:

- Do not use MS Word's "insert text box" feature to position text on the page. Scanners treat those boxes as graphics and won't read any of the contents.
- If you are including charts, graphs, or other visuals on your resume, be aware that the scanners will ignore them. You will need to describe your achievements in words as well as graphics.
- Scanners look for keyword matches. It makes sense to review each posted opening and edit your resume, if needed, to be sure that you have included most or all of the essential keywords.

From our point of view, even *better* news is that with our accelerated four-week job-search plan, described in Chapter 1, you won't be spending the bulk of your time and effort applying to posted openings. You'll be pursuing targeted search strategies that are much more effective and much less dependent on robo-reviewers. So our expert advice is not to worry about automated resume scanners, beyond those few factors just mentioned above.

Draft Your Resume

Now that we've dealt with the basics, we can jump right into the process of creating your resume. In the sections below, we cover all of the eight elements mentioned at the start of this chapter.

Of course, it's quite possible that you already have a resume but are looking to update and/or improve it. Old versions of your resume can be quite valuable as records of past employment dates, details, and accomplishments. But before simply tacking new information onto the old framework, we recommend that you work through all of the guidelines in this chapter and critically review your old content to see if it meets the standards for a modern resume, or can do so with just a bit of judicious trimming. If so—great! If not, you can modify based on our recommendations and then move on to crafting the newest, and most strategically significant, material.

Contact Information

This section is very straightforward—but you might be surprised at the questions that crop up.

Put your name on the top line of your resume, followed by your contact information. Specifically:

- Your personal cell phone number.
- Your personal (NOT work) email address. We suggest a gmail email address or, if you have your own domain, use that. To avoid dating yourself, do not use AOL, Hotmail, Yahoo, or other much older email providers.
- Your LinkedIn URL. We strongly recommend that you customize the URL so that it is not the string of random alpha-numeric characters that LinkedIn arbitrarily assigns. See Chapter 4 for instructions.
- *Consider* including your city/state/zip or metro region, especially if you will be searching primarily in the same geographic area. It's fine to omit location altogether—you will see samples of both in this book. Do not include your street address or mailing address.
- *Consider* adding a link to your personal website, portfolio, or blog, if any of those will complement and enhance your professional image.

*Please see the **Special Situations** section at the end of this chapter for recommendations on addressing androgynous names and other moniker questions.*

PRO TIP: Write from the bottom up. Now that you've started at the top of the page, we recommend that you move to the bottom!

Many professional resume writers develop the content of a resume starting at the bottom. We think this tactic will work for you, too. It helps you to move quickly and easily through a number of straightforward sections and will get you in the flow of writing...rather than staring at a blank page and struggling with how to write a concise, powerful, laser-focused executive introduction.

Starting at the bottom, roughly outline your civic and community involvement...fill in military experience, if applicable...add affiliations and professional memberships...enter educational details... determine the most relevant examples of presentations and/or publications to include. Next create an outline for your employment—employer name, city and state, job titles, and dates, working from the oldest to the newest.

Don't worry (yet) about paring down the oldest content or cutting coursework, organizational involvement, and the like. This material can be trimmed later (remembering you will have the opportunity to be more expansive with this content on LinkedIn). You'll also address resume design and final formatting further on in the process.

Once the preliminary sections are complete, you will be ready to focus on the two most critical sections of your resume: your professional experience and executive summary.

Presentations and/or Publications

This section (or sections) of your resume can be used to highlight the most important of your presentations and publications. Organize these in a reverse-chronological list. Be selective—you want to impress readers, not overwhelm them. You might combine presentations and publications into a single section or, if you have more than a few of each, create two separate sections. Include the following information.

For presentations:

- Formal title of your program
- Audience/platform/conference/organization addressed
- Number of attendees (if notable—i.e., you would omit the number if it were only 18...but certainly include multiples of 100 or 1,000)
- Location (city/state/country)
- Month and year of event

For publications:

- Title of your article/book/etc.
- List your name as sole author; name co-authors, if any
- Publisher (skip if self-published)
- Periodical name (if published as article in journal or magazine)
- Date of publication (year for book; add month or month/date for periodical)

If you speak or write extensively, consider an addendum page that is a running reverse-chronological listing of all talks delivered and/or all items published. Select those most applicable and important for the abbreviated listing on your resume.

Example...

Presentations and Publications

Breaking Down Silos, February 2020—Presentation at Butler Health National Quality Conference

Increasing Usability of Ambulatory Surgery Centers, March 2019—Panel Presentation, Seattle Healthcare Forum

"Optimizing Ambulatory Surgery Resources: Increasing Use, Maximizing Physician Resources, Boosting Profitability." T Smith, J Johnson, L Watkins. *Journal of Western Healthcare Providers,* Volume VI, 2018.

"Driving Change in Today's Healthcare Environment: Bringing Physicians On Board." T Smith. *Today's Healthcare,* April 2017.

Civic and Community Background

This section of your resume allows you to highlight extra information that can set you apart from others and reveal additional facets of your character, skills, and personality. Key questions to prompt your memory:

- On what boards, commissions, or organizations do you sit?
- What positions of leadership do you hold?
- Were you elected or appointed?
- Did you lead any significant initiatives during your tenure?

Example ...

Civic and Community Involvement

City of Boston Police Department

- **Board Member, Community Partnership Program** (2017–Present)

Jamaica Plain Neighborhood Task Force

- **Member, Traffic Safety Advisory Committee** (2015–Present)

- **Chair, Strategic Planning Committee** (2010–2015)

While it is usually adequate to name just the organization, location, position(s) held, and timeframe, you might choose to add details in those instances where you provided above-and-beyond leadership or managed a particularly significant project.

Example...

Philadelphia Society for Multiple Sclerosis

- Committee Chair, 2019–2020: Directed annual black-tie event that attracted 900 attendees and raised >$85K each year.

Be selective in choosing the items you list in this (optional) section of your resume. You don't want to place too much emphasis on extracurriculars, nor do you want to age yourself by showing dates from long ago. Do include items that support your executive leadership skills.

And here's a quick tip for handling dates: If you were extremely active in a particular organization but ceased membership more than a few years ago, instead of showing the actual timeline (1990–1999), indicate number of years:

> Elected City Council Member, Springfield, GA (9 years)

> *See the **Special Situations** section at the end of this chapter for recommendations on addressing religious and political affiliations.*

Military Experience

If this category applies to you and you choose to include it, list your branch/field of service, highest rank achieved, significant honors or recognition earned, and honorable discharge status. If your experience directly links to your current goal, a brief highlight or two is fine. Otherwise, nothing further is needed unless, of course, your military background comprises the bulk of your career. If that is the case, rather than including it in a separate "military" section, list it under Professional Experience and include all of your relevant accomplishments.

Example ...

UNITED STATES AIR FORCE—Dyess Air Force Base, Abilene, TX   1994–2000

Master Sergeant, Grade E-7 *(honorable discharge)*

- Managed maintenance production team of 15 on $280M B-1B aircraft.

Affiliations and Professional Memberships

Separate from community involvement, these will relate to your industry and field. It is optional whether you include number of years affiliated or timeframe of your affiliation; you may choose to omit year/date information altogether. The important thing is to be consistent.

Example ...

Affiliations

Global Security Advisory Council

National Society for Industrial Security

American Health Care Anti-Fraud Association

International Security Management Association

Atlanta Community Partnership Foundation

Example ...

Professional Memberships

New Haven Chamber of Commerce—President, Entrepreneurial Division (3 years); Member (7 years)

Quinnipiac Bureau of New Business Owners—Founder/Co-President (4 years)

Association of Manufacturing Excellence—Member (2 years)

PRO TIP: When space is tight, it makes sense to consolidate these typically brief sections at the end of the resume and create one solid entry that illustrates stature and thought leadership through a variety of activities—publications and presentations, board positions, professional association memberships, community leadership, and so forth.

We recommend that you first spell out everything, as we've suggested above, and then decide if a single section will allow you to gain the benefits of these entries without taking up quite so much space. The examples in Chapter 6 show a variety of combinations and formatting styles that can inspire you.

Education and Professional Development

For the Education section of your resume, remember it's "just the facts." List degree earned, institution, city/state, and—perhaps—year of graduation.

There are many schools of thought on whether or not to include years. If the potential for age discrimination is not a concern (and, frankly, for a senior-level executive, it is *expected* that you have years of experience), by all means show years. If, on the other hand, you are concerned about age perceptions, eliminate the dates of your degrees and be sure to truncate your work history as well. It does no good to eliminate the years in which you earned your degrees, but show employment beginning in 1979!

Here's the bottom line: Be consistent. Don't mix-and-match—show dates for *all* of your education or *none*.

PRO TIP: Highlight a recent MBA. Recent, top-level business education is worthy of emphasis. One way you can do that, without also dating your long-ago bachelor's degree, is to add a line to your Executive Summary, showing the recent date of your master's degree: "MBA, Kellogg School of Management, 2019." Then, in the Education section, list all of your education but *without* dates.

While you might be proud of your academic honors, we don't recommend detailing these on your resume unless they were truly stellar (for example, Rhodes or Fulbright scholar). Your achievements in your career are of greater value today. You may mention that you graduated with honors (*cum laude, magna cum laude, summa cum laude,* or other designation that appears on your diploma).

Do not mention any collegiate extracurricular activities (okay, if you were the star running back for three years and earned the Heisman trophy, you can be permitted that indulgence).

Do not list high school; one exception would be if you plan to network with alumni of an elite secondary school. For instance, if you are a graduate of Connecticut's Choate Rosemary Hall and you're using the alumni office to assist you, by all means list the connection on those resumes only.

*Please see the **Special Situations** section at the end of this chapter for recommendations on addressing no formal education, incomplete degree, and other education-related concerns.*

You may also choose to include relevant **Professional Development** as part of your Education section. Highlight two or three significant programs or seminars that add value to your portfolio of skills and abilities. Timeliness is important—you generally don't want to show programs completed more than 10 years ago.

Example …

Education and Professional Certification

M.S., Business Administration — Boston University • Boston, MA (1993)
B.S., Engineering — Northeastern University • Boston, MA (1990)

Executive Lean Manufacturing Program (2017)
Certified Zenger Miller Leadership Trainer (2016)

Professional Experience

You have many options for titling this critically important section of your resume. Here are a few:

> Executive Performance
> Experience and Accomplishments
> Career Overview
> Senior Management Experience
> Professional Management Experience

We don't recommend "Work History," a caption that we believe connotes other-than-executive experience. Ultimately, the decision regarding the heading is yours; select the one you feel most comfortable with.

In writing this section, it's essential to focus on those pieces of your background that indicate your value, predict your future success, and are relevant to your current career goals.

Start by creating a chronology beginning with your first professional role. Initially, don't worry about "how far back" you are going to go along the timeline—get the rudimentary outline into the document first. Concentrate on having correct names of companies, location (city/state), years of employment, and your title. If you held multiple roles within the same organization, break out the specific titles (for now) and years of each. The example below depicts this first chronological draft.

Example ...

Professional Experience

ALPHA CORPORATION • Denver, CO   2015–Present
Vice President of Field Operations *(2018–Present)*
Director, Northeast Area *(2015–2018)*

CARDINAL HEALTH SYSTEM • Boston, MA   2011–2015
Director, Network Planning and Integration

AC NIELSEN COMPANY • New York, NY   2001–2011
Regional Operations Manager *(2007–2011)*
Senior Field Operations Manager *(2001–2007)*

TECHNICAL EQUIPMENT CORPORATION • Hauppauge, NY   1995–2001
Field Service Branch Manager *(1998–2001)*
Field Service Unit Manager *(1995–1998)*

DELCOURT SYSTEMS • Norwalk, CT   1990–1995
Senior Project Engineer *(1993–1995)*
Project Engineer *(1990–1993)*

As we've mentioned, many professional resume writers start with the bottom of this section and move forward, leaving the current or most recent position for last. So we'll do the same as we walk you through the process of creating your resume.

At this point, you can begin to consider just how far back in time to go when culling material for your resume. As a sliding general rule, you probably won't want to include much detail for anything beyond 15 or 20 years ago; you don't want to overwhelm the reader with dated, detailed material, particularly at the expense of more recent and more relevant experience.

Let's assume our hypothetical job seeker, whose chronological career history appears above, graduated with a bachelor's degree in 1990, went to work immediately at Delcourt Systems, and now has 30+ years of professional experience. Using a yardstick of 20 years, we would consider going back to 2001 and detailing only Alpha, Cardinal Health, and AC Nielsen in the resume.

We might omit those earliest two employers entirely, or we might mention them briefly, without dates, as a simple listing or a brief paragraph—perhaps something like this:

> **Prior Professional Background** includes progressive engineering and management positions in high-technology manufacturing with Delcourt Systems and Technical Equipment Corporation.

Another option is to list titles and employers, but without dates—here is an example:

PRIOR EXPERIENCE

Field Service Manager—TECHNICAL EQUIPMENT CORPORATION • Hauppauge, NY

Senior Project Engineer • Project Engineer—DELCOURT SYSTEMS • Norwalk, CT

A final consideration, as you trim down your earliest experience, is the value of those early years. You might want to highlight a major accomplishment, notable accolade, or specific expertise that is relevant to your current goals. You can add a line or two using either the paragraph format or list format shown above. But keep any additional details brief, on point, and high impact.

> **PRO TIP: Let's put all of this discussion about age and dates into context.** In some cases and in some industries, younger perceived age may be a competitive edge—at least for first-impression resume screening. In actual fact, when interviewing begins age takes a back seat to experience, accomplishments, and fit.
>
> Our goal is not to have you focus undue energy on age but simply give you a few scenarios and strategies to evaluate your own situation. Think about the perception you're creating by including—or omitting—dates and perhaps early experience, and make sure that your resume is painting the right picture without distracting readers with irrelevant details.

Now, let's continue writing the Professional Experience section of your resume. If you follow our recommendations, you'll start by writing about your oldest positions and move forward from there. As a general rule, devote more space to more recent (and presumably more senior and more relevant) roles and decrease the amount of space allotted as you go backward in time.

As you begin to write, think about the purpose of your resume: to capture the interest of potential employers, position you for the roles you're seeking now, and differentiate you from other candidates. Your readers are not interested in your job description; they want to know *what you did* in that job, not what the "duties" or "responsibilities" were.

This is great news because it means you can focus on your most important and impressive achievements. Your unique success stories will definitely distinguish you from others and will create a narrative for your career that you can expand on during interviews.

And if you've followed our guidelines in Chapter 2, you have already prepared the raw material for a powerful and distinctive resume! The CAR stories you developed—perhaps three, four, or even more for each position—are the foundation for the bulk of the content in this Professional Experience section of your resume. Your challenge now is to condense those stories into concise, high-impact achievement statements (most often formatted as bullet points).

PRO TIP: For maximum impact, start with results. Your CAR stories begin with the challenge you faced, then go on to describe your actions, followed by the outcome. That's a clear and logical storytelling format that allows readers to grasp context, nuance, and the variety of skills you used in tackling that challenge.

However, people reading your resume are forming impressions and making decisions very, very quickly—perhaps 10 seconds or less in a first review. They may not take the time to read the entire story to get to the results. So it's imperative that you extract and highlight those results, followed by a bit of context and detail to add meaning to the achievement.

Consider the difference in immediate impact between these two bullet points that describe the same achievement:

- Saved $3.2M in annual operating expenses by developing, manufacturing, testing, and implementing cutting-edge data collection technology.
- To meet increasing need for customer and prospect information management, led team in developing, manufacturing, testing, and implementing cutting-edge data collection technology that replaced outdated systems, eliminated paper records, and saved $3.2M in annual operating expenses.

Notice, also, how a lengthy CAR story was distilled into one concise sentence. Obviously there's more to the story—and you can expand on it during the interview. But your first challenge is to capture attention, and beginning many if not most of your bullet points with a strong verb and high-impact results is a great way to do that.

Example...

ALPHA CORPORATION ($750M leader in voice and data solutions) • Denver, CO • 2015–Present
Vice President of Field Operations *(2018–Present)*

Promoted to strengthen field operations and manage team of 10–12 in Eastern U.S. Oversee multiple virtual teams, 25–30 members each, handling installation, network, and analysis services. Direct post-sales activities throughout operational span with complete P&L responsibility (on track to expand from $23M to $40M).

- In 12 months, grew services revenue from $1.8M to $5.5M per quarter through focus on service sales.

- Reversed 30%–40% turnover trend to zero by executing revitalization plan capitalizing on staff's unique strengths.

- During 12–18 month period of limited resources, increased capacity 20% by establishing strategic alliances with 3rd parties to augment implementation capability.

- Revamped business model to focus on implementation services, streamline maintenance agreements, and eliminate lower-end services with small profit margin yield.

Director, Northeast Area *(2015–2018)*

Stabilized organization experiencing widespread change; managed effectively during technology sector volatility while staff increased from 14 to 21 direct reports.

- Drove active and effective recruitment strategies to service a business increasing at 16% annually.

- Assumed additional responsibility for managing both pre- and post-sales engineering for Northeast.

- As Alpha transitioned out of large enterprise business, retained key talent through multi-pronged plan providing training opportunities and stay-on bonuses to ensure completion of all project requirements.

CARDINAL HEALTH SYSTEM ($37B healthcare services company) • Boston, MA • 2011–2015
Director, Network Planning and Integration

Brought on board to spearhead complex integration initiative for leader in healthcare products, services, and technology. Challenged to direct development and rollout of voice and data network in 6,000-node multi-protocol data environment and 13,000+ voice environment.

- Increased network performance through enterprise-wide design and implementation of TCP/IP routing (RIP and OSPF) as well as link-state routing of IPX/SPX (NLSP).

- Delivered 99% uptime through management of design/installation project providing redundant routers and communication links.

AC NIELSEN COMPANY • New York, NY   2001–2011
Regional Operations Manager *(2007–2011)*

Promoted to direct regional operations comprising 20 managers, 4 engineers, 135 employees, and $15M budget for Nielsen's household television meter service: 7,000 households across 12 markets.

- Saved $3.2M in operating expenses annually by developing, manufacturing, testing, and implementing cutting-edge data collection technology.

- Preserved strategic account relationship valued at $2.5M through effective leadership of customer service focus team.

> **Senior Field Operations Manager** *(2001–2007)*
>
> Managed team of 5 managers and 40 employees, $950K budget, and all field activities (installation, maintenance, service support) in 5 branch offices.
>
> - Transformed faltering Chicago branch, one of the company's worst performers, into a top-5 field office.
> - Recognized as Manager-of-the-Year with President's Award.

PRO TIP: Use context to add power and aid understanding. For greatest impact, frame your career history and accomplishments within the context of specific challenges, market conditions, or other circumstances that existed when you took each job or during your tenure.

In the example above, note how each introductory paragraph includes language that "puts the reader in the picture" as to what this executive was expected to do or specific challenges that existed. We then read accomplishments that tell us what this person *did* do in those circumstances. This structure and context make it easier for readers to understand career activities and achievements.

While the above format—introductory paragraph followed by achievement bullets—is extremely popular, it is not the only way to describe the activities and accomplishments of your career. As you look through the portfolio of sample documents in Chapter 6, you'll see many creative and effective approaches.

For example:

- **Willa Robinson resume,** page 131: Each position starts with a quick "Snapshot," a big-picture achievement statement. Next, subheadings introduce specific areas of activity and are followed by concise bullet points stating specific accomplishments. Job details are minimal and folded into achievements if needed for context.

- **Matthew Pearson resume,** page 158: Job scope details are briefly listed in a shaded box, and the introductory paragraph is used to describe context and challenges. Hefty bullet points include multiple related achievements distinguished with bold type.

- **Angela Davis resume,** page 137: This resume is designed for quick skimming. Job scope is summarized in one line under job title; context paragraph is followed by bold "Key Impact" statement; and achievements often include sub-bullets for easy reading.

As you translate your raw material into a concise and powerful resume, use the samples—all written by professional resume writers who specialize in working with executives—as inspiration and guidance while creating something uniquely your own.

PRO TIP: Control length to captivate readers. To keep your resume readable and your readers interested, keep your content concise and avoid large blocks of text.

- Limit paragraphs to three or at most four lines.
- Strive for bullet points no longer than one or two lines—although the occasional longer bullet point may be warranted to fully convey an achievement.
- Curtail bullet lists to no more than four or five items. If you have more, and it's truly important, consider ways to break up what would otherwise be a dense block of text:
  - Use second-level bullets to break down an overly long accomplishment into multiple smaller "bites" of information.
  - Add subheadings, grouping several bullets under a meaningful category such as a functional area or leadership strength.
  - Create an Executive Leadership Brief (an addendum to your resume). Described in Chapter 5, this document allows you to expand on the most significant accomplishments of your career without bogging down your resume.
- Add white space between bullets, between paragraphs, and anywhere else on the page where you want to create an opportunity for readers to pause and absorb what they've just read.

Executive Profile/Summary

Your resume should begin with a well-written executive summary—an introduction to what follows and a critical opportunity for you to position yourself exactly as you want to be perceived.

The summary can take many forms, as you'll see throughout the samples in this book. In selecting the material for your summary, think about the small handful of facts that you want readers to immediately see, understand, and absorb. You might consider this section of the resume your "highlights reel," in that it should be snappy, interesting, and brief while still conveying relevant and differentiating information.

Rather than leading off with a heading such as "Professional Profile" or "Executive Summary," we strongly recommend that you begin your summary with a headline—a meaningful title that creates immediate context for the career story you are going to tell in the rest of the resume.

Your summary should be concise, perhaps one-fourth to one-third of the page, before you begin your professional experience. Readers glancing at your resume can then quickly get to the heart of the matter—your employment history—without having to search or flip pages to find it.

In a well-developed business plan, the Executive Summary appears first, but it is always written last, after all components of the plan have been developed. Your resume summary will come together the same way.

To begin creating your profile, give careful consideration to questions like these to tease out your own unique value proposition:

- In what areas do you have special expertise?
- What are your core competencies?
- What areas of performance have distinguished your career?
- What do you do differently or better than others?

- What would others say about you?
- What are your most significant achievements?
- What specific technical proficiencies (if relevant) do you possess?
- What other defining information about you could be important to impart in the quick 5-second read your Executive Summary may garner?
- What additional distinguishing characteristics do you possess (e.g., multiple language proficiencies, key industry credentials, prestigious board of directors' roles, name-brand MBA)?

As you are gathering information and ideas for your Executive Profile, you'll find it helpful to refer to the exercises in Chapter 2, particularly your responses in the Signature Strengths section of that chapter.

> **PRO TIP: Be crystal-clear right from the top.** It is absolutely essential that in your Executive Summary you immediately communicate your career focus. In those first few seconds, readers *must* be able to tell who you are so they can place you in context and have the right expectation for what you will present in the rest of the resume.

Here are four sample Executive Summaries. You'll note that they don't follow a formula—they don't all present the same types of information in the same sequence or style. In each case, the resume writer chose distinguishing and relevant facts and assembled them into a unique presentation for that particular executive. Your own Executive Summary should do the same.

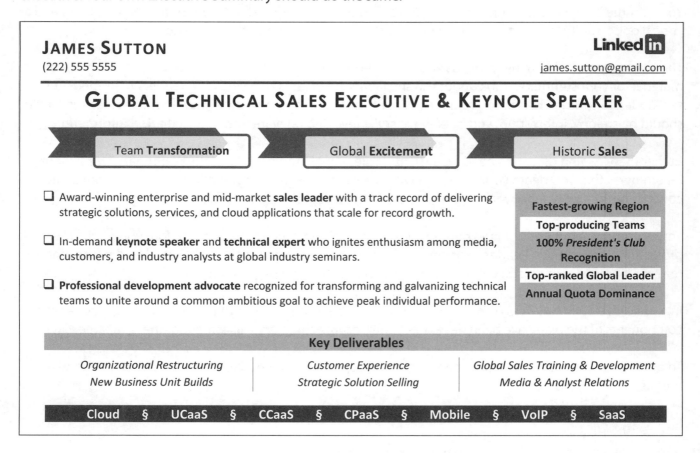

Kristofer Nagy

kristofer.nagy@gmail.com ■ 555-876-1234 ■ LinkedIn/com/in/krisnagy

Senior Sales Executive: Software/Technology

- **Growth catalyst** for technology sales—15-year history of opening doors to new business opportunities in areas never before penetrated.

- **Business strategist** who devises meticulous processes, structures, and checkpoints in sales planning for complex products.

- **Sales team champion,** developing top performers supported by proven sales methodology that identifies, qualifies, and delivers.

B2B Consultative Sales

Strategic Business Development

Enterprise SaaS Market

Fortune 500 Accounts

Milestones

- Added $3.5M new revenue to a $20M company in first 9 months post-acquisition.

- Nearly doubled software revenue ($4M to $7.6M) through partnerships/sales to Fortune 500 accounts.

- Created $10M life sciences business of a $25M entrepreneurial enterprise software firm.

- Spearheaded strategy that propelled startup sales from $500K to $6M.

VINCE BREWSTER

503-453-1724 | brewster@email.com
www.linkedin.com/in/brewster

SENIOR EXECUTIVE: GENERAL MANAGEMENT, FINANCE, OPERATIONS

HOTELS | HOSPITALITY

Operational and Financial Excellence: Build brand-driven value by evaluating business processes, establishing best practices, upgrading systems, and securing the right talent. **Approachable Leadership:** Cultivate empowered, service-oriented teams in an environment of originality and respect. MBA.

$750M consumer-driven businesses. Multimillion-dollar budgets. 1000+ employees.

- Improved customer service, check-in, and room ratings by roughly 20% in first 6 months. *The Westerly Hotel*
- Introduced a new vision for the financial/operational growth of a $750M organization. *NG&E/Parisienne Hotel*
- Oversaw financial operations, reporting, and compliance for $475M revenue. *BE&C/Grandview Hotel*

Connie Sutherland

919-999-1234 | conniesutherland@gmail.com
Raleigh, NC 27605 | LinkedIn.com/in/connie-sutherland

GENERAL MANAGER | PLANT MANAGER | DIRECTOR
Pharmaceutical/Biotech Manufacturing & Engineering

Unparalleled record of success improving business and optimizing manufacturing processes; driving individual performance gains; championing and executing turnarounds; and leading cross-functional teams.

Management Skillset	Technical Expertise	Global Mindset
• cGMPs/Best Business Practices • Green Belt Training • Lean Six Sigma—DMAIIC, DMADVC	• MS, Global Management of Technology • BS, Chemical Engineering	• Bilingual English/Spanish • Conversational fluency in French • Lived/worked in 4 countries

Special Situations

There are probably as many special challenges that can occur in resume writing as there are innovative strategies for addressing them. We'll walk through some of the more typical cases we face as resume writers…and provide some suggested solutions for your consideration.

Problem #1…I'm concerned about my age. What's the best way to handle that on the resume?

*Solution…*Earlier in this chapter we mentioned that age may not necessarily be a bad thing. In fact, we daresay that *most* savvy, accomplished senior-level executives are not 26 years old. However, from our work with candidates, we do know some have concerns about their age—or, more specifically, that they will *appear* to be "too old." (We've never met an executive who feared he or she *was* too old!)

We see this most often in executives who have established decades-long careers within one industry (and sometimes one company) who find themselves unexpectedly unemployed in their late 40s, 50s, or even 60s and 70s. The vast majority of candidates in this situation have tremendous expertise and experience to offer. Yet, for some, their job searches become mired in self-doubt for a variety of reasons.

The primary root cause can often be attributed to a lack of experience *conducting an executive job search* and perhaps expecting too much too soon. (If this describes you, refer back to Chapter 1 for proven strategies and a quick-start action plan.)

Although each situation is unique, you can expect to spend at least six months in active job search, reflecting the scarcity of top positions and an often protracted interview process. Of course, this is just a guideline. We have seen $500K–$1M+ executives land a new position in two or three months, while others in the low-six-figure range search hard for a year or more. Still, keeping this as your guideline will help you from becoming too impatient after just a few weeks or months of searching!

However, let's assume that your expectations are realistic but that for any number of reasons you wish to disguise your age on your resume. Here is a recap and further explication of the strategies we recommended under the Education and Professional Experience sections earlier in this chapter:

1) It is okay to omit years of graduation from your degrees—provided you do so consistently.

2) It is permissible to not tell the *whole* story. Your resume is not a complete autobiography. You do not need to go "all the way back." In some instances you may be asked to complete an employment application/form that does require virtually all employment, so have that information ready. However, at the point in the process that this may become necessary, you are usually through all of the gates.

Problem #2…I never completed my degree, although I did attend college for a few years. How do you recommend handling this on the resume?

*Solution…*Our number-one solution is never to lie on your resume; don't give in to the temptation to turn your college studies into a college degree. In the first place, it's unethical; in the second place, it can be cause for immediate dismissal if it is ever found out (and it's extremely easy for employers to check); and finally, have the confidence that your expertise, experience, and proven accomplishments are of most interest to employers.

One caveat: If you do not have a degree, you will probably find that executive recruiters are not a viable channel for your career marketing activities. Because they are programmed to fill "specs" that almost universally include a bachelor's degree or, in many cases, an MBA, recruiters will not be inclined to bend the rules for you when they (typically) have so many other candidates. This is not a problem, of course, if you follow our ROI strategies and action plan in Chapter 1.

Here are several different approaches for downplaying lack of a degree on your resume. Consider the following:

Examples…

University of Massachusetts • Amherst, MA
Pursued Bachelor of Science, Business Management (1995–1997)

Connecticut College — New London, Connecticut
- Matriculated in B.S., Accounting
- Completed all but 9 credits toward degree with cumulative GPA of 3.7.

University of California at Berkeley: Completed coursework toward a degree in Sociology

---

Why include this information when you haven't completed a degree? Generally speaking, *some* college is better than *no* college. In fact, you may have a great story to tell about why you never finished your degree. Another factor is resume-scanning software that will be looking for degree details such as B.S. or Bachelor of Science. Including those terms in your education section—while being entirely truthful that you did not earn a degree—may help you get through that gate.

Problem #3…I have never attended college. What's the best way to address "Education" on the resume?

*Solution…*Our recommendation is to omit the Education section altogether—and be prepared to address it in the interview. You might consider providing examples of continuing professional education that you have completed over the years as well as a very brief indication of why you did not go to college conventionally at age 18—perhaps a tremendous work opportunity was offered to you…perhaps financial circumstances did not permit. The key is to make no apology and, instead, demonstrate through wealth of accomplishments and success how this has not impeded your progress.

Problem #4…What's the best way to talk about my work in the community with my temple. I've heard it's not always a good idea to reveal religious background.

*Solution…*While there are exceptions to every rule, it is probably wise for most candidates not to mention specific religious affiliation. Instead, you can simply speak about leadership experience in a general context within the civic section of your resume—*Quarterbacked fundraising project that raised more than $300,000 for a charitable organization in Dayton.*

Caveat: If your faith is an extremely important part of your life—playing a role that helps to define your professional work—then it is appropriate to specifically list actual religious affiliations. Likewise, if you make your living in a field of work that has a religious connection (for instance, a director of development for a large, faith-based organization), it is again appropriate to be specific.

Problem #5…I've been very active in town government for many years. I've held a number of appointed and elected offices—all in my free time and on a volunteer basis—for the past two decades. How do I show this on my resume without offending someone of a different political leaning?

*Solution…*Similar to Problem #4 above (religious background), political ties can be potentially problematic. We generally advise using the generic approach: Elected Chairman of Town Committee, Town of Binghamton, NY—4 years (omitting your specific political party).

*Note…*The same advice as provided for problems #4 and #5 (religious and political affiliations) would hold true for any memberships in what might potentially be construed as controversial organizations—such as the NRA, Planned Parenthood, Gay & Lesbian Alliance Against Defamation, and so forth. In fact, we generally recommend omitting such memberships altogether. In general, while it may be an important cause to you, the affiliation is typically not germane to your job search and you don't want readers becoming overly hung up on such details.

Problem #6…I've moved around quite a bit, especially over the past seven or eight years. How do I deal with this on the resume so that I don't look like a job-hopper?

*Solution...*We recommend showing years only (and not months) on your resume; this approach can reduce the job-hopper perception. If a position was very short-term and relatively unimportant, feel free to omit it entirely. And finally, it is not necessarily considered a negative for you to have moved around a lot. As we recommended earlier in this chapter, include context in your job descriptions…were you recruited to a specific role based on prior career successes? Did a former boss leave to start a new company and take you along? You can send the message that you have been constantly in demand rather than signaling that you "couldn't hold a job."

Problem #7…I made a career change several years ago, but ended up being recruited back to my original company. How do I show this on the resume?

*Solution...*You have two options. One is to show each position in the usual chronological order. Another is to combine the two stints in one employment section, showing both sets of dates. Your content should emphasize the more recent role and accomplishments with perhaps a brief bullet or two at the end of the segment to address any noteworthy accomplishments from the prior tenure. Here's an example:

XYGen Systems, San Diego, CA *($75M solar-energy technology company)*

Senior Vice President, Sales, 2018–Present
Senior Sales Manager, 2010–2014

Recruited to return to XYGen in 2018 to rejuvenate entire national sales division…

Problem #8…Following a meteoric rise to power with a Fortune 100 company over a 20-year period, I was terminated with a severance package following a takeover. Despite serious attempts to secure a similar level position with another top company, I was unsuccessful after 18 months—and now I am the store manager of a Staples. How do I handle this?

*Solution...*Our recommendation is to be open and candid, citing every accomplishment and how you've leveraged your experience in this new opportunity. Take nothing for granted. If you put in place a new staffing model, reduced absenteeism, boosted productivity, be sure to highlight it. There's no shame in honest, gainful employment, and for any number of reasons people (even senior-level executives) have taken positions at lower levels and with less compensation.

Another approach might be to omit this position altogether, provided it does not leave too much of a gap. If you are currently a clerk at Home Depot, for example, it could be more detrimental to add this to your resume than to show a year or so unemployment. Or, if you want to list the employment to cover all gaps, be as brief as possible rather than trying to make a truly stop-gap job into a significant career experience.

Problem #9…I was caught in industry-wide cutbacks nearly two years ago. I searched diligently, but was unsuccessful finding anything remotely appropriate. So I've gone into commissioned sales. While I have achieved some good successes, this is not what I want to be doing. How do I reflect this on the resume?

*Solution...*As with problem #8, lead with your strengths in this role. A strategically written cover letter will best address the timeline and decisions you've made. And as much as possible, emphasize any strategic activities and company-wide contributions during your sales role.

Problem #10…I've been out of work now for more than a year and a half. I know that putting the title "consultant" on a resume is a quick giveaway to unemployment, but the fact is, I have been doing some consulting for pay, though certainly not on a full-time basis. What do you recommend?

Solution…Provided that it is accurate and that you have been working in some capacity as a consultant (whether for pay or not), it is fine to reflect this on your resume. It shows initiative that, while seeking a permanent post, you applied significant skill and knowledge to helping other organizations build, turn around faltering performance, and so forth. Be sure to highlight specific engagements and success stories and do mention types of industries and problem scenarios faced. The fact that this work has been part-time or unpaid is not relevant, so don't mention it.

Problem #11…How should I handle confidentiality when it comes to presenting numbers that are proprietary?

Solution…This is actually a common scenario. You may have an incredible success story to tell about turning around a division or a company, but you need numbers for credibility. The problem? The company is privately held and this information is proprietary; you can't reveal the numbers.

One approach is to use percentages to reflect change and success, as in these two bullet points:

> • Generated 10% annual revenue growth while industry as a whole declined at least 5% per year.
> • Grew market share 50%, boosting customer base through innovative product development, a pioneering customer-care hotline, and new customer support centers.

Another option would be to illustrate performance using a graph—without including the specific numbers. Here's a powerful example of results that doesn't reveal confidential company information:

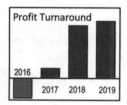

Problem #12…The sudden death of my spouse required me to re-prioritize, taking time off to handle the estate and care for our young children. Frankly, I needed some time, too, to get things clear in my head. Before my performance was affected, I decided that a resignation was the best way to proceed (rather than take advantage of family leave time). Now, eight months later, I am ready to go back to work on a full-time basis for a new company. How do I address this?

Solution…This is best addressed in a conversation; however, for the gap on the resume, it is appropriate to address the timeline openly and honestly. It is also important to convey—especially to a recruiter—that you have worked through the grieving process (difficult, we know) and are fully ready to bring your talents and broad expertise to bear for the right organization. A very positive outlook and approach is required; despite the tragedy you've experienced, you want to demonstrate strength and not appear to be desirous of any sympathies outwardly expressed (a simple "thank you" and move on).

For your resume, consider:

Family Care Sabbatical   10/2019–6/2020
- Since 5/2020, have been actively seeking appropriate executive opportunities.
- From 10/2019–4/2020, handled family matters.

Of course, if the gap is barely noticeable, you might prefer simply to omit any mention from your resume. But do be prepared to respond to the question, "What have you been doing since you left your last job?"

Problem #13…My name is gender-neutral. This sometimes leads to confusion and even awkwardness in telephone calls and interviews. What do you recommend?

Solution…This can certainly go both ways, for both genders. It can also be a problem for people with foreign-sounding names whose pronunciation as well as gender is not readily apparent. Here are some strategies you might consider:

- For names such as Tracy, Dana, and Sandy that could be used for both men and women, a common strategy is to spell out the middle name in the contact line (Dana Joseph Bisceglia).

- For names that do clearly denote gender but are sometimes confused (for instance, Frances for the female gender and Francis for the male gender), the same approach can be considered (Frances Anne Capella). If Francis prefers to be addressed as Frank, the resume contact line can read Francis "Frank" E. Donovan.

- For foreign-sounding or unusually spelled names, consider adding a nickname if appropriate (Nadezhda "Nadia" Gurov) or a phonetic equivalent (Thanh [Tom] Nguyen). If you are most comfortable with your nickname, feel free to use it in place of your given name (Tom Nguyen).

Problem #14…For several decades I have used as my first name a nickname by which everyone in business knows me. There is no connection whatsoever to my given name. What's the best strategy for ensuring clarity?

Solution…For those who use a nickname in virtually all business dealings completely unrelated to their given name (for instance, Julian Hummell Knox is widely known as Bill), the contact information on the resume can read Julian "Bill" H. Knox.

Problem #15…I've changed my name [and my gender]. Should I include both present and past names on my resume?

Solution…Your resume is a first introduction, not a detailed life history. Whether you are recently married, recently divorced, have transitioned to a different gender, or taken on a new name for any other reason, we suggest that you use only your current name on the resume. At the point when you are asked to provide references or granting permission for a background check, you should indicate any prior names you have used.

Problem #16…A major company I worked with for a number of years (and produced well for) is no longer in existence. How do I handle this on my resume?

Solution… If the company was well-known, as "major" would suggest, it is not necessary to indicate that the company no longer conducts business. If responsibilities ultimately included disposing of assets, you can reflect this in a bullet point (usually one of the last points in the section on this position, possibly ending with "Company ceased operations in 2012").

Problem #17…A company I worked for in the past has changed its name (once, twice…). How should I address this?

Solution… Generally we recommend listing both current and prior company names on your resume—for example:

> FORTERRA (formerly Hanson Building Materials…merged with X-Con Products to form Forterra in 2019)

However, if the name change occurred some years ago and the new name is well established, it's not necessary to explain; you can simply use the current well-known name.

Final Thoughts on Your Resume Content…

Keep the Big Picture in Mind

No matter your specific circumstances or unique challenges, keep the following points in the forefront when preparing your resume. They will help you to make good decisions about how (or whether) to position specific items within your document.

- **Your resume is a marketing piece,** *not* an autobiography. Your objective is to entice the reader into calling you for more information (an interview), not to share every detail about yourself and your career.

- **Your resume must clearly communicate your career focus** and paint a strong, compelling picture of a top-flight executive. Omit or downplay information that does not support your current objectives or might create a negative first impression.

- **Your resume must convey your value in the career marketplace**—the ROI you have delivered to past employers and the value you promise to your future employer. When deciding what information to include, always choose value-packed statements and quantified results over less-relevant details or generic "job duties" that could be written by anyone else who has held similar jobs.

- **Your resume must resonate with your executive brand and your "authentic self."** All of the material in the resume must be congruent, and you must be able to support the resume with relevant stories, examples, and amplifications at every stage of your job search.

Polish Your Draft

Now that you've drafted the content of your resume, it's time to review, edit, proofread, and polish it into a top-quality document.

PRO TIP: Save your draft. Before you start editing, use the "save-as" function to create a new file. You can then cut and edit to your heart's content without losing details from the original file.

Your comprehensive, rough-draft resume can be useful when filling out job applications that require specific dates and other details. It can help you refresh your memory before interviews. And it can be source material for additional documents—such as publication or presentation lists, executive leadership briefs, or 30-60-90-day plans—that you might want to share with recruiters or employers at some stage during the hiring process.

Resumes have certainly evolved from the dry CV format of several decades ago, but one thing that hasn't changed is the need for your resume to be error-free. The only way to ensure that your resume contains no mistakes is for you to proofread and fact check—multiple times.

Have a trusted friend or two read it critically and "red-pen" any questions or errors they see. As you review your bullet points, think about how you would expand on each briefly stated accomplishment. Are all the numbers and results accurate and consistent with the stories you'll tell?

Next, assess your resume for readability. Consider font size (neither too large nor too small), white space, and overall appearance of each page. The resume should look professional and be appropriately formatted for an executive appearance. There are no hard and fast rules about format, but the examples in Chapter 6 will give you some good ideas. Most executive resumes will fit nicely on two or possibly three pages.

Design Your Resume

What used to be verboten is now commonplace! That's as true in resume design as in many other areas of business and culture.

One of the changes that we, as professional resume writers, find most exciting is the growing acceptance of color, graphics, and other design elements—even in executive resumes. We do want your resume to exude good taste and professionalism. But we also want it to project a fresh, modern appearance and avoid appearing stodgy and outdated.

Following are some guidelines for spicing up your resume design with color and graphics.

- A standout design cannot overcome poorly written content. Focus first on your content, then determine how best to enhance it.

- Colored borders and shading are easy to add and create a distinctive look while still exuding professionalism and maintaining an executive look and feel. We generally recommend conservative colors (blue, green, gray) and occasional use of brighter colors such as red, gold, or orange. Although you can't see them in this black-and-white book, nearly all of the resume samples contain some color elements.

- If you choose to use graphics, make sure that they support and enhance your prime message and don't distract from it.

- Graphs and charts are powerful tools used in most business presentations, so why not in your resume?

- Avoid creating an appearance that is too busy, cluttered, or amateurish-looking. Err on the side of doing *less* rather than too much.

- Graphics are attention-getting, so make sure that yours are calling attention to your most impressive career information.

Create Your Final Formats

All of the resumes in this book were created using Microsoft Word—still the standard for business documents. We recommend that you do the same, as this will be the most useful document throughout your search and can be easily edited or customized for specific opportunities.

When emailing or uploading your resume, you can send the Word file or—even better—a PDF, which is more stable than a Word document. Just be certain to follow instructions so that you are sending or uploading the preferred format.

For interviews and in-person meetings, print your resume on high-quality paper in an "executive" color (white, off-white, or gray). Use the same paper for all of your career marketing documents. Visit the stationery/resume paper section of your local office supply store and choose the one that you like best, or visit an online stationery retailer such as Crane & Company (crane.com)—their pearl white, 32-lb. paper is a personal favorite.

As we've discussed, your chronological resume—even with color and graphics—should be perfectly readable by most resume-scanning software. But if for some reason you have an unusual structure or highly designed format, you should also prepare a stripped-down version for uploading. If your content can't be read by the ATS (applicant tracking system), you may never make it past the first step in the process.

Your Resume Is Just the Beginning

Congratulations! You've completed your resume—the traditional document for career transition. Following our guidelines, you've created a value-packed, fairly concise summary of your career experiences and achievements. You'll find it to be a truly essential document for many of your activities during the weeks and months of your job search.

In the next two chapters, we share strategies and examples of additional career documents, starting with your LinkedIn profile and continuing through letters, leadership addenda, executive bios, and more. Combined with your resume, these documents will prepare you for many different scenarios and stages of an executive search and will give you a true competitive edge.

CHAPTER 4
Your LinkedIn Profile

Which is more important…your resume or your LinkedIn profile?

We believe that they are equally essential in establishing your executive presence and positioning you for your next career opportunity.

The resume, of course, is the traditional job-search document, a necessary part of just about every application process and an invaluable networking tool. In Chapter 3, we walked you through the process of creating a resume that clearly communicates your unique value. But before you begin the active phase of your job search by circulating that resume, make certain that your online image is equally powerful, positive, and aligned with your current career goals.

With your new resume—your foundational document—in hand, along with the exercises you completed in Chapter 2, you have everything you need to build a LinkedIn profile. This chapter guides you through it.

> **PRO TIP: LinkedIn is constantly changing,** adding new features and updating others. So don't be surprised if what you find differs just a bit from what we've described in this chapter. What won't change, we are confident, is the importance of your *content*, the need to build a complete profile, and the usefulness of LinkedIn in managing your search.
>
> In Chapter 1 we described the incredible value that LinkedIn brings to your targeted, networking-based search process. In this chapter we guide you through building your content. Don't be concerned if a few details are different—the essential purpose and value of LinkedIn remain the same.

Before we begin, let's address a few fundamental questions about LinkedIn.

LinkedIn FAQs

What is LinkedIn and why is it important?
LinkedIn is the premier online social network with a professional focus. For executives in career transition, it offers immense value. LinkedIn's size, diversity, and many features mean that it can function as your:

- **Contact database.** You will undoubtedly choose to maintain your own private directory of contacts, but LinkedIn offers multiple means for getting in touch with people you know. It can also help you track down individuals you've lost touch with—people who could be instrumental in helping you find your next opportunity.

- **Personal website.** As you work through the sections in this chapter, you'll see our recommendations for creating a rich collection of content on LinkedIn that starts with your profile but doesn't end there.

- **Top-ranked search result.** Unless you have a robust public image (and perhaps even if you do), it's likely that your LinkedIn profile will be at the top of the list of "hits" when individuals search for you online. And because you control the content on your LinkedIn page, you can make sure that this easily found source says exactly what you would like it to say.

- **Network-building tool.** In Chapter 1, we discussed the importance of securing referrals into your target companies. LinkedIn makes it easy to go beyond your known contacts to find connections at those companies.

How does LinkedIn differ from a resume?
Some people, it's true, simply paste content from their resume into the relevant sections on LinkedIn. Certainly that's better than nothing. But we believe they're missing an opportunity to provide more comprehensive, meaningful, and insightful information to people who visit on LinkedIn.

Consider when and why people look you up online. They might have seen your resume or met you at a networking event. Perhaps you got together for coffee. Maybe you were referred to them by one of your contacts. They're curious, and they want to know more. If your profile simply rehashes your resume, those visitors haven't learned anything new about you, and that would be a shame.

LinkedIn lets you go beyond the resume. You can talk about what you love to do—what drives you in your work. You can give readers your "origin story"—how you got where you are today. You might mention your family or how you spend leisure time. Above all, you can connect your personal attributes to your professional skills so that readers understand the intangibles that you bring to work every day.

Bottom line: A well-written LinkedIn profile paints a personal, in-depth portrait that will further distinguish you from every other candidate and help you find opportunities that are the right fit.

LinkedIn is encouraging me to upload my resume to complete my profile. Should I?
As we advised in Chapter 1, you should *not* upload your resume as part of your profile—despite LinkedIn's admonishment to "get to 100% by uploading a resume." For many reasons you want to quickly shift the conversation offline for a deeper and more personal connection. You can provide your resume—customized if need be—based on the contact.

I'm worried that if I update my profile, my colleagues (even my boss!) will notice and assume that I'm job hunting. I'd rather not call it to their attention.
Before beginning your update, adjust your settings so that your network is not notified of changes. To do this, go to "Me," choose "Settings and Privacy," and scroll down to "Share job changes, education changes, and work anniversaries from profile." Set control to "off." You can switch it back on later if you like, once you've completed your update.

While you're in the Privacy settings, scroll up to "Microsoft Word" and disable the "Resume Assistant" feature. Otherwise, other LinkedIn users can capture language from your profile to write their own.

Draft Your LinkedIn Profile

You will need to write content for three primary sections of your profile: Headline, About (summary), and Experience.

Headline: The headline appears just below your name at the top of your profile. As a default, LinkedIn will insert your most recent job title (pulled from your Experience section). But you can change that—and we think you should. Here's why:

- Headline content ranks high in keyword searches.
- A unique headline will distinguish you from others with similar or identical job titles.
- The recruiter version of LinkedIn (a very powerful tool with expanded search capabilities, used by thousands of search firms) presents an abbreviated snapshot of the profile when a match is found. The headline and first few lines of your About section are part of that snapshot, so you want it to be as relevant and compelling as possible.

We recommend a headline that conveys your unique value while also clearly communicating career context details such as function/level/industry. And, oh yes…do all of that within 220 characters. (After being limited to 120 characters for many years, LinkedIn increased this count to 220 in 2020.)

The character limit, which includes all spaces and punctuation, can certainly be limiting. But why not embrace the challenge! It can be fun to play around with different options that get your message across within that tight allocation.

In crafting your headline, always think of your target audience. What few key facts do you want them to retain from a brief scan? We, just like you, are challenged with the need to be concise, specific, and tuned in to the needs of our audience. Here is what we came up with:

> Jan Melnik, M.A., MRW, CCM, CPRW
> Career Strategist & C-Level Resume Writer | Job-Search/Interview/LinkedIn Coach | Keynote Speaker | Let's Target the Role of Your Dreams!

> Louise Kursmark
> Career Storyteller | Master Resume Writer | Interview Coach | Partnering with Senior Executives to help you land your next great opportunity

Just like a traditional newspaper headline, your LinkedIn headline is designed to draw readers to the main article (your profile below). It should be clear, specific, and interesting enough to pique their interest and make them want to read more. Here are a few examples from senior executive job seekers.

Examples:

> Director/VP Facilities, Maintenance & Construction—Delivering superior results and high ROI: "Whatever it takes."

Senior Executive, Financial Services and Investment Advisory: Building business by building relationships

CEO/COO | Aerospace Executive—Aftermarket and OEM | Business Development and Operations Optimization | Board Leadership

Hands-on Operations Executive—A solid hand at the tiller, steering early-stage and entrepreneurial companies to success

PRO TIP: Write several headline options for yourself. When working with clients, we typically provide two or three different headlines for consideration. Each one might focus on a slightly different point that we're trying to get across...perhaps industry expertise, blue-chip employer names, leadership style, or a major achievement. The character limit forces us to focus on just a few tightly written terms or phrases.

After you've written several potential headlines, go back and review them all. You might find that you pull something from one option, something from another, and create an entirely new headline that gets the key message across and feels right.

Once you've completed your headline, here are two additional changes you should make to transform the default LinkedIn page into a personal, customized profile.

1. **Include a photo.** Profiles without a headshot appear somewhat anonymous and might even be perceived as sketchy. A photograph instantly customizes your profile and establishes a personal, friendly tone.

    Your photo should be a headshot, full face (so that your face takes up most of the space in the frame), with a pleasant and professional expression. (Smile!) It does not have to be a professionally taken, formal headshot, but do experiment with several different photos so that your selection is clear, has good lighting, and does not have any distracting details or backgrounds.

2. **Add a custom banner/background.** While not required, a custom background will create an individualized appearance for your profile. Choose something that links to your professional expertise or your executive brand. Here are a few examples of background photos that accompany some LinkedIn sites we've seen:

    - Digital strategy expert—well-designed banner stating "Make Digital Real"
    - Blockchain/IT consultant—logo of his consulting business
    - Commercial development executive—cityscape
    - Multiple people in different professions—beautiful nature shots that likely represent a view that has personal meaning for them

About: This first section of your profile allows you just under 2,600 characters to tell an engaging story about yourself, your qualifications and experience, and your value to your next employer. Because LinkedIn is a social/professional network and not a resume, we recommend that you write the About section in a narrative format, sharing interesting details about yourself and a few success highlights from your career.

Here are a few guidelines for writing the About section:

- Write in first person using "I."
- Use short paragraphs so the page has ample white space—essential for online reading.
- Strike a conversational tone and avoid "resume language" and resume structure, for the most part. (It's fine to include bullet points, use subheadings to organize and differentiate content, and briefly list key achievements.)
- Use storytelling techniques for a personal tone, to spark interest, and to share different content than what's in your resume.
- Don't be afraid to express emotion, using words like "love," "passionate about," or "excited," injecting a bit of humor, or occasionally sprinkling in an exclamation point!

Do keep in mind, however, your primary purpose in creating this online profile: to enhance your professional image, attract inquiries from recruiters, build your network, and advance your career. Your profile and your career story should perfectly align with your current professional goals. As you are deciding what to include, think about the attributes, experiences, and accomplishments that are your greatest assets. The stories and details you share should reveal those assets and not distract with extraneous information.

For example, if you are a sales executive, you might mention that you have been a top sales performer since third grade, when you set a new record for sales of Girl Scout cookies. The business you started from your dorm room could reveal a longtime entrepreneurial bent. A challenge you faced in managing people early in your career could be the springboard for your present-day leadership style. Your stories need to serve your purpose, revealing insights and information that are relevant in your current situation.

As you are writing, ask yourself these questions to be certain that your About section is on point and not simply a storytelling exercise:

- Have I clearly conveyed my professional expertise?
- Have I mentioned my most notable and relevant career achievements?
- Do stories reveal traits that are intrinsic to my professional success?
- Does it relate my talents to the challenges and environment that I'm seeking in my next job?
- Does it show how I solve problems that are relevant to my target audience (top executives, board directors, VC/PE firms, recruiters)?
- Does it feel authentic to who I am?

In Chapter 6, you will see LinkedIn samples that show a variety of styles and structures for creating the About section. There is no formula. Experiment to create content that feels genuine, a structure that highlights information that will be meaningful to your audience, and details that reveal the assets you bring to your job.

PRO TIP: Use discretion in revealing numbers on LinkedIn. Numbers that you are comfortable sharing in a resume or interview may not be appropriate to announce on the public platform that is LinkedIn. Even if you set tight privacy settings, your first-degree contacts and most recruiters will be able to see your entire profile.

If you've worked for privately held companies...if you don't want to reveal the depths of corporate losses...if market-share numbers are closely held...in all of these instances and more, think of ways to describe your successes without revealing actual dollar amounts or other sensitive content. You might use percentages, or choose a round number ("more than $xx"), or use adjectives such as "best" or "worst" to describe an accomplishment.

Experience: The Experience section of your profile is similar to the chronological experience in your resume. Here you will detail each of your jobs, showing scope, challenges, and achievements. Many people—including professional resume writers—struggle with how to make this part of your profile different from the resume. In addition to using a more conversational/narrative writing style (yes, it is okay and encouraged to use the pronoun "I"), we think the secret lies in the strategy and structure that you create for your experience.

In your resume, quite likely you've followed the tried-and-true structure of first describing job scope/challenge, followed by bullet-point achievements. Here in your LinkedIn profile, change things up. Here are a few different approaches you might try:

- Lead off with a short list of notable achievements, followed by a narrative that fills in the details.

- Explain the scene that existed when you took the job—get into a bit of detail about the challenges and obstacles before describing (perhaps in paragraph form rather than bullets) how you resolved them.

- Tell a single "signature" story about each job rather than the broader overview you give in your resume.

- Include, at the bottom or top of each job description, a list of keywords to cover the ground of what your job entailed without having to detail multiple projects and programs.

- Use consistent headings for each job description…for example, CHALLENGE or OPPORTUNITY (followed by a brief scene-setting story), ACTIONS AND RESULTS (followed by bullets or paragraphs describing your key achievements), and IMPACT (a big-picture view of your contributions).

- Consider less "resume-like" headings to reveal personal traits and emotions—for example, WHAT I'M PROUDEST OF or WHAT I DO AND WHY I DO IT.

The CAR stories and other materials you developed in Chapter 2 are an outstanding resource for creating a distinctive experience section in your LinkedIn profile. You can write in a more leisurely fashion than in your resume and reveal more of the story—but do be careful not to present big blocks of text. As prescribed for your About section, keep your paragraphs short to allow ample white space so that readers can absorb each thought before moving on to the next. Consider adding carefully curated images, clips from trade publications, YouTube links, and other media (more below under "Supplemental Material").

The LinkedIn profiles we share in Chapter 6 show a variety of effective ways for writing Experience sections, as well as Headlines and About sections. Use them for inspiration and ideas.

Add to Your Profile Content

As you move through building your LinkedIn profile, you will be prompted to fill out each section and add new sections as appropriate. As a general rule, it is wise to make your profile as complete and comprehensive as possible. The following guidelines will help you move confidently through the process.

Education: To add your educational credentials, begin typing the name of your college or university and choose the correct match (if available) from the drop-down menu. If appropriate, you should also include the specific school within the university that you attended. For example, "University of Pennsylvania" may be your main entry; "The Wharton School" should also be included if you studied there.

You can and should also list schools where you took classes but did not earn a degree. For example, if you took an executive workshop at Stanford or an innovation seminar at MIT, be certain to list it.

It is not necessary to include dates of attendance or graduation year. Use the same strategy that you used in your resume—disguise your precise age if that is a concern for you, or avoid questions regarding a gap between education and employment history. Otherwise, include dates.

If relevant, feel free to include details of a dissertation, capstone project, or other major educational achievement, even if you did not mention it in your resume.

Licenses and Certifications: If you have earned any pertinent credentials other than your college degree(s), include them in this category.

Volunteer Experience: This section is a great place to showcase your involvement in causes you believe in and organizations you support. As with many of the "extras" in your profile, it can create a connection, spark a conversation, and reveal insights about who you are as a person.

List your volunteer experience in a similar fashion to your work experience, showing title/role, name of organization, dates of involvement, and any major accomplishments or relevant activities.

Skills and Endorsements: You may select up to 50 skills to be included on your profile. We suggest that you add as many as are relevant—the quantity and variety of skills is a factor in keyword searches. Your skills will be endorsed by your contacts, and the top three (having earned the most endorsements) will be visible at first glance. Readers will have to click to "see more."

We recommend that you visit your page periodically, view your top three skills, and rearrange them if needed so that they represent what *you* consider to be the most relevant to your career objectives.

Recommendations: Recommendations must be created by others—you cannot add them to your profile yourself. These third-party endorsements are extremely valuable in validating your expertise and providing insights into your personal brand. We suggest that you ask several close colleagues, prior bosses or direct reports, and others in your network to write recommendations for you, if they haven't done so already.

Strive to capture four to ten endorsements. Ideally, at least one or two should be from people you worked with quite recently so as to reflect the most senior level of your career.

As with your skills, you can rearrange your recommendations so that the top two that are visible are the most relevant and impressive.

Accomplishments: This catch-all section on LinkedIn includes eight different categories that you can populate to enrich your profile:

- *Projects:* For the most part, you will include significant projects in the experience section. However, if you have completed an important or impressive project, perhaps on a volunteer basis or outside the scope of your regular work, feel free to include it here. It could be a nice differentiator, a further enhancement of your personal brand, or an interesting conversation topic.

- *Patents:* Include any that you have earned. Even if they are not entirely relevant to your current career goals, patents are prestigious and demonstrate innovation and rigor.

- *Honors & Awards:* Be sure to showcase any special recognition that you have received. If it is not a well-known award, feel free to elaborate just a bit to describe the circumstances or criteria.

- *Publications:* Authorship indicates expertise, so you should provide the details of any books, book chapters, white papers, professional treatises, or other publications that you have written or co-written. If you publish a personal or professional blog, you may mention it here and provide a link.

- *Organizations:* In addition to your professional organizations, you might add any volunteer associations you've been affiliated with—unless, of course, you have created a separate "Volunteer Experience" section, as described above. If that's the case, no need to repeat here.

- *Courses* and *Test Scores:* For most executives, these two categories are not relevant. Keep any prestigious coursework within the Education section, as mentioned above, and don't include test scores, no matter how stellar!

- *Languages:* Do include your language proficiency—and don't think you must be fully fluent to list a language. It's fine to indicate "basic Spanish" or even get a bit more descriptive—"learned conversational Japanese for business/social occasions."

Interests: The "Influencers," "Companies," "Groups," and "Schools" that you are following are important because they open you to new connections, ideas, and opinions. Posts from these "Interests" will populate your daily LinkedIn feed. "Groups" may give you opportunities to connect with like-minded professionals and position yourself as a thought leader.

We suggest that you branch out beyond the companies you've worked for. Add influencers whose work or image you admire; add your target companies; and join groups that represent your professional interests. All of this activity will make your profile more vibrant and relevant—and more searchable.

LinkedIn Profile: Supplemental Material

Now that we've covered the fundamentals of your LinkedIn profile, let's go a bit deeper and consider two ways that LinkedIn allows you to enhance your profile with extra material.

Featured allows you to pin posts, articles, photographs, links, or media (such as video) to the top of your profile, immediately below the *About* section. If you view our profiles, for example, you'll see that Jan has included more than a dozen photographs of presentations she's delivered to job seekers and career professionals (linkedin.com/in/janmelnik). Louise has included a video bio—a self-introduction (linkedin.com/in/louisekursmark). These "featured" items remain permanently at the top of the profile.

Because video is such a powerful medium, we recommend that you add a video clip to your profile if at all possible. It does not have to be a professionally produced video, but it should show you at your professional best and add to your credibility.

Activity: Here you can post updates and publish articles. If you comment on another post, that post will appear in this section as well. We recommend that you maintain steady involvement on LinkedIn so that a fresh "activity" will appear at least once a week.

As mentioned above, the "Interests" that you've selected will influence your daily feed, often providing excellent articles and opportunities for you to comment and share with your own network—thereby increasing your "activity" and building your visibility and influence.

> **PRO TIP: No need to redesign your profile for phone viewing.** A few years ago, LinkedIn very wisely adjusted the site so that the desktop/laptop view is substantially similar to the way a profile is seen on a tablet computer or smartphone. The only difference is that the smaller screen truncates some of the material. For example, on a desktop or laptop, two third-party endorsements are visible; on a tablet or phone, just one.
>
> At the same time, LinkedIn expanded its use of the "see more" feature, wherein brief content is shown and a link provided for those who want more details. What this means is that you should write your content for both audiences: those who want a quick overview and those who will spend the time to delve a bit more deeply. With your two audiences in mind, take a critical look at your completed profile from both laptop and phone views and see if you can (1) improve comprehension for your quick readers and (2) provide more detail for those who want to "see more."

Ready, Set, Go!

Now that you've completed your LinkedIn profile and your executive resume, you are ready to jump into a targeted job search, using the accelerated four-week plan that we detailed in Chapter 1. As you do, you will find valuable materials in Chapter 5 (*Additional ROI Documents*) to augment your core resume and LinkedIn profile—guidelines and examples for writing cover letters and email messages, scripting for that all-important elevator pitch, additional resume versions and addenda, and much more.

We know that the process can feel overwhelming, but if you proceed one step at a time, and dip into this book as needed for guidance, examples, and inspiration, we are confident you will master the "job-search dance" and quickly uncover new opportunities.

CHAPTER 5
Additional ROI Documents

While the Executive Resume and LinkedIn profile are the core elements of your career-search plan, you'll want to give careful consideration to some additional strategic tools. Several will be absolutely necessary. Others, while optional, may provide significant value in your search.

Here are the recommended add-on tools senior-level executives find most useful in their career transition:

- Cover letters (traditional and email)
- Email messages
- LinkedIn messages (invitations to connect, introductions)
- Networking card
- "Elevator" pitches
- Networking scripts
- Executive leadership brief
- One-page executive resume
- Board resume
- Professional biography
- Detailed "mulligan" thank-you letters (post-interview)
- 30-60-90-day plans (or Q1/Q2/Q3/Q4 Plans)

In this chapter, we'll explore each of these tools and provide examples you can pattern in your own messaging.

Cover Letters

Almost no search can be conducted effectively without a cover letter. Optimally, a cover letter is uniquely created for each opportunity. Practically speaking, provided that your search is for similar positions in the same or a related industry, a well-developed cover letter should serve you well for most communications with just minor revisions to customize it for the audience and the specific opportunity, if any.

Generally speaking, your cover letter should be one page in length and include these components:

1) *Opening*—your reason for writing, referral or source, and a clear link to the opportunity

2) *Body*—the strongest section of your letter—a few paragraphs, or paragraphs plus bullet points, clearly demonstrating your fit with the opportunity at hand, matching your proven skills and attributes to the desired traits, and highlighting the key distinguishing characteristics of your career

3)   *Closing*—a compelling closing paragraph that includes the classic "call to action," spelling out steps you'll take next and providing important contact and follow-up details

An alternative approach to the "body" component is to create a T-brief format—a bit dated, but still an effective technique for replying to specific openings. In this format, a two-column list shows hiring needs and challenges on the left, with your relevant strengths and experience on the right. For each qualification listed, you should show specifically how you meet that requirement—or, better still, how you exceed it.

Today, most of your cover letters will be transmitted electronically—as an email message, an attached document, or an uploaded document. Regardless of the way it is sent, the content can be similar and the purpose remains the same: to capture attention, invite readers to learn more about you, and prompt some action—a referral, a conversation, an in-person meeting, an interview.

However, the tone, length, and detail of each letter will differ according to the audience and the circumstances, which will vary widely throughout your search. Consider these very common circumstances:

- A cold letter to a recruiter without knowledge of a specific opportunity…or to a hiring manager, again without a specific opportunity
- An application letter to a recruiter who has posted a relevant position
- A response to a posting on an employer website or aggregate job board such as Indeed, Glassdoor, or LinkedIn
- An exploratory letter to a company
- A letter for your contacts to share when forwarding your resume

Let's look at each of these scenarios, the similarities and differences in how to write and format each letter, and additional guidelines pertinent to the situation and the audience. In addition to the sample letter(s) that we provide for each scenario, you will find a diverse collection of additional letters in the portfolios in Chapter 6.

Cover Letter to Recruiter without Knowledge of Any Opening

Format: Email, with letter comprising the body of the email message

Guidelines:

- Clearly identify "who you are" in your opening and/or the subject line of your email. Recruiters will not take the time to read your message unless you spark an immediate interest—in this case, when you identify that you fit the profile of the candidates that this recruiter typically sources.

- Strive for a "wow" effect by including a few impressive achievements that would be considered valuable for your ideal next position.

- Briefly summarize your career history, areas of specific knowledge and expertise, and leadership attributes that have contributed to your success.

- Provide details and parameters regarding the types of roles you are most interested in, geographic preferences or restrictions, relocation availability, and other relevant factors.

- Consider including a target salary range—again, to provide context so that the recruiter considers you for appropriate opportunities.

Example: Sam Lee Letter, page 86

Cover Letter to Hiring Manager without Knowledge of Any Opening

Format: Email, with letter comprising the body of the email message—OR—traditionally formatted letter sent by US mail if you have been unable to determine the recipient's email address (Often you can find that information in LinkedIn's "contact" section.)

Guidelines:

- Follow guidelines for Recruiter letter, above, but omit details regarding geography and other preferences or restrictions.

- Do *not* provide a salary range, salary requirements, or any other compensation details.

Example: Sarah Marie Rodriguez Letter, page 87

Cover Letter to a Recruiter for a Specific Opportunity

Format: Email, with letter comprising the body of the email message—OR—traditionally formatted letter uploaded to the recruiting firm website

Guidelines:

- Use the subject line and/or your opening sentence to clearly identify why you are writing—the particular opportunity to which you are responding.

- Carefully align the content of your letter to the requirements of the position—highlight the specific experiences, skills, knowledge, and attributes you have that the employer is seeking.

- If the job posting requests compensation information, you should provide it. We suggest providing a range, not an absolute salary or compensation number.

Example: Stan Nakajima Letter, page 88

> **PRO TIP: Always include a cover letter—even if the upload site does not specifically allow for it.** If you are uploading your resume on a recruiter or employer website in response to a posted opening, carefully follow directions regarding the preferred file type and other details.
>
> In some cases, you won't see an option for uploading a separate cover letter. Rather than omitting this clarifying and distinguishing document, we recommend that you combine it with your resume file, adding an extra page at the front.
>
> And, of course, as described in Chapter 1, we highly recommend that you go beyond simply responding to an ad. When you can identify the employer, try to find a connection who can refer you to the hiring manager or other individual at the company. Remember—when you are a recommended candidate, you are practically guaranteed the opportunity for an interview. When you are one of hundreds of anonymous responses, you have a minuscule chance of being selected.

Re: C-Level Operations & Supply Chain Executive—Unilever Background, Global Product Launches, Turnarounds

In senior leadership roles with Unilever and a PE-funded global CPG company, I have been the driving force behind business strategies and supply chain innovations that have delivered profit, productivity, and revenue gains for more than 15 years.

A few examples:

▶ **Transformation of The Sterling Group.** In 2 years, we improved productivity 20% at US factories, cut costs by right-sizing global operations, and instilled a new culture of high performance and best practices.

▶ **Reinvention of the global manufacturing/supply network** for Unilever's XO business line. Fueling growth after 4 years of shrinking sales and margins, I then led divestiture of the business to Berkshire Hathaway.

▶ **Supply chain innovation** for Unilever's Walmart account—a $5B business.

▶ **Leadership of a complex, low-cost supply chain** across 40 countries to launch the Dove Men's brand that grew from zero to nearly $1B in 5 years.

At my best when leading organizations and collaborating on teams to create breakthroughs, my expertise positively affects both the top and bottom line by improving cost structure, customer service, and competitiveness while building new partnerships, penetrating new markets, and expanding global footprint.

My goal is a senior-level operations/supply chain role with a mid- to large-size company focused on global growth and innovation. I have lived in Asia and worked in many countries throughout Asia, Europe, and Latin America. I am location flexible.

My resume is attached. I would appreciate the opportunity to speak with you regarding any current search assignments that call for a supply chain expert and decisive leader who will deliver on all directives.

Sincerely,

Sam Lee
>>>>>>>>>>>>>>>
555-321-9876
sam.lee@email.com
LinkedIn.com/in/sam.lee

Dear Mr. Andrews:

I am a well-qualified Vice President of Sales with a track record of consistent achievement of all performance objectives. My purpose in writing is to explore potential career opportunities with Optimum Financial Systems to which I could immediately apply proven skills in building top-performing sales organizations, cultivating key accounts, and building new business.

Sales success is easily measurable: increased dollar volume, added accounts, improved account penetration, consistent base retention. As detailed in my resume (attached), I have been recognized for sales leadership—my teams have always produced numbers that significantly exceed aggressive goals in virtually every sales management position I've held.

To truly assess these accomplishments, however, it is necessary to look *behind* the numbers. And this is what I can immediately bring to OFS. Through a leadership style that emphasizes a professional, persistent, and thorough sales planning approach, an emphasis on consultative selling, and a real talent for mentoring my team in managing key accounts and relationships, I have built the foundation for both *current* and *future* business growth.

I have a reputation for taking initiatives that are successful … and proposing changes that take them to the next level. Managing sales professionals is the work that I love, and my enthusiasm is apparent to all who know me, particularly to my sales staff and our customers.

What I believe sets me apart is my record of developing new business in uncharted territories or untapped market sectors. My energy is unflagging, and the results my teams have been able to achieve speak for themselves. I would value the opportunity to speak with you regarding the value I can bring to OFS. Thank you for your consideration.

Sincerely,
Sarah Marie Rodriguez
633-339-6948 • smrodriguez1@gmail.com

Dear Ms. Hofstaetter:

Having recently completed my fourth sequential success in building companies and creating shareholder value, I am looking to add a fifth.

As CEO and President of Diamond Enterprises, Inc., I led the transformation from 8 years of losses into profits, delivered industry-leading revenue growth, and attained #2 market share in our 2 primary lines of business. Simultaneously, I completed the sale of this "un-saleable" company to a strategic buyer— all in one year.

As Chairman, President, and CEO of American Properties International, I increased enterprise value from $0 to $300 million, in 4 years building API from a debt-burdened company into the largest and most successful in its marketplace.

Previously, I delivered similar successes for both public and private companies in diverse sectors, repeatedly building revenue, improving operations, controlling costs, enhancing cash flow, and creating high-performance cultures.

I am very proud to have executed these transformations with existing management teams who earned, and were paid, full performance bonuses every year since 2012.

The attached performance chart and resume outline my record. If you know of a company or investment group seeking a CEO or board member with my expertise, I would welcome your call.

Sincerely,

Stan Nakajima
StanNakajima@mac.com | 555-334-6678

Cover Letter to an Employer for a Specific Opportunity

Format: Email, with letter comprising the body of the email message—OR—traditionally formatted letter uploaded to the company job site

Guidelines:

- Follow the guidelines for the Recruiter letter, immediately above, but do *not* include compensation information, even if requested.

Example: Padma Agarwal Letter, page 90

> **PRO TIP: Table the compensation question.** We don't recommend that you share your salary history with hiring authorities or state your salary requirements in your cover letter—even if requested in a posting. Reserve discussion until you've created desire, demonstrated your value proposition, and can negotiate from a position of strength—face-to-face.
>
> As we've mentioned above, however, it is acceptable to provide a target range to outside recruiters to help them evaluate your fit for appropriate opportunities.

Exploratory Letter to a Company—No Specific Opportunity

Format: Email, with letter comprising the body of the email message—OR—traditionally formatted letter sent via US mail if you cannot obtain the email address of your recipient

Guidelines:

- If you have been referred, mention the referral source immediately so that your letter will instantly receive a favorable review.

- If you are writing a "cold" letter, clearly state your reason for writing in the opening paragraph.

- Identify specific problems, challenges, and opportunities that you know (or can reasonably assume) the company is facing—and how you can help them solve these problems, surmount these challenges, and seize these opportunities.

- Call out specific aspects of the company that you find appealing. Not only will you connect with your audience, you will show that you have done your homework and that you are writing specifically to *this* individual at *this* company.

- Use an assumed close—assuming that you *will* be granted the opportunity for a conversation—especially if you have been referred.

Example: Casey Simmons Letter, page 91

Re: Head of Customer Experience | Vision & Strategy

"Improving business performance by improving customer experience." This is the approach that I have brought to every challenge as a Customer Experience strategist for some of the world's best-known companies.

The challenges have been diverse, the solutions precise, and the results measurable:

➔ 50% growth in enrollment for FinBank's personal savings product
➔ 35% reduction in call-center volume for Microsoft ($12M savings in first year)
➔ 22% revenue above projections for the first paywall ever installed at Time, Inc.
➔ 130% surge in sign-ups of a specifically targeted market for LinkedIn

Most recently, as SVP Operations and Customer Experience at Artforms, I introduced a formal discipline around customer experience for the first time in the history of this nearly 300-year-old company. Among other results, within one year we increased sales leads 200% and direct-marketing response rates 25%.

In brief, my experience seems to be an excellent fit for your needs. As an executive with 15+ years of customer experience leadership and innovation, I bring a data-driven approach, strong influencing skills, and expertise leading large-scale transformations. By aligning vision with priority-based plans, I build support for change across the organization and instill a customer-centric culture that ensures results are sustainable.

I am very interested in learning more about this role and how my experience may be a fit. May we schedule a call to discuss?

Sincerely,

Padma Agarwal
Padma.Agarwal@mail.com • 555-345-6790 • LinkedIn.com/in/padma-agarwal

Dear Ms. Hampshire:

At the suggestion of John McAvoy, I am contacting you regarding leadership positions at PlanForms. John thought you would be interested in my record of implementing lean manufacturing and continuous improvement practices in fully integrated production businesses.

Improving results and executing to plan in highly competitive markets is what I do best. As a champion of lean/Kaizen principles, I have turned a traditional money-losing production business at publicly traded National Pallets to a modest gainer in one year by eliminating waste, reducing operating expense, increasing market share, and improving customer satisfaction. For example —

>> Improved revenue per employee 27% and reached profitability.
>> Implemented master scheduling and boosted on-time delivery 14%.
>> Created "flat" operating structure and eliminated 3 levels of indirect hierarchy.
>> Reduced OSHA recordable incidents from 127 yearly to 9.
>> Directed lean design for manufacturability on 2 new product lines to improve costs.

As an accomplished general management executive with the full scope of cross-functional business and leadership skills, I have a keen business sense and a strong understanding of how to effectively run P&L. I am driven to achieve results in the most challenging circumstances.

I am impressed with PlanForms' commitment to growth and improvement. From a recent news article, I understand that "execution" is a critical priority and that you are addressing this need "with a sense of urgency." Thus, it seems there might be a great fit with my proven strengths, my ability to execute, and my own deep commitment to excellence.

May we set up a time to talk?

Sincerely,

Casey Simmons
>>>>>>>>>>>>>
casey.simmons@email.com
555-345-6789

Cover Letter for Your Contacts to Share When Forwarding Your Resume

Format: Traditionally formatted letter sent to your contact as a PDF attachment to an email (The following section on Email Messages includes guidelines for your covering message.)

Guidelines:

- With this letter, rather than leaving it up to your contacts, you make it easy for them to share the most meaningful and appropriate information about you when forwarding your resume to their contacts.

- Provide a thorough overview of your most salient career information—what you have done and how well you have done it—so that readers understand your expertise and value.

- Because contacts may forward this without informing you, you must leave the closing somewhat vague—rather than following the best practice of keeping further action under your control.

Example: Joe Scarapace Letter, page 93

JOSEPH L. SCARAPACE

949-493-2041 | jlscarapace@gmail.com
www.linkedin.com/in/joseph-l-scarapace

Greetings! I'm delighted to have this opportunity to be introduced to you and pleased that our mutual contact has forwarded this letter along with my resume. To give you an idea about my background and current situation, I'll share the following points:

While successfully employed with Trilium Design Corporation, I am confidentially commencing a search to identify a C-level role with greater opportunity to grow business both organically and through acquisition, provide greater strategic impact, and deliver exceptional returns to shareholders. I believe you will find my background reflects a unique blend of visionary leadership, strategic planning and execution, new product/business development initiatives, and process improvements/operational optimization—all leading to top- and bottom-line margin improvements and revenue growth.

Briefly, key areas of leadership and managerial excellence that I can bring to the right organization include these highlights:

> **Strategic Planning and Execution ...** Defined and executed a pragmatic and strategic business plan that delivered $20M in annual growth over 6 years with Trilium. Key contributors to this success story include: Introduction of 2 innovative product lines, 3 strategic partnerships with vendors, and increased revenue on existing product lines by improving product quality and eliminating underperforming SKUs.

> **Accountability and Performance Metrics (KPIs) ...** Created accountability through visibility of metrics. Most notably, introduced "Core 6 Metrics" in production, technical, and customer service departments, addressing target quality levels, production output, safety (lost time), warranty and claims, productivity, and efficiencies.

> **Customer Relationship Management ...** Built dynamic relationship with sales VPs and their customers by performing routine annual visits with 6 of the top-tier and 6 of the bottom-tier customers. The goal? Determine where performance was optimal as well as identify opportunities for improvements.

> **Prime Characteristic Underlining a History of Leadership Success ...** I am highly accountable and committed to personally moving a company forward—always seeking to exceed performance measurements, targets, and expectations.

I'd appreciate an opportunity to speak with you for 10 minutes or so and explore any connections you might share that could prove mutually beneficial. Of course, if your organization is seeking the type of candidate I've described, I'd be delighted to have a deeper conversation.

Sincerely,

Joe Scarapace

Email Messages

Your email messages can, of course, be your actual cover letter, as discussed in the previous section. In this section we address other circumstances when you will be writing to existing and new contacts during the course of your job search.

It may seem obvious what to say in an email that accompanies your resume. However, our experience has shown that many executives, while highly competent in communicating about business matters either verbally or by email, tend to freeze when sending an email with their all-important resume. So we present, for your consideration, several flavors of email communications to give you ideas for tailoring your own email correspondence.

> **PRO TIP: Create a standard email signature block and include it on all of your emails.** It should include your full name, phone number, and email address (to be certain this important information is shared in the event that your message is copied or forwarded). You might also include links to your LinkedIn profile, personal website, blog, or any other relevant sites. You may wish to also add a tagline or branding statement (no more than one line).
>
> You can precede the signature block with a friendly first-name-only sign-off if you like.

When Sending a Resume to a Colleague

Guidelines:

- Strike a friendly tone, but tailor the level of formality to the relationship—when writing to a close colleague or friend, you can be more relaxed.
- In all cases, keep in mind that your message might be passed along, so always keep a professional tone, and pay close attention to spelling, grammar, and formatting.
- Whenever possible, keep the ball in your court by promising a follow-up call in the closing paragraph of your message. (Of course, be certain to place that call!)

Examples: Tom Chrabascz, Stan Nakajima

Priscilla —

I'm reaching out to share some news and ask for your assistance.

After more than 20 years of running operations as the President at The Platinum Company, I have decided to actively (and confidentially) pursue a change in direction. I am seeking opportunities where I can turn around a faltering operation or contribute to continued growth of an existing well-run company—in the capacity of President, General Manager, or even VP/Director of Operations of a large division. As you know, manufacturing is my forte and optimizing operations, utilizing lean/best-practice principles, is my approach.

I'd be interested in hearing any ideas, leads, or referrals you might have. I'll call you next week to see what comes to mind. I appreciate any assistance you can offer.

Best regards,
Tom Chrabascz
508.385.5726 | tchrabascz@platinum.com

Ron—

Thanks for taking a few minutes to speak today. As promised, I am forwarding my performance charts showing the most notable results of the four performance turnarounds I have led for diverse companies facing a variety of challenges. I will be happy to expand on these highlights when we next speak.

The two company investments your firm has recently made are high stakes—you need big results and need them quickly. Given my record, I am a strong candidate for the CEO role at either organization. I'd like to learn more about their operations, obstacles, and opportunities and will call you on Friday to follow up.

Best —
Stan
Stanley Nakajima
StanNakajima@mac.com | 555-334-6678

Networking Followup

Guidelines:

- Be clear about your purpose in writing.
- Provide a brief overview of your career.
- Confirm next steps, meeting time and place, or other details.

Examples: Derrick Delacamera (new contact); Derrick Delacamera (existing contact)

Ms. Garofalo, I want to thank you for scheduling time to meet with me next week. I appreciate your willingness to share your perspectives and insights.

Let me emphasize that my purpose in asking to see you isn't to request employment. Nor do I expect you to know of an opening for me. At this point, I am seeking information to help me focus my job-search efforts and broaden my visibility in the job market.

As briefly mentioned, my background is in finance with high-tech manufacturing companies. I'm quite interested in exploring how this background might translate to different industries—what the specific challenges are for companies/industries like yours and where my skills would be of value.

As agreed, I'll arrive at your office at 10 a.m. on Wednesday. I look forward to the conversation.

Best regards,
Derrick Delacamera :: 922-683-2899 :: ddelacamera@gmail.com
linkedin.com/in/derrickdelacamera

Judy, thanks for getting back to me so quickly.

The reason for my outreach ... several people have mentioned that the start-up of your new division might create a need for someone who can manage a full set of financial and accounting controls. If that's true, I'd like to express my interest.

If my friends are mistaken and there's no prospect for employment here, then perhaps we could go to Plan B: that is, I'd welcome the opportunity to informally network about the market for controllers and CFOs in high-tech manufacturing in this region.

I will call you tomorrow morning to follow up and see if we can set up a time to meet. Thanks!

Best regards,
Derrick Delacamera :: 922-683-2899 :: ddelacamera@gmail.com
linkedin.com/in/derrickdelacamera

Networking Cards

Your networking card is your job-seeker business card. It gives all of your contacts an easy way to stay in touch with you, and it allows you to share specific information that can help them steer their efforts toward the kind of help that is most valuable to you.

As you see in this example, the card can include simply your contact information:

Jennifer O'Donnell
413.449.3069 | jodonnell@gmail.com
www.JenODonnell.com
www.linkedin.com/in/jtodonnell
Transforming organizations through optimized business practices!

But you have many options for including additional information that could be beneficial in your job-search efforts. Here are a few ideas:

- In place of or in addition to a tagline at the bottom, you could use keywords (i.e., Change Architect | Lean Expert | COO/Lead Operations Manager).

- Consider printing on the reverse of the card, letting others know precisely how they can help, the type of leads you're most interested in obtaining. Consider these examples:
  — Seeking opportunities to contribute to (manufacturing companies, not-for-profit organizations, *state what is right for you*) in an (operations management, financial/accounting, etc.) role
  — Job Targets: Accountant | Controller | Finance Manager *(whatever suits your expertise)*
  — Exploring roles as (title) with opportunity to optimize operations and turn around lackluster performance

PRO TIP: Always keep a few of your networking cards in your pocket or wallet. You never know when you might encounter someone who could be instrumental in your search. Share your elevator pitch (see next section), offer your card, and seek ideas and advice from this new contact or chance encounter.

"Elevator" Pitches

Called elevator speeches for their ability to be delivered in the 25-second span of an elevator's ascent, these are useful introductory summaries for a number of situations:

- Networking events
- Chamber of Commerce meetings
- Exploratory "cold" phone calls
- Holiday and other social events (weddings, block parties, graduations, retirement dinners, and so forth)
- Referral and follow-up phone calls
- Impromptu get-togethers of colleagues/vendors/neighbors at community functions; kids' sporting/scouting events; at the theatre, mall, golf club, or restaurant; and other unanticipated opportunities

For the executive job seeker, a powerful elevator speech must memorably communicate signature strengths and convey with clarity, "sizzle," and speed four key elements:

1) who you are
2) what you do
3) what you are seeking
4) other key information that can be imparted in a few seconds

These short, pithy snapshots provide key differentiation—an abbreviated branding statement, if you will—and can often be used in email messages to recruiters and hiring managers. It is essential to zero in on what you believe your listener will find of most value and interest.

Emphasize in clear, easily understood language what it is you can do (deliver… provide…). Avoid using jargon and industry acronyms that may not be clearly recognized. Think visually in terms of what you can say that is truly memorable and will be retained after the encounter.

Be sincere in your delivery. Never try to memorize your pitch. Definitely ensure your tone is engaging, low-key, and conversational.

Examples follow.

> Hello. I'm David Harris, a senior finance professional with 20 years of experience leading finance organizations of Fortune 500 companies. My specialties are in the aerospace and high-tech industries. Most recently, as CFO of Jayson Aerospace, I led the M&A efforts that resulted in 3 acquisitions that doubled the company in size. I'm targeting CFO opportunities presenting challenges related to growth.

> I'm a senior operations management professional in the manufacturing industry with a track record of restoring profitability and achieving growth. For the past 18 years, I have produced exceptional results for 3 organizations: a privately held high-tech composites company, a start-up injection-molding plastics company, and a publicly traded $1 billion electronics component manufacturer. I'm targeting opportunities where I can add value through improved operations management, lean manufacturing methods, and a practical approach to cross-training and staff alignment.

> What I do best is build revenue by building relationships. Most recently, as Global Sales Director at FlashTech, I developed relationships at Intel and grew the business from a $50K trial account to more than $20M in annual sales. Previously, I've led sales teams at several Silicon Valley companies, from emerging players to high-tech giants. I understand their world and I know what drives them to action. If you know of a technology company that is looking for a sales leader, I'd be very interested in the referral. I'm ready to start building new relationships and new revenue.

> Hi. I am a human resource vice president with expertise in career management, training, and team-building. I've worked with a broad range of industries, and in every case I've been able to improve the performance of sales and customer-service teams. My greatest strength is my ability to build rapport with people from a wide range of backgrounds and identify talent. I am looking for human resources VP/director opportunities with middle-tier to large firms.

For nearly 20 years, I have managed high-growth pharmaceutical and medical device manufacturing companies. As a CEO or President, I bring a hands-on style of leadership to a company—quickly identifying key team members and determining areas of strength, opportunity, and outage. With a sharp focus on what needs to be done, we have been able to consistently grow revenue, market share, and profitability. Now I'm looking for a new opportunity that demands an innovative, collaborative leader and rainmaker.

LinkedIn Messages

Use the LinkedIn message feature to reach out to people with whom you would like to connect.

Here are a few sample scenarios and scripts to inspire you in crafting your own personal notes.

Invitation to Connect

As we mentioned in Chapter 1, you should not simply hit the "connect" button to send an automated message; instead, go to the person's page and click the blue "Message" button.

Hello, Jerry. I was pleased to find you on LinkedIn. It seems like you've been very busy since we last worked together! I'd love to connect here on LinkedIn and would enjoy catching up with you sometime soon. Is there a good time to chat briefly?

Message to Someone within Company of Interest for a Specific Opportunity

Good morning, Maryann. I hope this finds you well—we haven't chatted in a few months. I'm very seriously exploring an Executive Customer Experience VP position with Hartford HealthCare, posted a week ago. Are you by any chance connected with the hiring or HR manager who is recruiting for the position? If so, would you be willing to refer me...or can you suggest the best way for me to proceed?

Introductions

You can either reach out directly to people with whom you are not connected—but share a connection in common—or ask your shared connection for an introduction.

Hello, Marcy—I learned of you from my former colleague, Jack Williams, who worked with you at Delancey Studios and had some very nice things to say about you. I would love to connect with you here on LinkedIn and, if possible, meet by phone or in person as well. I'm considering an opportunity with HMS and would greatly appreciate an insider's perspective.

> Jack, I see that you are connected with Marcy Daniels at HMS Productions. Would you feel comfortable introducing me to her? I've just submitted my resume for the position of Senior Creative Director there and would love to gain some insider information about the company and culture. Thanks, as always, for your support!

Networking Scripts

For many executives, it helps to craft a networking script prior to picking up the phone. While each approach is highly individual, here are some ideas to get you started.

Warm lead (someone you know)

> "Hi, Steve, this is Joe Figueroa. *(then insert something that connects: my wife and I really enjoyed spending time at the golf tournament with you and Ellen...I want to tell you again how pleased I was to read of your promotion in the xyz journal...wasn't that a great game the kids played over the weekend?).*
>
> "Listen, have I caught you at a good time? The reason for my call is that I'm beginning to explore senior-level operations and general management opportunities in the high-tech manufacturing sector. As I know you're aware, I've been the VP of Operations for Midwest Components Company for the past five years...I know, it doesn't seem possible, does it?! (pause) My strengths are building and leading lean, optimally performing manufacturing organizations...driving productivity...and positioning a company for rapid, sustained growth and market leadership. With your connections—and your sphere of influence—I knew you'd be an excellent person to share my plans with. I'm very interested in picking your brain—who you know, what contacts you have, where you think my skills might best be utilized."

Referral lead (you haven't met yet)

> "Hello, Mr. Druga. This is Joe Figueroa. I was referred to you by Stephen Pitkin, who was very complimentary about your leadership skills when you were both at Technical Solutions. I met Stephen when I joined Midwest Components, where I've been the Vice President of Operations for the past five years.
>
> My strengths are building and leading lean, optimally performing manufacturing organizations... driving productivity...and positioning a company for rapid, sustained growth and market leadership. I am confidentially exploring senior-level operations and general management opportunities in the manufacturing sector.
>
> I understand from Stephen that you might be interested in someone with my background there at Anodized Products...or, if that's not the case, that you might be able to put me in touch with other key contacts in the industry. Would you have a few minutes to meet with me to discuss?"

Other add-on questions and points to consider in crafting your message include the following:

- "What ideas, leads, or suggestions do you have for me?"
- "Who, among your network, might be interested in someone with my leadership experience and background?"
- "What related industries can you think of, and contacts do you know, where these skills might prove valuable?"
- "I have a short list of companies I'm trying to crack. Who do you know at (name any specific target companies you've identified)?"
- "I've also been thinking about some other manufacturing areas myself. Who do you know in pharmaceuticals? Any key contacts at Pfizer? How about Lee Manufacturing? (etc.)"
- "What about people you might know outside of business? Who in your church (temple) might be able to refer me to someone in these areas? Who do you know from your health club who might know someone in these companies or industries?"

Continue to edit and rehearse your networking script until it is completely natural. When you begin speaking, do not go too fast. Just because you know it well (and you will know it very well!), remember that the listener is hearing it for the first time. Develop a pleasant, comfortable cadence and delivery…don't rush.

> **PRO TIP: Always have your resume printed out right beside you** as you make these calls so that you can quickly refer to something as you are speaking. You can also highlight points on your resume that don't come out in the abbreviated call for reference in your follow-up email.

Closing

> You've been a great help, Bob. These leads sound very promising. I'll let you know if anything comes out of this. Listen, I'd like you to keep your eyes and ears open for me. Are you going to be in town next week? Great. I'll call you on Friday to see if you've heard anything new or thought of anything else. I really appreciate this and, if I can return the favor, you can be sure I will.

-or-

> Bob, you just know so many people in this business. Would you mind if I call you once every week or two until I land the right position? You're bound to hear something on the grapevine sooner or later. If you don't have any new leads, you don't even need to take the call. I'll just leave a message and if you don't ring back, I'll know it's because you haven't heard anything. I don't want to inconvenience you.

Keep in mind that the more purposeful networking you do, the more skilled you will become. It is like anything else—with practice, you will perfect a totally natural delivery.

Executive Leadership Brief

The Leadership Brief is a relatively new tool in the cadre of professional search documents for the executive. It is typically one or two pages in length. Most often, three to five CAR stories (see Chapter 2 for in-depth assistance in creating your own) are expanded to provide a very clear indication of the results an executive is able to deliver.

Remember, the CAR (Challenge-Action-Result) approach should focus on the accomplishments in your background that are most meaningful, most relevant to your current career goal, and ideally represent what you are most capable of achieving and what you will be able to accomplish in your next position. They are predictors of your future success.

The Executive Leadership Brief can be effectively used as a companion document as well as a standalone tool. The most useful ways to employ it are:

1)   As a leave-behind document following a discussion with a recruiter and/or meeting with a board or decision-maker ("You may find these additional details regarding several specific accomplishments relevant in assessing my ability to make a difference in your organization.")

2)   As a follow-up piece to a resume already provided to a recruiter, board, or decision-maker (Similar transmittal message: "In addition to the information already conveyed in my resume, you may find the enclosed document that highlights several specific accomplishments relevant in assessing my candidacy.")

3)   As an advance document with a recruiter during initial stages of conversation

4)   As a component in your complete resume/cover letter package

On the next two pages, you will see a sample Executive Leadership Brief that powerfully describes executive achievements in much more detail than is feasible in a resume. The structure makes the document clear, consistent, and easy to skim. You'll find an additional sample in Chapter 6 on page 134.

Example: Richard Morales Executive Leadership Brief

Richard T. Morales

Seattle, WA 98116 | 206-810-3081 | richardtmorales@gmail.com | www.linkedin.com/in/rtmorales

EXECUTIVE LEADERSHIP BRIEF: Experienced Law Enforcement Executive
Visionary Leadership | Innovative Community Policing | Exceptional Talent Management

Visionary Leadership—Organizational Transformation   CHIEF OF POLICE

Challenge   Develop model and institutionalize a plan to provide 21st century policing and professional law enforcement services to Greater Seattle.

Action   Demonstrated a need for 150 incremental police officers from tactical units by illustrating demands/return on investment from increased regulatory requirements and preventive community outreach programs. Researched force structure constraints and analyzed staffing models. Designed plan using established manpower and operational data. Established payroll/logistical budgets to initiate transformation. Garnered stakeholder support through briefing community leaders.

Result   Secured authorization and funding for 150 police positions and implemented a sustainable foundation for a robust police department fully staffed by dedicated officers committed to providing superior, community-oriented policing.

Strength   I leveraged logical thinking with a visionary ability to identify root causes of problems or shortfalls, recommend viable courses of action, and take necessary actions to produce outstanding results.

Media Relations & Communication   PUBLIC INFORMATION OFFICER

Challenge   Broaden appeal and scope of primary information tool without significantly increasing cost.

Action   Researched and obtained new vendor for augmented existing print newspaper while rolling out robust website version with mobile access.

Result   This initiative increased the newspaper's appeal to its audience, thus broadening reach. At the same time, produced significant cost savings through improved operational practices and distribution strategies.

Strength   I showcased my ability as a communicator and an innovator—initiating business practice changes that consistently enhance productivity. I can effectively communicate key messages to a broad audience and am able to maximize the potential of available resources.

Driving Organizational Excellence   CHIEF OF POLICE

Challenge   Promote best practices in law enforcement and bring departmental operations above industry standards.

Action   Researched methodology for earning accreditation from the Commission for Accreditation of Law Enforcement Agencies (held by just 5% of police departments nationwide) and gained stakeholder buy-in for value. Established pathway for achieving accreditation. Contracted with an agency that reviewed, revised, and republished policies reflecting industry's best practices. Managed process and implemented transition to best practices throughout entire department.

Result   Instilled best practices in law enforcement on a department-wide basis, putting in place consistency and excellence. Department is on track to earn accreditation in 2022. Earning CALEA accreditation reduces liability and risk, increases accountability, and demonstrates professional excellence. At the same time, implementation reduces time spent dealing with litigation, citizen complaints, and employee misconduct.

Strength   I demonstrated my commitment to optimizing an organization's operations, brokering positive change, earning support across the board, and executing a successful strategy.

Richard T. Morales / Executive Leadership Brief / page 2 of 2

Turnaround Management   DEPUTY PROGRAM MANAGER

Challenge   Instill discipline, professionalism, and pride in a group of employees who had been neglected by local and corporate leadership for more than a year.

Action   Established written guidelines to set parameters for success and failure. Developed policies on all aspects of operations—from counseling and discipline to handling promotions and evaluations that required leaders to provide subordinates with continual feedback on their performance and ways to improve. Set high performance standards and rewarded people who exceeded standards while holding those who failed to meet standards accountable for results.

Result   Improved employee performance and organizational results across the board. Strong performers were moved to increased positions of responsibility and non-performers were coached and performance improved (or they were removed from operation if standards were not attained). Achieved considerably increased positive feedback from customers and a reduction in complaints from 2 per week to 1 per quarter.

Strength   I confirmed my ability as a change agent, leader, and motivator—someone who can turn around poorly performing operations and weak performers and instill individual and team pride.

Community Outreach & Perception   CHIEF OF POLICE

Challenge   Enhance image of police department and earn status of police department personnel as cherished, trusted, and respected members of the community.

Action   Launched multi-faceted plan that expanded bike patrols, doubled number of School Resource Officers, involved police in afterschool activities, provided a presence (booth, demonstrations) at all community activities, published weekly column and frequent feature stories/photos in local newspaper, made regular television/town meeting appearances on issues of community importance, and published 12+ brochures on safety and crime prevention topics.

Result   The department earned community respect, police were considered more approachable as integral members of the community, the community as a whole was safer (juvenile crime dropped 40%), and involvement of residents in community-based policing increased substantially.

Strength   I am an experienced team builder and communicator as well as an assertive leader of unquestionable integrity. I am able to effectively use a myriad of media formats to inform internal and external audiences. I am able to quickly develop rapport and gain public trust—critical when faced with inevitable crisis management issues.

One-Page Executive Resume

A pared-down version of your full executive resume, this document can be very helpful in informal networking. It presents a succinct, one-page summary of salient experience in chronological order with educational background and an abbreviated summary.

As well, it is a non-threatening "read" for first-time networked contacts when a two- or three-page executive resume might appear intimidating or "over the top." Of course, the one-page networking/abbreviated resume is always presented as just that—with the promise of a full resume as desired or requested.

Your one-page resume can also be an effective companion to the Executive Leadership Brief, offering the reader adequate information on which to base a decision to proceed to the next phase in the candidate pre-selection process.

In the following example (Teresa daSilva resume), you can see how each position still retains important accomplishments, even in abbreviated format.

The second example (Edward Justice resume, written by one of our Chapter 6 portfolio contributors, Marie Zimenoff) is a bit different. It is very specifically a networking resume, used when meeting with contacts and very clearly spelling out target jobs, companies, and even precise contacts. Note also several blank bullet points—designed so that any ideas that arise during conversation can be quickly jotted down in the appropriate spot.

Examples:
Teresa daSilva Resume, page 106; Edward Justice Resume, page 107

Teresa da Silva

330-456-7890
teresa.dasilva@gmail.com | LinkedIn Profile

MANUFACTURING INDUSTRY EXECUTIVE—U.S. AND INTERNATIONAL

High-Quality Products | Niche Markets | Automated Manufacturing

➔ **Versatile Executive:** Broad leadership experience across manufacturing operations, finance, sales, and marketing.

➔ **Global Business Leader:** 15+ years of experience working for international companies located on 3 continents.

➔ **Systems Expert:** Deep knowledge of business workflows and processes for efficiency and accountability.

➔ **Relationship Builder:** Respected by customers and staff, trusted by senior leadership, known for inspiring loyalty.

➔ **Steady Hand at the Tiller:** Leadership through growth and contraction, focusing on customer needs and business strategies to maintain stability and profitability.

MIDWEST RESINS | PARTY PRINTERS | ERNST & YOUNG
Languages: Portuguese (fluent), French and Spanish (conversational)

PROFESSIONAL EXPERIENCE

MIDWEST RESINS, Akron, OH   2008–Present
Manufacturer of styrene acrylic resin for toner production; $25M revenue at peak; subsidiary of Global Resins, Inc., of Sweden.

President, 2015–Present | **VP Finance,** 2009–2015 | **Director of Finance,** 2008–2009

IMPACT: Captured and retained critical business for U.S. manufacturing company in intensely competitive global environment. Built an efficient operation, a positive work culture, and an exceptionally customer-oriented team.

SCOPE: Full operating and P&L authority for U.S. Manufacturing, Sales, Finance, Operations, IT, Purchasing, and Logistics. Member of 3-person Management Committee setting strategic direction for the business. 18 reports (3 direct).

HIGHLIGHTS:

➔ **Sales and Marketing:** Captured major new account ($2M annual sales) through outreach and relationship building.

➔ **Manufacturing:** Reduced headcount 20% by restructuring shift schedules—while meeting 100% of production goals.

➔ **Negotiations:** Secured 40% reduction in cost of transitioning underused plant back to land owners.

➔ **Corporate Culture:** Set a tone of teamwork, respect, and customer focus—retained 100% of employees for 10+ years.

PARTY PRINTERS, INC., Cleveland, OH   2005–2008

Financial Controller

IMPACT: Brought accounting and finance expertise to innovative e-commerce/printing company during early, high-growth years. Designed and installed the company's first general ledger system.

SCOPE: Accounting, Finance, and IT for early-stage company with operations in U.S. and headquarters in Hong Kong.

ERNST & YOUNG, Lisbon, Portugal | Cleveland, OH   2000–2005

Senior Auditor, 2002–2005 | **Auditor,** 2000–2002

SCOPE: Member of audit teams for large public companies in Financial and Manufacturing sectors. Chosen for rotation to Cleveland office in 2002; earned CPA designation on first attempt.

EDUCATION AND PROFESSIONAL CERTIFICATION

BA Honors in Business Management, 2000 | University of Coimbra, Portugal
Certified Public Accountant, 2002 | Member, AICPA

EDWARD JUSTICE

Fort Collins, CO 80526 | 303-973-6278 | www.linkedin.com/in/edwardjustice | edwardjustice@gmail.com

GLOBAL DIRECTOR OF MARKETING & BUSINESS DEVELOPMENT

Translate customer insights into highly differentiated products and programs for leading brands.

Key Accomplishments:

✓ **Captured market segments for global enterprises and startups,** planning and executing social/new media marketing to increase solution sales, secure venture capital, and position companies for sale.

✓ **Secured multimillion-dollar contracts in Europe, the US, and Asia,** leveraging a gift for languages to negotiate business customs in 50 countries and build relationships to springboard new opportunities.

✓ **Turned around profitability in key business segments,** using financial background to focus on the bottom line and co-location with R&D/manufacturing to create integrated teams within matrix organization.

✓ **Rejuvenated direct report and matrix teams to produce top results** across multiple segments and geographies, energizing teams, partners, and suppliers to track and capitalize on technology trends.

PREFERRED ROLES / FUNCTIONS	TARGET MARKET CHARACTERISTICS
Market Entry & Penetration	Geographic Location
Increasing market share and revenue	*Northern Colorado*
Business Development	Industries
Closing new accounts and delivering top results	*Technology, Green Energy, Healthcare*
Global Leadership	Size / Type of Organization
Transforming global organizations to restore profitability	*Start-up / Small Business / Nonprofit*

TARGET LIST

Target Organizations

- Honeywell
- Covidien
- Hach
-

- Tolmar
- Beckman Coulter
- McKesson
-

Contacts of Interest:

- Karey Jamison, HR, Hach
- Scott Jessup, CMO, Tolmar
-
-

CAREER HIGHLIGHTS

Marketing Director (HP)—Turned around 3-year declining US and European revenue to grow business, winning long-term supply contracts with 3 major OEMs to ultimately position company for sale. Refined and implemented business strategies to deliver "Lowest Total Lifecycle Cost" equipment systems to global customer base.

Business Development Manager (Waterpik Stream)—Transformed business from product focus to solution approach, directing marketing strategy, value-based solution mapping, and sales analysis/plans for 5 global regions. Managed technical assistance group and market analysts. Gained traction in global market segment as leader for product management, manufacturing, and European business development from regional HQ in Germany.

Worldwide Product Manager (Waterpik)—Led total lifecycle management for 6 portfolios with 185 products, reining in suppliers worldwide and coming up to speed quickly on products. Saved millions by standardizing suppliers, training, and logistics. Increased profitability of $75 million business 10% in 2 years through manufacturing consolidation, portfolio reduction, and regional pricing alignment.

Board Resumes

A board resume, typically one page, is a strategic document showcasing a candidate's highest and greatest value to serve on a board of directors.

When developing the document, it's useful to start with your polished resume, preserving design features such as font, style of headings, and so forth. Your education and community background are typically at the bottom of the one-page board resume, and you may have to truncate some of these details, retaining just the most prestigious or relevant to the board opportunities you are pursuing.

Once the education and community sections are complete, move up to the body of the document—your experience. Obviously, your traditional resume is packed with many exceptional examples of leadership, visionary management practices, actions, and quantified results. You won't be able to fit all of these onto the one-page board resume.

For this tool, try to isolate the top handful of examples that best demonstrate what you believe to be the capabilities sought in the new board member. Capture those stories from your experiences and include the best ones that make the cut. Create an abbreviated career chronology showing, typically, your job titles and growth/advancement, company names, and dates.

As with your traditional resume, you'll want to consider tweaking your board resume based on the target audience and details for a specific board opportunity. Who will be on the selection committee? What expertise do they bring? Use your network and LinkedIn to ferret out details about their experiences and gain insight into the elements of your background that will be most valuable. It's crucial to try to determine what you can bring to the board that complements the assets of other board members.

The top section of the board resume—just like your regular resume—is where you present and refine your value proposition. Using appropriate keywords, highlight your industry expertise and key differentiators that likely will separate you from other candidates. Share a few precise details to create a compelling story.

Positioning for board opportunities—whether volunteer roles or those with stipends—enables an executive to further demonstrate expertise, knowledge, and in-demand leadership talent. A board appointment can be instrumental in promoting your personal brand and appeal within an industry or broader community.

In addition to the sample that follows, you will find a board resume in Chapter 6 (page 133).

Example: Thomas Pinkerton Board Resume

Thomas L. Pinkerton   Board Director Candidate

513-826-2071 | tlpinkerton@gmail.com | linkedin.com/in/thomaslpinkerton

TARGET OBJECTIVE: Board of Directors' Role
Aerospace & Automotive Manufacturing Industries

M&A | Global Business Development | Strategic Vision & Growth | Turnaround Expertise | Optimizing Operations
Experienced Board Member and Catalyst for Organizational Development, Transformational Change & Leadership

➢ Deep experience optimizing business operations, integrating new acquisitions, and positioning companies for growth and expansion. Senior Board Leadership: Start-up, Pre-IPO, Turnaround — Succession Planning — Interim CEO/COO.

➢ P&L management and financial acumen: Consistently generating profitability and sustained improvements to margin.

➢ Outstanding reputation for cultivating top talent and leaders: Creating climate that values innovation and collaboration.

BOARD OF DIRECTORS' EXPERIENCE

AMERICELL DYNAMICS | Cincinnati, OH   2017–Present
Member, Board of Directors

- Chair, Compensation Committee
- Co-chair, Six Sigma Program implementation

ABBOTT TECHNOLOGIES | Blue Ash, OH   2018–Present
Member, Board of Directors

- Author, Abbott Tech Succession Plan
- Chair, Search Committee (new President)

PROFESSIONAL HIGHLIGHTS

PRECISION FABRICATORS, INC. | Cincinnati, OH   2012–Present
President / Founder

- Grew startup from $50K investment to $50M contract manufacturer specializing in customized plastics and composites, primarily for global aerospace industry.
- Executed successful IPO and public launch, retaining top organizational talent as well as role as President.

JUPITER DYNAMICS | Covington, KY   1998–2012
COO / Senior Vice President

- Held progressively challenging roles over 14 years, ultimately leading overall operations across 12 plants throughout Midwest for $300M automotive components manufacturer.
- Introduced Kaizen, JIT, and Lean concepts throughout all manufacturing cells, improving margin by double digits while cutting costs by 35%.

EDUCATION & PROFESSIONAL DISTINCTION

Master of Science, Business Administration — NORTHWESTERN UNIVERSITY | Evanston, IL
Bachelor of Science, Political Science — NOTRE DAME UNIVERSITY | Notre Dame, IN

Northwestern University: Keynote Address, Tomorrow's Leaders Conference (May 2019)
Harvard University: Invited Panelist, Harvard Sustainability Summit (October 2018)
Exchange Club: Past President, Active Member (Since 2010)

Professional Biographies

Bios are storytelling documents that help to brand, position, and market an executive and are especially useful in augmenting a resume.

As you are networking with new contacts, you might share your bio when you don't want to send the "job-seeker" message that inevitably accompanies a resume.

In the initial stages of job search, a recruiter might share your bio when recommending you to the hiring company, without having to go to the trouble of editing your resume for the specific opportunity.

Further into the process, your bio might be used to introduce you to other decision-makers within the organization and to members of the board of directors.

Finally, at the conclusion of the hiring process, your bio can serve as the basis for a press release and internal announcement of your selection. By sharing this document immediately prior to the start of new employment, you establish the tone and content of these important communications.

Separate from job search, a professional biography will also serve you well for public speaking opportunities, professional appearances and appointments, press releases, and other occasions when you need to share your professional background.

The following examples illustrate diverse ways that bios can be written and structured to best showcase each individual's background, expertise, and executive brand. You'll find several more biographies in Chapter 6.

Examples: Daria Wolf Bio, page 111; Stephen LaFountain Bio, page 112

Transformational Chief Executive — Leading Global Excellence in Women's Retail While Delivering Proven Value

786-933-1856 | dariawolff@gmail.com

www.linkedin.com/in/dariawolff

Value Proposition

➢ Extensive transformation experience in women's retail
➢ Global market expansion
➢ Talent recruitment/development
➢ M&A and integration
➢ Stellar expertise boosting top and bottom lines
➢ Visionary innovation

Education

MBA, Goizueta Business School
Emory University

BACHELOR OF ARTS, Philosophy
Wesleyan University

EXECUTIVE LEADERSHIP
Management Training Institute
Yale University

Daria J. Wolff

Division CEO

A leader and innovator in retail women's softlines, **Daria Wolff** has built a career exemplified by excellence in growing product lines, building brands, and paving new pathways in the fashion industry. As Division CEO of Metrix Fashion (consistently ranked among the top 3 women's labels for more than a decade), Daria has transformed the organization and driven global expansion.

Daria's record of turning around underperforming units, rightsizing retail organizations, and staying ahead of the best trends in women's fashion is unparalleled. In her 12 years with Casual Corner, she upscaled the brand image and more than tripled retail outlets nationwide—delivering double-digit profitability at a time when retail was shrinking.

When tapped to reorganize Better Brands, she employed a talent-focused strategy and upended the status quo—instituting measures that gave division heads authority and accountability. The result? A record of sustainable revenue growth based on lean practices and a focus on customer engagement.

Daria has consistently delivered outstanding results in virtually every role she has held—leading to her present role as a catalyst for global expansion for Metrix, where she has built an outstanding presence throughout Eurasia that augments the brand's leading performance in North America. She has improved margin and grown market share since taking over as CEO 5 years ago.

Complementing her MBA (Emory) and BA (Wesleyan), Daria's professional development includes Yale's Executive Leadership program through the Management Training Institute as well as leadership programs at Columbia University and Harvard. Fluent in English and Spanish, she spent the first 2 years of her career teaching in Argentina with AmeriCorps.

Daria serves on several Miami boards and commissions, including the Community Fund of North Miami Dade and the Miami Commission for the Arts. She is an in-demand keynote speaker internationally, frequently tapped to address major supply chain conferences. As committed to her community as she is to her employer and industry, Daria is a Big Sister and United Way mentor, supporting young women and teens as they explore educational and career opportunities.

Stephen LaFountain

Senior Finance Executive
Strategy, Innovation, and Operational Excellence

Stephen LaFountain is an accomplished finance management professional with more than 20 years of senior-level experience in both municipal and corporate environments. He is currently the Assistant Superintendent of Rochester Public Schools, where his leadership in the past 3 years has delivered measurable benefits to students, administrators, and taxpayers:

- $1 million annual savings through elimination of underused and duplicate outside services;
- 13% reduction in IT cost while delivering an expanding array of technology services to students;
- 50% reduction in time and staff required to complete month-end close and provide financial reports to the Board of Education.

Previously, as Director of Finance and Information Technology for the Syracuse Housing Authority, he identified and recovered more than $500,000 in overlooked payments and upgraded financial systems to eliminate duplication and reduce fraud.

Stephen's corporate background includes positions as Chief Financial Officer and General Manager with New Abacus Technologies, Ace Computer, and General Dynamics. His responsibility has included broad financial and operations management with organizations producing annual revenues exceeding $250 million. His expertise ranges from oversight of Finance, Human Resources, and capital budgets to effectively managing operations, developing municipal budgets, directing organizational growth, and facilitating complex negotiations in both union and non-union environments.

A proactive, senior-level manager, he has been recognized throughout his career for a keen business acumen, strong strategic planning and project management skills, and excellent negotiation and communication abilities.

Stephen earned his undergraduate degree in finance from Cornell University and his Master's degree in Business Administration from Rensselaer Polytechnic Institute.

Active in the community, Stephen has been a long-time booster of the Rochester Falcons Football Gridiron Cub and currently serves as the club's President. He coached recreational basketball and soccer for middle school boys for 7 years and has served as a Project Graduation volunteer for more than 10 years.

Combining a strategic mindset with innovative problem solving, Stephen is laser-focused on operational excellence to deliver value to all stakeholders—whether taxpayers or shareholders, students or customers, corporate or municipal colleagues.

Detailed "Mulligan" Thank-You Letters

Of course you are sending a thank-you letter following every interview. In addition to showing courtesy and good manners, a thank-you letter gives you a golden opportunity to *reiterate, reinforce, recap,* and *recover* following an interview.

We call it taking a mulligan. Golfers know the strategy. In job search, a mulligan is the do-over that can make all the difference, both for building pre-interview confidence (heading into the interview knowing that you can use a mulligan "no matter what happens") and for recovering any missteps after the interview.

Send your thank-you by email the same day or the day immediately following each interview. You might be thinking that a traditionally mailed letter or card is more personal, but those options have a serious disadvantage: They don't have the benefit of immediacy. Often, decisions regarding which candidates move on to the next stage happen quickly. An email ensures the decision-makers at this stage know your seriousness and professionalism.

Besides expressing the normal courtesies of a typical thank-you, use your mulligan to *reiterate* key points made in the interview that align with the opportunity, *reinforce* how you are a match, and *recap* the next steps. The mulligan also provides a perfect opportunity for *recovery*. Here are some examples of how to introduce a mulligan and add your valuable content.

> "When you asked me about global expansion, I wanted to go a little deeper to describe some of the synergies I produced by partnering with..."

> "In our discussion about designing new compensation plans, I neglected to mention the work I did in spearheading a total overhaul of LMN's commission structure…"

> "We talked about vision and examples of overcoming obstacles. In my role as president with RST, one of the strategies I used with my executive team each Friday morning was…"

Within reason (you don't want a dozen!), use as many short mulligans as necessary. Keep them to two or three lines each and format as separate bullet points or paragraphs. Close with a solid, enthusiastic restatement of interest and anticipation of moving to the next steps in the process.

30-60-90-Day Plans (or: Q1/Q2/Q3/Q4 Plans)

Job searches require a considerable amount of time, from candidate sourcing and prescreening through the multiple stages of interviewing, the final candidate selection, and a job offer. What used to be a timeframe of perhaps a few weeks to a month can easily extend across several months.

As the hiring cycle has become increasingly protracted as well as competitive, savvy candidates look for strategies that will help them gain an advantage. One that we recommend is the 30-60-90-day plan. (Depending on the level/scope of the role, it might be a Q1/Q2/Q3/Q4 plan.) Using this tried-and-true tool, you can uniquely position yourself by detailing specifically *what you will do* in the first weeks and months in the new position.

Format: The 30-60-90-Day Plan

Formatted like a business letter, your 30-60-90-day plan might range from two to five pages in length. We recommend that you attach it to an email as a PDF…and also paste the entire contents of the plan into the body of the email. This way, recipients can easily read the content on smartphones and tablets without having to download the document.

The following outline describes the structure we most often use in creating these plans for our executive clients.

Open

Lead off with a short paragraph expressing appreciation for the interview and making a strong initial pitch for your candidacy. Include the usual pleasantries, recap people met during the interview, and highlight a few takeaways.

Recap

The next section of the plan should briefly reiterate the top features of your background that are most relevant to the opportunity, followed by key, transferable skills that align directly with the position requirements. After a short introductory paragraph, recap these important qualifiers in brief paragraphs or bullet points. They might be a little longer than those in a cover letter—three to five lines in length and no more than five or six bullet points altogether.

Pitch Your Plan

Start with a brief segue, then move immediately into the body of your plan—three timeframes (30 days, 60 days, 90 days) showing specific goals, followed by the initiatives, steps, and actions that you anticipate taking. Be as specific as possible, but use language that suggests these are *working* ideas and *preliminary* concepts.

The details in the plan should dovetail as much as possible with information you learned in the first few interviews. Where there is a lack of clarity, ideas can be couched in terms that include "for possible discussion," "for potential consideration," and "from a preliminary standpoint."

Close

Close your plan with one or two short paragraphs that solidify the concepts, reinforce your brand and suitability for the job, and reiterate that the document reflects preliminary ideas, inviting further discussion.

Strategic Use of the Plan

We recommend 30-60-90-day plans be used following the *second* job interview and not the first. This is because the field of candidates can still be too wide following the first round of interviews for there to be a good ROI on the time you'll invest in developing the plan.

The other reason for delaying till round two is that most candidates will not be able to fully glean the level of pain, problems requiring solutions, and "lay of the land" in just one interview. However, a second interview provides opportunities to ask more pointed questions; it may very well involve meetings with multiple stakeholders, further deepening your ability to understand opportunities and challenges faced by the organization or department. All of this background knowledge serves as the ideal foundation for crafting the 30-60-90-day plan.

Variations of the plan can be extrapolated for use following subsequent steps in the interview process. Sometimes it is just a matter of referencing a few strategies or tactics from the plan in a post-third-interview follow-up. For instance, following the initial thank-you language, you might add, "I was gratified to learn that the points I'd postulated in my 30-60-90-day plan mirror the direction you envision for this company. Of course, these were preliminary ideas, but I'm excited to see we're on the same page with the opportunities that are available to achieve this year's objectives…"

There will nearly always be additional layers of information to bring into the plan that can be expanded and sent back to the original interviewers from round two as well as funneled up the pipeline to the executive team and even the board of directors.

Be sure to capture key ideas immediately after your interview before attempting to draft your 30-60-90-day plan. You'll also want to quickly do some additional research, which should include media coverage, YouTube and social media visibility, business journals, annual report, and other sources. Weave any salient points into some of the recommended actions or strategies.

To maximize the efficacy of the plan, it's essential that the document be written and provided within 24 to 48 hours of the interview. Part of the success of the plan (measured by getting to the final interview stage—and/or to the offer—as well as serving as an effective roadmap for the first 90 days in position) is its ability to demonstrate your skill in promptly synthesizing a great deal of information, encapsulating it in a meaningful and strategic manner, and effectively showing an "above-and-beyond" approach that proves your professionalism and fit for the opportunity at hand.

The bottom line is that few, if any, individuals will go to this length to reinforce their candidacy for a particular position. When used for a highly coveted position for which there is strong competition, the plan can be a key differentiator with tremendous power in moving your search forward to a successful conclusion. It can give you a superb leg-up over the competition.

In the following example, you can see the introductory section and the structure of the actual plan along with a few specifics that will serve as a starting point for writing your own unique plan.

Example: Beverly Davidson 30-60-90-Day Plan

Proposed 30-60-90-Day Plan

July–August–September 2021

Candidate: Beverly J. Davidson
Chief Operating Officer, ABSOLUTE DYNAMICS

Presented to: Mr. Jeffrey Schwartz, President & CEO
Absolute Dynamics
May 2, 2021

Dear Jeffrey:

I appreciate the opportunity to have spoken with you in three formal meetings over the past few months to explore my candidacy for the COO position heading up North American operations for Absolute Dynamics. I am confident of my ability to make a significant contribution to the organization in this capacity and deliver a fresh vision and effective turnaround plan.

In our last meeting, I committed to providing you with a proposed blueprint for the first 90 days in position, detailing my initial recommendations and strategies—subject, of course, to further discussions around resources, funding, timelines, and other factors.

Foremost among my goals will be focusing attention on the most critical organizational initiatives spanning all divisions. Once in position and with key leadership support, a comprehensive set of plans and detailed timeline can be developed to support this direction and further develop a yearlong plan of objectives as well as three- to five-year projections.

Recapping some of the most crucial areas where I can play a pivotal leadership role contributing to the overall success of Absolute Dynamics in my first 3 months in this position, I present the following:

MILESTONE: Month 1 (through July 31, 2021)

Initial priorities within the first 30 days in position include the following highlights:

Priority #1 … Within the first 30 days, I will meet all direct reports and tour facilities, shadow critical operational leaders, review current leadership, and understand what is and is not working within each of the divisions. In addition, I will meet with the executive leadership team (you, as President & CEO, plus CFO, CHRO, CIO, and Senior VP of Sales & Marketing) and gain an understanding of short- and long-term objectives, strategies, and tactics as well as clear insight into where outages exist presently in the overall operations.

I would also establish a leadership counsel that includes the GMs of each division plus my senior staff; of course, my goal will be to promote a collaborative structure and provide representation of all areas of the business to foster strategic goals and actions.

Priority #2 … Play leadership role in developing, planning, and executing build-out of the …

- 1 -

Priority #3 … Advance launch of new service line in aerospace composites …

Priority #4 … Spearhead efforts supporting development of new …

Priority #5 … Partner strategically with stateside vendors …

Augmenting the priorities articulated above, I would conduct meetings with all stakeholders and core team members in the first few weeks and months as I assume the COO role. Talking with stakeholders throughout the organization, building relationships with new and existing vendors, and meeting with strategic partners and customers will afford opportunities to listen-and-learn to identify opportunities, issues/concerns, and areas for future development and implementation. These in-depth discussions would ensure a solid foundation for working together strategically and effectively.

MILESTONE: Month 2 (through August 31, 2021)

Priorities within the second 30 days in position include the following highlights:

Priority #1 … Design …

Priority #2 … Present …

Priority #3 … Lead …

Priority #4 … Drive …

MILESTONE: Month 3 (through September 30, 2021)

Subsequent objectives to undertake within the third 30 days (end of my first quarter) in position as COO include the following highlights:

Priority #1 … Invigorate …

Priority #2 … Spearhead …

Priority #3 … Execute …

Priority #4 … Lead …

Consistent with specific milestones established in the first 90 days, I would continue to prioritize areas of oversight and leadership for multiple initiatives, advancing a smooth operations management transition and ensuring highest emphasis on the top priorities. Bottom-line, I would be demonstrating my value through ongoing accountability, focus, and strategic vision/execution of the objectives we agree upon to position Absolute Dynamics for exceptional performance in the next 5 years.

I am very excited about the prospect of leading Absolute Dynamics as its new Chief Operating Officer and look forward to the next steps in the process. Thank you, again, for your consideration.

Sincerely,

Beverly J. Davidson

- 2 -

Inspiration and Examples

We've covered a lot of ground in these first five chapters, providing executive-specific strategies, tactics, exercises, guidelines, and examples for creating career-marketing documents and launching an accelerated job search. As you move on to Chapter 6, you can take a breather! Browse the diverse portfolios, fictionalized from career documents written by professional resume writers for real executive clients. We think you'll be inspired and energized as you put the final polish on your own preparations.

CHAPTER 6
Transition Stories and Portfolios

Thus far, we've shown you examples of every component of your resume, the key sections of your LinkedIn profile, and a wide array of additional ROI documents. We've given you guidelines and recommendations for creating your own unique and powerful messages, along with exercises to help you uncover and express your career stories. You should be well on your way to developing the foundational career documents you'll need before launching an accelerated job search.

Now, we go one step further and present complete transition stories and portfolios so you can see how numerous senior executives positioned themselves and executed their searches. On the following pages you'll find stories and samples for 19 executive job seekers, each package containing:

- **Backstory**—Background information explaining the individual's career goals along with the strategies used to create the marketing messages and documents. When possible, we also let you know the outcome—the conclusion of that specific search.

- **Executive resume**—The complete 2- or 3-page document written to position each executive for his or her current objective.

- **Additional ROI documents**—An assortment of LinkedIn profiles, cover letters and thank-you letters, executive biographies, executive leadership briefs, board resumes, and other materials created for that particular job seeker.

Read the backstories and leaf through the samples to gain additional ideas for preparing your own documents.

> **PRO TIP: Let your authentic self shine through.** As you review the following portfolios, notice that every document is different. Every strategy takes into account the strengths of each executive, the current career objective, and potential challenges. In a similar vein, your own documents must position you to achieve your specific goals.
>
> We encourage you to get ideas and inspiration from these samples and scenarios, but be sure that all of your messages—your resume, LinkedIn profile, letters, addenda—reflect your unique value and authentic voice.

In presenting these portfolios, we are proud to feature the contributions of a handful of executive resume writers, hand-picked because of their expertise and the consistently high quality of their work. At the top of each backstory you will find the name of the resume writer; and here we provide their complete contact information for those of you who wish to partner with the best in the industry.

Authors

Louise Kursmark, MRW, CPRW, JCTC, CEIP, CCM
Best Impression Career Services | Emerald Career Publishing—Greater Boston
774-404-7829
louise@louisekursmark.com
www.louisekursmark.com | www.emeraldcareerpublishing.com
www.linkedin.com/in/LouiseKursmark

Jan Melnik, M.A., MRW, CPRW, CCM
Absolute Advantage—Siesta Key, Sarasota, FL & Portland, CT
860-349-0256
jan@janmelnik.com
www.janmelnik.com
www.linkedin.com/in/JanMelnik

Recommended Executive Writers/Coaches

Darlene M. Dassy, CMRW, CERM, MYFRCW, CEIC
Dynamic Resume Solutions—Sinking Spring, PA
610-678-0147
info@dynamicresumesolutions.com
www.dynamicresumesolutions.com
www.linkedin.com/in/darlenedassy

Melanie L. Denny, MBA, CPRW, NCOPE
Resume-Evolution—Kissimmee, FL
888-765-8515
info@resume-evolution.com
www.resume-evolution.com
www.linkedin.com/in/melanieldenny

Wendy S. Enelow, CCM, MRW, JCTC, CPRW
Enelow Enterprises, Inc. | Emerald Career Publishing—Holden Beach, NC
434-444-4714
wendy@wendyenelow.com
www.wendyenelow.com | www.emeraldcareerpublishing.com
www.linkedin.com/in/WendyEnelow

Marjorie Sussman, MRW, ACRW, CPRW, ACCS
Dover Productions NYC—Greater NYC
201-941-8237
marjoriesussman@outlook.com
www.linkedin.com/in/marjoriesussmanmrw

Adrienne Tom, CERM, MCRS, CCS, CES, CIS
Career Impressions—Calgary, Alberta
587-332-6806
adrienne@careerimpressions.ca
www.CareerImpressions.ca
www.linkedin.com/in/adriennetom

Stephen Van Vreede, MBA, ACRW
ITtechExec—Rochester, NY
585-586-1385
stephen@ittechexec.com
www.ittechexec.com
www.linkedin.com/in/stephenvanvreede

Martin Weitzman, NCRW, RBPS, JCTC, CPRW
Gilbert Resumes—Englishtown, NJ
800-967-3846
marty@gilbertresumes.com
executiveresumewriter.com
www.linkedin.com/in/gilbertresumes

Emily Wong, MIM, ACRW, CPRW
Words of Distinction—Greater San Francisco
425-269-5549
emily@wordsofdistinction.net
www.wordsofdistinction.net
www.linkedin.com/in/emilyfithianwong

Marie Zimenoff, M.Ed., CHJMC, CPBS
Resume Writing Academy & Career Thought Leaders—Salt Lake City, UT
800-517-2080
marie@careerthoughtleaders.com
www.resumewritingacademy.com | www.careerthoughtleaders.com
www.linkedin.com/in/mariezimenoff

BACKSTORY: Mark S. Yee (Writer: Jan Melnik)

TARGET ROLE: Chief Executive Officer
CURRENT TITLE: President
INDUSTRY: Electronics Engineering

WRITER'S COMMENTS

Mark's executive career spans more than 20 years and includes top roles with brand-name companies in the electronics engineering, circuit board technology, and semiconductor space. Most recently he accepted a 1-year opportunity as interim President for a key industry player in need of rejuvenation and turnaround. He delivered—as has been characteristic of each of his senior leadership roles throughout his career.

Now poised for his next gig, Mark would like to leverage both executive management and leadership and exceptional speaking/mentoring capabilities for a high-potential, well-funded start-up (so VC/PE opportunities are welcome) or within a company or division that is seeking accelerated growth. Ideally, he'd prefer a highly visible CEO role where he isn't hiding in the glass tower—but putting his unique brand of leadership on an organization through global influence and advocacy.

WRITING/DESIGN STRATEGY FOR DOCUMENTS

Resume: The stories present the numbers and tell bottom-line results Mark has produced throughout his career. "High I" on the DISC, he has a turbocharged personality, and the language selected for outcomes in each of his roles brings this out.

LinkedIn: Mark's headline, his About section, and his Experience present an accomplished and highly capable Chief Executive Officer/President—one who has clearly talked the talk and walked the walk. His personality is robust and he has built a reputation for optimizing every organization and leadership team as a high-energy catalyst.

Bio: A somewhat unique bio focuses on key coaching and speaking expertise while amplifying corporate career growth. Mark has augmented resume distribution to each of his networking contacts as well as recruiters using this tool that helps to demonstrate his brand and what differentiates him from others.

UNIQUE CHALLENGES

As with many highly qualified executives with numerous turnaround success stories, selecting the optimal highlights to showcase Mark's talents presented the greatest challenge. He is very interested in developing a 30-60-90-day plan that would include significantly more detail if he becomes a finalist for the right position.

OUTCOME

Mark is currently meeting with industry headhunters and vetting potential opportunities for which he'd be a candidate when he wraps up his 1-year interim role.

MARK S. YEE

415-345-6789 | mark.yee@gmail.com | www.linkedin.com/in/mark-yee

CEO/PRESIDENT | VISIONARY LEADER | CHANGE AGENT

> Engineering & Technology > Strategic Operations > Executive Management > Board Leadership

Exceptional performance leading teams and transforming organizations—driving growth, profitability, business development, operations, sales, integration, and turnaround.

➢ **Secured 3 deals valued >$150M for Algard** while championing long-term aftermarket strategic plan.

➢ **Positioned Avalon to grow revenue at 12+% CAGR next 3 years,** retain valued customer relationships, and achieve lower cost targets while ensuring profitability.

➢ **Catapulted MMN division from $9M to $65M revenue** via strategy to capture long-term agreement with Ace Mfg.

Turnaround & Transformation | Talent Development | P&L | Global Leadership | Strategic Partnerships
Program/Value Stream Management | Engineering Leadership | DOD Security Clearance | Lean Manufacturing

EXECUTIVE EXPERIENCE

ALGARD SEMICONDUCTOR | SAN FRANCISCO, CA   2020–2021
Contract manufacturer of highly engineered electronics products.
President

Delivered rapid performance gains and set the company on a path to sustainable long-term growth.

Tapped for unique interim executive opportunity, leading $375M global business (full P&L, 800+ employees) during year-long sabbatical of permanent President. Achieved every financial performance measure during 1-year tenure.

➢ Developed aggressive, long-term strategic plan, pivoting from historical approaches with focus on long-term partnering fueled by organic growth as well as via acquisition. Presented to and garnered CEO support.

➢ Executed turnaround of unprofitable/underperforming site, resulting in first positive P&L in 3 years. Improved on-time delivery from mid 50s to >95% and turnaround times by ~20%.

➢ Crafted OEM transition plan and recruited key management resources for major growth in Asia with heavy focus on Apple relationship. Aggressive schedule included substantial CapEx procurement and installation in <1 year.

➢ Enacted business accountability drivers, optimizing team performance and achieving every Scorecard parameter.

➢ Drove technology development on new processes to secure new strategic business deal with electronics manufacturer valued at >$100M over 7 years.

➢ Negotiated new life for high-margin, pay-to-play spare parts deal with a major US defense contractor.

AVALON ELECTRONICS | HOUSTON, TX   2018–2020
Supplier of printed circuit boards and other engineered electronics products.
Chief Operating Officer

Hired to turn around post-acquisition organization, transform operations, and position for double-digit growth.

Within 1st year, fully integrated acquired business, rebranded to "One Avalon," and launched organizational redesign based on Centers of Excellence. Led 10 direct reports/1,600+ indirect reports across 15 US sites and Mexico.

➢ Championed organization-wide business transformation: Created business case, garnered Board buy-in, assembled team, and made multimillion $ investment to replace 6 disparate MRP systems/substandard infrastructure with SAP.

➢ Streamlined operations, closing 4 facilities and expanding 2. Realized $10M YOY cost savings, a 150K+ s.f. reduction in manufacturing space, and 19% productivity improvement.

...continued

AVALON ELECTRONICS | CONTINUED   **Mark S. Yee** | PAGE 2

➤ Reinvigorated languishing "design & build" program for a major European electronics manufacturer.
  — Led engineering teams through risk assessment using DFMEA model and tools to mitigate gaps in performance to design specifications.
  — Worked with customer senior management, negotiating work-scope changes to meet new EU regulatory issues.
  — Negotiated financial resolution to historical non-recurring cost overruns due to changes to technical scope.

➤ Strengthened strategic planning/forecasting process and instilled culture of accountability, instituting KPIs and scorecard/metrics across all business lines as well as bottom-up budgeting. Doubled win ratio of bid proposals.

➤ Spearheaded campaign that substantially improved working capital, reducing inventories >12% and improving free cash flow. Reduced debt ratio from 8.5 to 4.75 (targeting <3.5) while ensuring strategic CapEx investments.

➤ Achieved >98% on-time delivery and 99.9% quality while transitioning thousands of part numbers for a "right parts/right place/right equipment" strategy. Slashed costs by $13M in year 1 and $6M in year 2.

➤ Created Technology & Innovation Department, balancing low-cost/commodity strategies with in-house production.

MMN ELECTRONICS | PORTLAND, OR   2011–2018
Swedish-owned $4B manufacturer of complex, large-scale composite and metallic structures and assemblies.
EVP/GM, North America, 2015–2018

Rejuvenated underperforming operations, slashed costs, and grew profitability. Led >420% business growth.

Handpicked to lead turnaround of company's largest subdivision; full P&L for $600M business with 1,300+ employees.

➤ Developed 10-year strategic plan balancing existing business with emerging opportunities.
  — Consolidated 18 sites into 6 subdivisions.
  — Streamlined workforce for 22% cost savings.
  — Led bid for >$850M in new, long-term business, offsetting declining legacy programs.
  — Led campaign that secured formal partner position for MMN on new Ace Manufacturing product line.

➤ Optimized MMN's competitive posture through footprint rationalization and outsourcing using Lean/value stream approach. Progressive phased plan resulted in potential >30% savings on cost structure.

➤ Improved on-time delivery performance to >97%.

VP/GM, Portland Operations, 2011–2015

Directed operations and R&D with P&L oversight for $50M site with 135+ staff. Diversified technology and production programs and maturing product families. Consistently met or exceeded financial-operational budget goals.

➤ Developed long-term strategic plan for >30% YOY growth, including supplier co-location/vertical. Collaborated in developing technology JV agreement with key strategic customer. Improved market share from 60% to 100%.

➤ Championed 50% facility expansion as integral element of growth strategy. Helped secure $4M government funding.

➤ Secured 10-year program ($900M+) with Ace Manufacturing. Maintained operating profit margins and cut costs 38%.

PRIOR CAREER ADVANCEMENT

General Manager/Strategic Advisor, MacDonald Group (3 yrs.)
VP, Operations/GM, Monomoy, Inc. (3 yrs.) | **Director, Engineering & Tooling,** Monomoy, Inc. (2 yrs.)
Director, New Business Development/Engineering Director/Engineer, Maxima Engineered Products (7 yrs.)

───────── **EDUCATION & CIVIC** ─────────

GEORGE WASHINGTON UNIVERSITY | Washington, DC … MBA and B.S., Electrical Engineering
Training: Black Belt Six Sigma | MMN Lean Master Continuous Improvement Leadership Programs

Board Member: San Francisco Institute of Engineering & Science (2020–Present) | Houston Food Bank (2018–2020)

Mark S. Yee

CEO/COO | Highly Engineered Products/Electronics | Business Development & Operations Optimization | Supplier to Apple, Ace Manufacturing, Samsung | Board Leadership | Executive Coach

Algard Semiconductor
George Washington University MBA

Greater San Francisco Area • 500+ Connection

About

How do successful C-suite leaders distinguish themselves? What differentiates them from other senior executives? At the top of the list are likely such exceptional skills as engaging talent, driving individual and team performance … establishing accountability-focused goals … ensuring a consistent record of delivering results … and catapulting an organization to the next level. These same capabilities help to define my leadership style.

I have demonstrated numerous successes as an organizational leader and someone who cultivates and retains deep relationships over the course of my career. My reputation reflects an ability to set sights on "making it happen" and promote a culture where contributors can contribute and thrive. Combining strategic leadership with keen coaching skills, I am passionate about managing people and teams to maximize profit margins and generate impressive results.

My record also reflects leadership of enterprise-wide initiatives that build value and result in sustainable growth. Whether it is driving turnarounds and optimizing businesses, creating and leading business development initiatives, or championing transformational programs, I know how to leverage technology and innovation while never losing sight of the end game.

With C-suite experience spanning business development, sales, engineering, organizational management, and general operations, I have achieved strategic positioning for rapid, sustained growth and consistent market leadership. This is especially the case in the development and manufacturing of highly engineered electronics products. Bottom-line: I have a solid track record of transforming operations and sales—leading teams to deliver profitability and sustainable results.

A strong believer in giving back, my background has also enabled me to deliver value as a Board member, contributing to Boards of Directors at both the San Francisco Institute of Engineering & Science and the Houston Food Bank. I'm always interested in exploring Board opportunities to help companies enact strategic plans and achieve operational excellence.

Experience

PRESIDENT
Algard Semiconductor
2020–2021

I was brought on board to lead the organization during a planned 1-year sabbatical of its President. I held full P&L responsibility for the ~$375M business with 800+ employees.

In this short timeframe, I balanced the need to continue with existing programs that were highly successful while also creating a clear path to future growth.

Select performance highlights:

>> Developed aggressive, long-term strategic plan, pivoting from historical approaches with focus on long-term partnering fueled by organic growth as well as via acquisition. Presented to and garnered CEO support.

>> Executed turnaround of unprofitable/underperforming site, resulting in first positive P&L in 3 years. Improved on-time delivery from mid 50s to >95% and turnaround times by ~20%.

>> Crafted OEM transition plan and recruited key management resources for major growth in Asia with a heavy focus on Apple relationship. Aggressive schedule included substantial CapEx procurement and installation in <1 year.

>> Enacted business accountability drivers, optimizing team performance and achieving every Scorecard parameter.

>> Drove technology development on new processes to secure new strategic business deal with electronics manufacturer valued at >$100M over 7 years.

>> Negotiated new life for high-margin, pay-to-play spare parts deal with a major US defense contractor.

CHIEF OPERATING OFFICER
Avalon Electronics
2018–2020

I was hired to turn around Avalon Electronics following its acquisition of XYZ—the goal being to integrate and transform operations and position the company for major organic and acquisition-based growth at 10%+ CAGR. My team comprised 10 direct reports (including 2 VP-led P&Ls) and 1,600+ indirect reports, allocated across 15 US sites and Mexico.

In concert with the acquisition integration, I led a corporate-wide rebranding to create a "One Avalon" image both internally and externally.

In addition, I introduced a new culture of executive development, building bench strength for the future, and personally served as executive coach to the leadership team.

Select performance highlights:

>> Championed organization-wide business transformation: Created business case, garnered Board buy-in, assembled team, and made multimillion $ investment to replace 6 disparate MRP systems/substandard infrastructure with SAP.

>> Streamlined operations, closing 4 facilities and expanding 2. Realized $10M YOY cost savings, a 150K+ s.f. reduction in manufacturing space, and 19% productivity improvement.

>> Reinvigorated languishing "design & build" program for a major European electronics manufacturer.

>> Strengthened strategic planning/forecasting process and instilled culture of accountability, instituting KPIs and scorecard/metrics across all business lines as well as bottom-up budgeting. Doubled win ratio of bid proposals.

>> Directed campaign that substantially improved working capital, reducing inventories >10% and improving free cash flow.

>> Reduced debt ratio from 8.5 to 4.75 while ensuring strategic CapEx investment.

>> Achieved >98% on-time delivery and 99.9% quality while transitioning thousands of part numbers for a "right parts/right place/right equipment" strategy. Slashed costs by $13M in year 1 and $6M in year 2.

EVP/GM, North America
MMN Electronics
2015–2018

Following a 4-year stint as VP/GM of the Evanston operation of this Swedish-owned company, I was singled out to lead a turnaround of the entire US division (North America). My leadership scope included P&L for the $600M business with more than 1,300 employees and manufacturing and distribution sites across the US, Canada, and Mexico.

We were faced with large legacy programs that had been highly successful, but several contracts were nearing their natural conclusion. I knew that I needed to capture major new contracts while also improving the operating performance of our sites. I rallied my team and set to work.

Select performance highlights:

>> Developed 10-year strategic plan balancing existing business with emerging opportunities.
…Consolidated 18 sites into 6 subdivisions.
…Streamlined workforce for 22% cost savings.
…Led bid for >$850M in new, long-term business, offsetting declining legacy programs.

>> Optimized MMN's competitive posture through footprint rationalization and outsourcing that promised >30% savings on cost structure.

>> Improved on-time delivery performance to >97%.

>> Implemented value stream management system.

VP/GM, Portland Operations
MMN Electronics
2011–2015

I first served MMN as a consultant/advisor, during my stint with the MacDonald Group. I brought a strategic long-range view to the challenge of growing the business and was subsequently recruited to put my ideas into action as VP/GM of the company's largest US site.

Select performance highlights:

>> Developed long-term strategic plan for >30% YOY growth, including supplier co-location/vertical.

>> Improved market share from 60% to 100%.

>> Spearheaded 50% facility expansion as integral element of growth strategy.

>> Helped secure $4M government funding.

>> Secured 10-year program ($900M+) with Ace Manufacturing.

>> Maintained operating profit margins and cut costs 38%.

GENERAL MANAGER/STRATEGIC ADVISOR
MacDonald Group
2008–2011

Primary clients included MMN Electronics and several other global electronics manufacturers. My specific expertise was developing future-focused growth strategies.

Previous roles included:
VP/Operations GM — Director, Engineering & Tooling | Monomoy, Inc.
Director, New Business Development — Engineering Director — Engineer | Maxima Engineered Products

Mark S. Yee, the Executive's Coach

Visionary Catalyst for Growth-Oriented Companies ... and Top Professionals Seeking to Significantly Uplevel Their Game

Outstanding performance leading teams and transforming organizations— driving turnaround, profitability, business development, operations, sales, integration, and growth.

What are your <u>organization's</u> challenges? Untapped potential ... languishing opportunities?
How about your <u>individual</u> workplace challenges? Potential you haven't tapped ... personal challenges and goals?

LEADERSHIP SOLUTIONS

Whether it is a high-powered, visionary keynote talk or a kickoff to an industry event or conference ... or an intensive program for a company's senior leadership team and, individually, with its top executives, Mark creates customized programs that specifically address an organization's needs. Examples of innovative programs to such audiences as Primerica, Algard Semiconductor, MMN, Northwestern Medical Center, and many others include:

- ➤ Achieving Championship Behavior
- ➤ What it Takes to Drive Change
- ➤ Setting & Attaining Standards that Work
- ➤ Authenticity, Risk, and Change

BACKGROUND

With more than 25 years' experience as CEO, President, EVP, and COO of top companies in the engineered products/electronics industries, Mark has brought leadership and vision to Algard Semiconductor, Avalon Electronics, and MMN Electronics along with numerous others. His record of transformational management includes leading diversification and significant global growth at 5 companies, driving multiple M&A ventures, directing major integration and rationalization of acquired businesses, and orchestrating 3 successful turnarounds as well as holding Board positions with 4 organizations throughout his career.

BUT, Mark's passion is as a speaker and presenter—delivering exceptional leadership and change management strategies to senior-level executives, C-suite leadership teams, boards of directors, and companies desiring a significant upleveling in performance and results. Trained as a Six Sigma Black Belt, Mark brings a motivational and pragmatic delivery style to three key concepts:

#1... Scaling and Growth: Helping individuals and organizations accelerate, scale, and achieve outstanding results quickly. Proof of performance with speed of results are hallmarks of his programs.

#2... Vision and Innovation: Defining a game plan for success—specific, measurable benchmarks and goals and proven techniques to achieve them. His programs include strategic tools to reinforce the learning.

#3... Turnaround and Optimization: Mark's unique and pragmatic approach works to deliver individual-performance and corporate-optimizing actions and results that are sustainable and endure.

For those clients seeking to personally enhance their own development and performance, he incorporates a customized executive optimization program that includes health/wellness, fitness, and nutrition coaching. Mark helps his clients move the needle, taking them from where they *want to be* to having the tools to *achieve* the results they desire. **Call to explore how Mark can elevate your team's performance—and yours.**

Mark Yee, the Executive's Coach: Building Better Teams and Top Performers.

mark.yee@gmail.com | 415-345-6789

BACKSTORY: Willa Robinson (Writer: Louise Kursmark)

TARGET ROLE: Chief Strategy Officer
MOST RECENT TITLE: VP Corporate Development and Strategic Planning
INDUSTRY: Automotive

WRITER'S COMMENTS

Willa's entire career has been in the automotive industry. After college she quickly moved from engineering to marketing, product development, and strategic planning. She is fascinated at the ways that automation, electronics, robotics, and other advancements have impacted the industry and will continue to do so—and how these changes affect corporate strategy.

During the past 10 years with a global supplier to the automotive industry, she has been the driving force behind strategy shifts, new corporate direction, and financial turnarounds. She has extensive international experience, working with Asian suppliers and manufacturers. And she has many specific examples of revenue growth, cost reduction, and opportunity capture that she can take credit for.

Willa is ready to move up to the role of Chief Strategy Officer, remaining in the automotive industry where she has so much knowledge. In addition, she would like to serve on a board of directors, ideally in the auto industry.

WRITING/DESIGN STRATEGY FOR DOCUMENTS

Resume: The focal point of Willa's resume is the three graphs that immediately call attention to her most recent successes. The story behind each of the graphs is detailed in the opposite text. Each of her positions is introduced with a "Snapshot" paragraph that quickly encapsulates her role and overarching achievements.

Board Resume: Willa's board resume is a stripped-down version of her executive resume. Her prior board experience appears immediately below the summary (rather than at the end), and details of her professional experience are limited to the brief snapshot—if included at all.

Leadership Addendum: Because Willa has so much experience with M&A, JVs, international growth initiatives, and other experiences related to corporate strategy and structure, I created this addendum that groups like-with-like and provides more detail than the resume could accommodate. She planned to use the addendum as an interview follow-up and while networking for board opportunities.

UNIQUE CHALLENGES

Because Willa wants to focus her future career on strategy, not operations, in her documents it was important to emphasize activities and achievements that showed her vision, innovation, and long-term planning ability—not simply her in-the-trenches operational leadership.

OUTCOME

Willa left her company and started a strategy consulting firm. She also secured a seat on the board of a startup that is developing very promising technologies for self-driving cars.

WILLA ROBINSON

willa.robinson@mail.com   555-765-4321   linkedin.com/in/willarobinson

SENIOR STRATEGY EXECUTIVE: GLOBAL AUTOMOTIVE INDUSTRY

Executive with 15+ years of success driving strategic growth for Fortune 500 companies worldwide. Intuitive strategist able to translate vision to action, build support for new direction, and deliver results in complex environments. *Strengths:*

- ↗ Positioning and leading companies through transformative global growth.
- ↗ Improving profitability, market share, and product competitiveness.
- ↗ Executing strategic deals and business expansions in North America, Europe, and Asia.
- ↗ Accelerating the pace of innovation.

Strategic Planning • Marketing, Sales & Business Development • M&A, JV, Divestitures
Restructuring, Turnaround & Transformation • Team Leadership & Development • P&L Leadership
Product Management • Portfolio Management • Board Presentations & Interaction

PROFESSIONAL EXPERIENCE

AutoModule, Inc. (NYSE: AUMI)   Akron, OH • 2013–Present
$28B Fortune 500 global supplier of components, systems, modules, and vehicles to the automotive industry

VP Corporate Development & Strategic Planning, 2015–Present

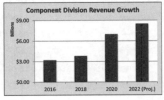

SNAPSHOT: Chief strategy executive and member of leadership team driving turnaround of component division. Redefined strategy, drove culture shift to global product orientation, spearheaded M&A, and steered company toward strategic growth: revenue +$3.5B and EBIT +$600M in 5 years.

CORPORATE STRATEGY

- ↗ Challenged traditional thinking and set new vision of a technology (not manufacturing) company.
- ↗ Revamped market approach and business structure. Created new role of 20+ Global Product Managers.
- ↗ Spearheaded portfolio management process and roadmap based on metrics and strategic fit.
- ↗ Exited non-strategic products, closed facilities, and drove higher growth, higher profit product investments.
- ↗ **Reversed negative EBIT to $500M positive and delivered 30% ROFE.**

INTEGRATION & TRANSFORMATION

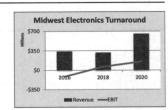

- ↗ Led integration of Midwest Electronics ($340M revenue, –$115M EBIT).
- ↗ Transformed business strategy, market approach, culture, and organizational structure.
- ↗ Exited unprofitable and non-strategic market segments and shifted focus to self-driving technologies.
- ↗ **In 4 years grew revenue 94% to $657M and improved EBIT $153M.**

M&A, CONSOLIDATION & TURNAROUND

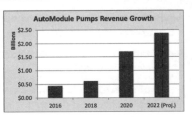

- ↗ Tasked with evaluating $440M (flat growth) commodity pump business being considered for divestiture.
- ↗ Identified growth opportunities requiring strategic refocus, technology acquisition, and diversification.
- ↗ Orchestrated 2 acquisitions and JV to expand global footprint. Integrated all entities into smoothly functioning global enterprise.
- ↗ **Grew sales from $440M to $1.7B; 5% market share to 20%.**

AutoModule, Inc. (CONTINUED)
Director Product Development & Marketing – AutoGlass Division, Shenzhen, China, 2014–2015

> **SNAPSHOT:** Created global strategy for $300M division, emphasizing product development, JV exploration, and engineering. Identified 9 acquisition/JV targets and divestitures in Asia and Europe. Performed due diligence, gained Board approval, and managed negotiations.

TURNAROUND & DIVESTITURE: CHINA JV——————————————————————————

- ↗ Took immediate action to address rapid performance decline when Chinese JV partner sold its shares to the Chinese government. Relocated to China as Senior Operating Executive and elected Board Member.
- ↗ Drove rapid operational improvements and pricing negotiations to improve profitability.
- ↗ Analyzed the business and recommended divestiture to our JV partner. Negotiated deal **($1.5M capital gain)** and shepherded sale through the complex government approval process.
- ↗ **Negotiated with SAFE Committee for release of $2.2M cash dividend virtually tax-free.**

Director Business Development & Marketing – AutoGlass Division, 2013–2014

> **SNAPSHOT:** Developed and executed turnaround and repositioning strategy that transformed $300M automotive glass division from 4% annual decline to rapid growth, new product launch, and international market expansion.

XYZ Industries, Inc., Automotive Glass Division (NYSE: XYZ)   Akron, OH • 2008–2013
$10B Fortune 200 global company, a diversified manufacturer of coatings, sealants, adhesives, glass, and chemicals
North American Marketing Manager, 2010–2013 • **Market Manager,** 2008–2010

> **SNAPSHOT:** Developed marketing, sales, program management, and R&D strategy to evolve organization from commodity producer to supplier of engineered and integrated systems. Vetted 3 international acquisitions: Merger that created $30M synergies; Greenfield for newly acquired technology licenses; and JV for $17M annual savings.

Xylon Automotive Systems, Inc.   Erie, OH • 1999–2008
Designer/manufacturer of driver control systems, a $1B global organization
Sales Manager: GMC Account, 2008 • **Sales Manager: Window Systems,** 2006–2008
Ford Account Manager, 2005–2006 • **Ford Sales Rep,** 2002–2005 • **Project Engineer,** 1999–2002

> **SNAPSHOT:** Progressed rapidly through Sales and Account Management roles, culminating as Sales Manager for the company's largest account ($450M).

EDUCATION

MBA, Ohio State University, Columbus, OH   2003
BS, Automotive Engineering Technology, University of Akron, Akron, OH   1992

BOARD POSITIONS

Advisory Board, Drive-Safe Technologies   2018–Present
Producer of an intelligent driver safety system that alerts drivers in real time of potential collisions and road hazards.

Vice Chair of the Board of Directors, Shenzhen/AutoGlass Window Systems   2014–2015
50/50 joint venture, half-owned by a Chinese government-owned enterprise.

Board of Directors, Akron Boosters Foundation   2012–Present
Nonprofit that advances the mission and goals of the university by generating and managing private financial support.

WILLA ROBINSON

willa.robinson@mail.com   555-765-4321   linkedin.com/in/willarobinson

BOARD MEMBER | STRATEGIST AND ADVISOR — GLOBAL AUTOMOTIVE INDUSTRY
Helping companies turn automotive technology into growth

Executive with 15+ years of success driving strategic growth: accelerating the pace of innovation, identifying evolving trends, and positioning companies to capture opportunities worldwide. Thought leadership in emerging automotive technologies: electrification, autonomous driving, connectivity, mobility. M&A and JV experience worldwide.

MBA, Ohio State University | **BS Automotive Engineering Technology,** University of Akron

BOARD POSITIONS

Advisory Board, Drive-Safe Technologies   2018–Present
Producer of an intelligent driver safety system that alerts drivers in real time of potential collisions and road hazards.

Vice Chairman of the Board of Directors, Shenzhen/AutoGlass Window Systems   2014–2015
50/50 joint venture, half-owned by a Chinese government-owned enterprise.

Board of Directors, Akron Boosters Foundation   2012–Present
Nonprofit that advances the mission and goals of the university by generating and managing private financial support.

PROFESSIONAL EXPERIENCE PROFILE

AutoModule, Inc. (NYSE: AUMI)   Akron, OH • 2013–Present
$28B Fortune 500 global supplier of components, systems, modules, and vehicles to the automotive industry
VP Corporate Development & Strategic Planning, 2015–Present

> **SNAPSHOT:** Chief strategy executive and member of leadership team driving turnaround of component division. Redefined strategy, drove culture shift to global product orientation, spearheaded M&A, and steered company toward strategic growth: revenue +$3.5B and EBIT +$600M in 5 years.

Director Product Development & Marketing – AutoGlass Division, Shenzhen, China, 2014–2015

> **SNAPSHOT:** Created global strategy for $300M division, emphasizing product development, JV exploration, and engineering. Identified 9 acquisition/JV targets and divestitures in Asia and Europe. Performed due diligence, gained Board approval, and managed negotiations.

Director Business Development & Marketing — AutoGlass Division, 2013–2014

XYZ Industries, Inc., Automotive Glass Division (NYSE: XYZ)   Akron, OH • 2008–2013
$10B Fortune 200 global company, a diversified manufacturer of coatings, sealants, adhesives, glass, and chemicals
North American Marketing Manager, 2010–2013 • **Market Manager,** 2008–2010

> **SNAPSHOT:** Developed marketing, sales, program management, and R&D strategy to evolve organization from commodity producer to supplier of engineered and integrated systems. Vetted 3 international acquisitions: Merger that created $30M synergies; Greenfield for newly acquired technology licenses; and JV for $17M annual savings.

Xylon Automotive Systems, Inc.   Erie, OH • 1999–2008
Designer/manufacturer of driver control systems, a $1B global organization
Sales Manager: GMC Account, 2008 • **Sales Manager: Window Systems,** 2006–2008
Ford Account Manager, 2005–2006 • **Ford Sales Rep,** 2002–2005 • **Project Engineer,** 1999–2002

WILLA ROBINSON

willa.robinson@mail.com   555-765-4321   linkedin.com/in/willarobinson

LEADERSHIP ADDENDUM

Following are specific examples that demonstrate leadership performance and success in planning and negotiating challenging acquisitions and joint ventures, promoting and implementing global growth initiatives, and orchestrating cost-effective organizational restructurings. **(This information is highly confidential.)**

ACQUISITIONS AND JOINT VENTURES

Advanced Auto Technologies (2020)

Most recently I led development of an end-to-end M&A strategy (target identification/qualification, due diligence, deal structure, negotiations, post-deal integration) for a $400M acquisition that provided access to new technology, diversified the customer base, improved our regional presence, and helped accelerate industry consolidation. I presented the plan to the Executive Committee and Board, projecting strong operating and financial results:

- ↗ New manufacturing footprint in Germany, Bulgaria, India, Brazil, and China.
- ↗ Immediate profitability—no restructuring needed, generating immediate cash sufficient to pay for the purchase in 5 years.
- ↗ More than $30M in synergies in addition to synergies from new sales opportunities.

The Board granted approval to proceed with the acquisition (currently in process) and later approved additional bolt-on acquisitions to expand technology capabilities.

Shimatsu JV — Japan (2012)

I oversaw business planning, valuation, and deal structure for a 50/50 JV with $2.5B automotive parts producer, predominately owned by Honda and Subaru, to produce all-wheel-drive (AWD) systems. Projected outcomes:

- ↗ Long-term supply agreement for all of Honda's and Subaru's AWD and 4WD systems.
- ↗ Projected booked business to hit $150M in sales by 2015.

Agarwal JV — India (2011)

I led the M&A process from target identification through negotiations for a 50/50 JV with a $285M automotive supplier to produce oil and water pumps in India. This was a Greenfield startup. Projected outcomes:

- ↗ Booked business expected to achieve $40M in sales by 2015 at an EBIT of approximately 10%.
- ↗ Expansion of JV with additional technology agreement for market that includes Thailand.

GLOBAL GROWTH INITIATIVES

Midwest Electronics (2016)

Charged with leading the integration of Midwest Electronics into AutoModule, I delivered a dramatic turnaround by instigating a cultural shift to a global product orientation focused on core technologies rather than manufacturing competencies. We restructured, divesting a profitable $100M lighting business into another AutoModule group. Further, we integrated the motor/actuator business into the Fluid Pressure & Controls Group and introduced the new role of global product manager to drive sales. Our efforts yielded positive results in first year:

- ↗ Sales – $439M to $621M; projected $688M 2022.
- ↗ EBIT – $115M loss improved $62M; projected $153M improvement 2022.
- ↗ Net Cash – negative $127M improved $50M; projected $147M improvement 2022.

LEADERSHIP ADDENDUM, CONTINUED

AutoModule Pumps (2016)

I was challenged to revitalize and grow this $440M commodity pump business. I immediately defined a new global vision and growth strategy, shifting to new fuel-efficient pump technologies, and established the new role of product manager to drive product development, business acquisition, and market growth. We re-directed our $30M CAPEX budget toward higher growth/more profitable products. As part of the growth strategy, I identified, evaluated, and recommended acquisition targets to the Executive Committee and Board. Financial and operating results included:

- ↗ Sales grew from $440M (2016) to booked sales of $1.5B with acquisition (2020).
- ↗ Global market share grew from 5%–6% market share (2016) to more than 18% (2020).
- ↗ $40M in new sales generated from 50/50 JV with Vietnamese manufacturer.
- ↗ Technology acquisition in Europe (Advanced Auto Technologies) will lead to additional sales of $400M.

DIVESTITURES | CLOSURES | EXITS

Midwest Electronics (2018/2020)

With the integration of Midwest Electronics into AutoModule, I developed a new business vision and conducted a thorough evaluation of the business portfolio. Subsequently I oversaw the exits of the $21M Ultrasonic product line and $30M Pedestrian Protection system and the sale of the Radar product portfolio to Ryder.

AutoModule Stamping Division (2016)

AutoModule decided to sell a $65M stamping manufacturing business in Michigan, but the sale was never completed due to the buyer's financial insolvency. Instead, I directed closure of the operation and relocation to two other facilities in less than one year, resulting in $4M annual savings; payback came in less than 1.5 years.

Shenzhen/AutoGlass Window Systems (2014)

When AutoModule purchased the AutoGlass business, the partner sold its interest to a Chinese government-owned enterprise. The $21M 50/50 JV had not had any active management for 10 years, was losing money, and required immediate action. I relocated to China to revitalize operations and was appointed Vice Chairman of the JV's Board of Directors. Launching an immediate evaluation of the JV, I determined it to be unprofitable and requiring divestiture. My negotiations through the complex government approval process, including the SAFE Committee, led to profitable results:

- ↗ $1.5M capital gain.
- ↗ Release of $2.2M cash dividend on virtually tax-free basis.

BACKSTORY: Angela Davis (Writer: Adrienne Tom)

TARGET ROLE: Vice President, Human Resources
CURRENT TITLE: Vice President, Corporate Services
INDUSTRY: Manufacturing and Industrial

WRITER'S COMMENTS

Angela wanted a portfolio of career tools for two unique purposes: first, to explore outside opportunities at the VP of HR level, after rising in the ranks over the past 15+ years in her current organization and seeking a new challenge. The other reason was that her team was putting forward her name for an industry award that required an executive bio and LinkedIn content.

In partnership with Angela, I created an executive resume, cover letter, LinkedIn profile content, and an executive bio—all designed with consistent branding, messaging, and appearance.

WRITING/DESIGN STRATEGY FOR DOCUMENTS

Resume: I highlighted Angela's brand of building highly accountable work cultures and strong teams. Her value-add is that she is not content with quick fixes and invests time in people and processes to bring about sustainable change. The resume is not flashy, yet is designed to help guide the reader's eye, with a strong emphasis on leadership strengths, HR skill sets, and positive organizational change. For interest and to help add credibility to content, supporting testimonials are featured.

Cover Letter: The letter was created to be customizable for a range of well-suited positions, expressing interest and sharing on-brand messaging. I included two sets of bullet points in the letter to make the file easy for readers to absorb and easy for Angela to tailor.

LinkedIn: Angela felt strongly about ensuring her profile appropriately reflected her leadership abilities, but she did not want to share detailed company stats or very specific results on this public platform. I aligned messaging and content with the executive resume and overall leadership story, sharing work history details and personal leadership strengths without releasing "all the facts."

Bio: To help make the bio more interesting, I structured the left side to highlight a few big impacts, skill sets, and value-add alongside a photo of Angela herself.

UNIQUE CHALLENGES

In recent roles, Angela has worked for a very traditional organization that hasn't changed its ways for some time, and she is proud of both the positive influence she has had on the organization, but also that she is the first female executive in the company's history. It was important to mention these details for her award application without overemphasizing them throughout the portfolio.

OUTCOME

Angela immediately submitted her documents for the award application and is awaiting word. She feels well equipped to manage a job search when she is ready to move that forward.

ANGELA DAVIS, CPHR

Toronto, ON M4B 1T4 ▪ 416-555-9711 ▪ angela.davis@gmail.com ▪ LinkedIn

VICE PRESIDENT | Corporate Services & Human Resources

Drive Change | Reduce Complexity | Develop People

Build Highly Accountable Work Cultures and Strong Teams

*Improve long-term health of corporate cultures by driving necessary business change through HR metrics.
Develop talent, culture, and leadership programs in alignment with business objectives to ensure operations deliver.
Fuel productivity by streamlining and simplifying complex tasks.*

☑ **Top Performer:** Streamlined diverse HR practices across multiple business units and geographies, introducing metrics that better aligned workforce demands with organizational priorities.

☑ **Team Builder:** Challenged teams to "up their game." Secured multiple team recognitions, including Service Excellence Awards 5 years straight.

☑ **Change Leader:** Facilitated department turnarounds, influencing critical business changes by compelling executive management and board buy-in.

☑ **Strategic Executor:** Elevated leadership, accountability, and talent through HR metrics, processes, and system advancements. Introduced first cloud-based system in company's 60-year history to support business decisions.

> *"Angela demonstrated success in quickly understanding the broad scope of the business and its drivers, speaking to her ability to deliver results and so gain the trust of the highly experienced executive team at Titan."*
>
> - CEO, Titan

Career Evolution

Titan Industries Ltd.—Toronto, ON | 2010–Present
Privately owned Canadian steel products company with over 6,000 employees across 6 provinces. Sales of over $2B.

VICE PRESIDENT, CORPORATE SERVICES | 2015–Present
Budget: $7M | Payroll: $95M | Procurement Managed Spend: $100M | Direct Reports: 9

Advanced within position to take on both HR and corporate services oversight. Reporting to CEO/President, continue to drive execution of operating plans and strategic organizational objectives with executive management team. Prioritize procurement spend to manage profitability and cash flow. Direct HR initiatives and infrastructure. Oversee communications plan creation and implementation.

KEY IMPACT: Progressed workplace culture and positioned company for profitable growth through strategic change and productivity enhancements.

▪ **Generated and implemented board-approved executive succession plan** in alignment with organizational goals to increase effectiveness of corporate communications and ensure consistent brand recognition.

▪ **Boosted employee engagement, reduced turnover, and raised staff productivity** through focused HR initiatives, people strategies, and targeted recruitment and sourcing campaigns.

> **Corporate Services Group Oversight: 65 Members**
> Corporate Human Resources, Procurement, Communications, Office Administration, Building Maintenance, and Leasing

  ✓ Escalated employee engagement score 68% in 3 years via competitive total rewards strategy.
  ✓ Lowered disability leaves from 62 days to 19 days per claim.
  ✓ Reduced trade turnover 54% in 1 year through location-specific compensation programs.
  ✓ Improved employee referrals from 2.2% to 36%.
  ✓ Decreased external search firm costs $800K/year through dedicated internal recruitment position.

▪ **Enhanced organizational profitability.** Introduced strategic procurement sourcing strategy and inventory management plan, mitigating risk through governance and standardization.
  ✓ Generated 26% annual savings on $100M managed spend and avoided $1M additional spend.
  ✓ Reduced overall inventory $1.5M in first year.

Angela Davis, CPHR | Page 2

VICE PRESIDENT, HUMAN RESOURCES | 2011–2015
Budget: $4.5M | Payroll: $85M | Direct Reports: 5 | Employees: 2,500 | Work Sites: 12

Stepped into newly created role as first female executive in company's history to develop and execute HR strategies, programs, systems, and practices in alignment with organizational operating plans.

KEY IMPACT: As member of executive leadership team, spearheaded turnaround of struggling HR department and escalated people development.

- **Implemented new organizational structure and compensation strategy,** positively challenging status quo to increase productivity and performance.
  - ✓ Produced succession program to filter down throughout company, creating pipeline for key roles.
  - ✓ Increased manager effectiveness 46% through in-house training.

- **Improved operating performance,** creating people plan to address turnover, team effectiveness, and recruitment.
  - ✓ Lowered turnover from 29% to 12% in 3 years and increased engagement 30% in 3 years. Broke multiple production records.
  - ✓ Created standard operating procedures and hired 150+ employees to start up new mill, which achieved 80% engagement score—highest in company.

- **Created additional competitive benefit and incentive programs.** Generated 30% reduction in costs while placing company in top quartile for competitiveness.

> *"Your group is of a higher calibre than what I see from your competitors in the industry; whatever you are doing with respect to recruiting, identifying high potentials, and developing them is working."*
>
> – External Industry Trainer

Local Power Corp.—Toronto, ON | 2005–2011
Ontario's leading electricity supplier.

GENERAL MANAGER, HUMAN RESOURCES
Budget: $12M | Payroll: $200M | Direct Reports: 6 | Team Members: 62 | Employees: 2,100

Reporting to President/CEO, directed all HR initiatives, including compensation and benefits, payroll, recruitment, employee relations, labour relations, and organizational development for staff across 4 business units and 6 support groups. Supported executive management with creative strategic business partnerships.

KEY IMPACT: Turned around poor union and management relationships, fostering trust to increase communications and generate new policies. Reduced filed grievances 65%.

- **Transformed HR into strategic business partner.** Increased accountability and performance by creating HR strategy with process improvements, technology advances, and metrics system.
  - ✓ Achieved recognition as one of top 15 employers in province and one of top 25 diversity employers in Canada.

Committee & Association Work

Member: Steel Product Association of Canada HR Committee, 2010–Present
Member: Titan Business Solutions Steering Committee, 2013–Present
Chair: Titan Compensation Committee, 2013–Present / Member: Titan Pension Committee, 2012–Present
CPHR/Member: Ontario Human Resource Association, 2010–Present

Education & Training

Bachelor of Commerce: Human Resources Management—University of Toronto, 2000
Advanced Trust Management Standards: International Foundation of Employee Benefit Plans, 2014
Master's Certificate: Project Management—Executive Education Center, 2010
Change Management Certificate—Prosci, 2010

ANGELA DAVIS, CPHR

Toronto, ON M4B 1T4 ▪ 416-555-9711 ▪ <u>angela.davis@gmail.com</u> ▪ <u>LinkedIn</u>

VICE PRESIDENT | Corporate Services & Human Resources

Drive Change | Reduce Complexity | Develop People

Build Highly Accountable Work Cultures and Strong Teams

DATE

NAME, TITLE
COMPANY
ADDRESS
CITY / PROVINCE

Dear SALUTATION:

As a **transformative HR executive with 15+ years of progressive leadership expertise,** I am now seeking a new challenge within human resources or corporate services. My preference is an executive leadership position with a strong people focus. Although I am open to working in a range of industries, my background includes recent experience in the manufacturing and resource sectors.

In my current leadership position with Titan Industries, I partner with the executive team to develop and execute on the strategic business plan, positioning the business for sustainable growth. I bring the following skills and leadership strengths to the table:

- **Revitalizing underperforming services and teams** and implementing highly accountable work environments and staff.
- **Developing streamlined HR strategies, programs, and systems** in alignment with business goals, leveraging metrics and technologies to support business decisions.
- **Strengthening continuity of leadership strategy** and establishing comprehensive succession plans for key business roles.
- **Bringing together divergent HR practices** across different business units and geographies, tying the HR function to business requirements and growth.

Highly dedicated to my work, with a laser focus on accountability and simplicity, I am most energized when my teams develop and excel. In addition to securing multiple team awards for service excellence over the years, I have delivered the following wins for Titan as both VP of Corporate Services and VP of Human Resources:

- ✓ Strong, accountable workforces of 2,500+ employees aligned with strategic business direction.
- ✓ Increased business profitability, productivity, and cash flow by as much as 30%.
- ✓ Solid corporation-wide succession programs with dependable pipelines.
- ✓ Drastic rise in employee engagement, retention, and management effectiveness—as much as 30%.

I am certain that my expertise would be of tremendous value to your organization as you seek to raise business productivity via sustainable HR and corporate services solutions. My attached resume details my experience, but I would welcome a chance to discuss things with you in greater detail soon. Can we arrange a time to talk?

Sincerely,

Angela Davis, CPHR
Enclosed: Resume

Angela Davis

VP Human Resources/ Corporate Services: Build accountable work cultures and strong teams to boost business performance

Titan Industries Ltd.
University of Toronto

Toronto, ON • 500+ Connections

About

My strength as Vice President of Human Resources & Corporate Services is stepping in to revitalize service departments and teams and improving organizations by designing and implementing strategic HR plans and management systems.

I like to get things done, but never with quick fixes.

Change takes dedicated focus. My leadership approach is to generate sustainable visions and plans, identify the culture required to support execution, and align teams and processes with organizational goals.

In my current role as VP of Corporate Services, I improved company profitability and cash flow with a strategic sourcing strategy. I enhanced internal communications, implemented HR strategies to attract and retain top talent, and created a leadership succession program.

Change also requires accountability. Known for introducing highly accountable work cultures that "up everyone's game," I'm proud of the people I've developed. My teams have been recognized with multiple Excellence in Service Awards and accolades over the years.

Finally, I have a need for simplicity. My current CEO tells me, "You make complex things simple," and that is because I believe that simplifying and streamlining systems, procedures, and policies is best achieved through strong, basic foundations to further build upon.

Highly dedicated to my executive HR work, with a well-rounded business acumen, my expertise spans the areas of:

● Building highly accountable work cultures and teams
● Driving business change through HR metrics and technologies
● Developing leadership, talent, and culture programs aligned with business goals
● Progressing clear deliverables
● Acquiring and retaining great employees

Please reach out to connect and discuss common interests—building business productivity through sustainable HR and corporate services solutions and leadership.

Experience

Vice President, Corporate Services
Titan Industries Ltd.
2015–Present

Evolved leadership position to include corporate services group, in addition to corporate human resources oversight. Areas of management include procurement, communications, and office administration. Direct team of 65.

As member of executive leadership team, support development and execution of long-term corporate plans and policies. Formulate and drive strategies to realize key goals. Build relationships between departments and stakeholders to improve efficiencies.

Establish department strategies, aligning systems, processes, and business practices with corporate strategic objectives. Report to CEO/President.

SELECT IMPACTS:

● Developed strategic sourcing strategy and inventory management plan, enhancing company profitability and cash flow.

● Implemented competitive total rewards strategy, disability management program, and defined learning strategy, boosting employee engagement and reducing turnover. Received Top 100 Ontario Employer Award in 2017.

● Championed introduction of innovative technologies and systems, including company's first HRIS cloud-based system.

● Restructured internal communications, creating plan with delivery dates and clear accountabilities. Increased information transparency and opened dialogues.

Vice President, Human Resources
Titan Industries Ltd.
2011–2015

In newly created position, stepped in to transform department and team, building leadership bench strength. Drove attraction, development, and retention of top talent to support long-term organizational success, aligning workforce plan with business requirements.

Partnering with executive team, worked collaboratively to interpret company's strategic and operating plans, and then developed tailored HR strategies, programs, and systems to support workforce demands.

Provided HR services to over 2,500 employees located at 12 work sites.

SELECT IMPACTS:

● Developed corporation-wide succession program with pipeline for key roles.

● Piloted first rapid mobile learning application and created in-house training program.

● Conducted detailed competitive benefit analysis to generate more robust, cost-controlled program. Negotiated new vendors and streamlined offerings.

● Created recruitment plan and SOPs to support new location start-up. Hired over 150 employees, executing recruitment plan under budget.

General Manager
Local Power Corp.
2005–2011

Directed HR initiatives, including compensation and benefits, payroll, diversity, recruitment, organizational development, employee relations, and return to work for 2,100 employees located in 4 business units and 6 support groups.

SELECT IMPACTS:

• Instituted organization-wide performance management system to align employee objectives with corporate priorities.

• Engaged union representatives to rebuild trust and communications. Achieved withdrawal of 200+ union grievances after analyzing and completing job evaluations.

Human Resources Country Manager
Water Inc.
2003–2005

Led integration and administration of HR best practices to strengthen and drive HR contributions across enterprise. Managed 11 employees.

SELECT IMPACTS:

• Implemented defined HR metrics and programs, reducing turnover and temporary labor costs.

• Collaborated with senior leadership to define and implement requirements for new sales compensation plan for Canadian consultants.

Director of HR / Manager of HR / Coordinator of HR
Big Box Technologies
2001–2003

Brought on board as HR Coordinator to solidify organization's first fully functioning HR department. Managed all facets of HR, including payroll, benefits, and related HR programs for 500 employees in multiple provinces. Promoted to HR Manager in 2002 and into director position in 2004, overseeing development of Canadian HR strategies and process improvements.

SELECT IMPACTS:

• Partnered with VP to facilitate negotiations of benefits program, selecting more cost-effective carrier.

• Redesigned, streamlined, and automated programs to deliver cost savings.

ANGELA DAVIS, CPHR

Toronto, ON M4B 1T4 ▪ 416-555-9711 ▪ <u>angela.davis@gmail.com</u> ▪ <u>LinkedIn</u>

VICE PRESIDENT | Corporate Services & Human Resources

Drive Change | Reduce Complexity | Develop People

Build Highly Accountable Work Cultures and Strong Teams

Millions in Cost Savings

5 Service Excellence Awards

2,500+ Employees | $7M+ Budgets

HR LEADERSHIP EXPERTISE:

Strategic HR Planning
Change Management
Continuous Improvement
Employee Engagement
Productivity Enhancement
Performance Management
Stakeholder Engagement
Team Leadership

"I LIKE TO GET THINGS DONE, BUT NOT WITH QUICK FIXES."

Angela Davis is a transformative executive leader who is never content with quick fixes. Beyond her talent for building accountable work cultures and teams, she develops strong foundations in processes and programs to align workforce plans with business requirements. She ensures that organizations and their people are well equipped and strongly positioned for results and sustainable growth—and she takes the time necessary to get it done right.

As the first female executive in Titan Industries' 60-year history, Angela, who has seen her role expand from Vice President of Human Resources to Vice President of Corporate Services, partners with executive leadership and the board of directors to shape and execute organizational strategic direction. Most energized when progressing deliverables, Angela creates clear targets and executes with firm expectations to achieve results.

Angela's leadership expertise spans a wide range of operational functions, including human resources, procurement, administration, payroll, and communications. Add to this her many years of leveraging HR metrics to influence corporate decisions, and she is a well-rounded business leader equipped and driven to manage critical change and strategic objectives.

Often described as someone who "ups everyone's game," Angela has generated substantial benefits for Titan. Managing $100M in procurement spend, she introduced a procurement strategy that drove up corporate profitability and cash flow. She also increased employee engagement, implemented a corporation-wide succession program, and transitioned HR into a strategic business partner.

In addition to her corporate leadership activity, Angela is blazing trails in the steel industry, developing a youth initiative and a women's strategy to encourage the participation of these key groups. She also shares her expertise and insights on numerous boards and councils, including as chair of Titan's compensation committee.

Driven to deliver, Angela steers the improvement of systems and efficiencies through simplicity. She is forward-thinking and innovative, bringing on board new technologies and fresh initiatives to boost productivity. Angela introduced the company's first cloud-based HRIS system, piloted a rapid mobile learning app, and spearheaded creation of a multilingual website—the first of its kind in the industry.

Along with revitalizing departments and teams, Angela is immensely proud of the people she has developed over the years. She coaches and mentors for success with clear expectations and reasonable timelines. As a testament to her leadership, her team and staff have been recognized with multiple awards, including Service Excellence Awards in each of the past 5 years.

Angela's affinity for acquiring and shaping talent, making complex tasks simple, and holding leaders and teams accountable has established her reputation for being dependable, hardworking, and purposeful. Critical change takes investment and focused direction. It also takes perseverance. Angela has proven her capacity to lead change initiatives in challenging work environments with a unique determination that always advances companies.

BACKSTORY: James Sutton (Writer: Emily Wong)

TARGET ROLE: Senior Vice President/Chief Sales Officer
CURRENT TITLE: Senior Vice President, Worldwide Sales Engineering
INDUSTRY: Technology (Cloud/VoIP)

WRITER'S COMMENTS

James is looking for a new position where he can continue to use his skills to turn around stagnant teams or build new ones, while continuing to speak at high-profile industry events. He came to me with a four-page, highly technical resume that was densely packed with every product and technology he had sold, dating back into the 90s.

I had to convince him that we could do a better job of showcasing his relevance as a leader by focusing on more high-level achievements, creating more white space, and limiting the timeline to this century.

WRITING/DESIGN STRATEGY FOR DOCUMENTS

Resume: James's unique trifecta of gifts: team transformation, global excitement, and historic sales (all of which feed into one another) served as the foundation of his success as a leader. The top section of the resume brands him in a way that is easily readable, with three quick snapshots of his value and legacy.

While I wanted to soften the edges of the overwhelming technical jargon in his original resume, it was also important to keep elements of those skills and products in the resume as proof of his background and experience, so finding that sweet spot of what to keep and what to let go was a challenge, but worth the effort.

Cover Letter: Typically, the cover letters I write are shorter, but with James I felt this was an opportunity to communicate how virtually every move he made to challenge and energize his teams led to some outstanding result. Also, the greater detail gives James leeway for customizing to different opportunities.

LinkedIn: I see the "About" section of LinkedIn as the best place to convey James's humanity, highlight his skills as a keynote speaker, and call out his ability to make strong connections with teams, customers, and media analysts—in essence, build a narrative around the "why" of his success. To add color to this section, I uploaded rich media clips from his keynotes and demos.

In the Experience section, I chose to use subheadings to showcase content in three distinct areas: Challenge, Results and Recognition, and Keynotes and Other Presentations.

UNIQUE CHALLENGES

For a detail-oriented person in a highly technical profession, it was a challenge to embrace documents with less detail, less tech-speak, and more personality. But James trusted my recommendations and moved forward confidently into his search.

OUTCOME

James landed a role as the VP of Global Solutions Engineering at a global company on an accelerated growth trajectory. He continues to post about his keynote addresses and add dynamic media to his LinkedIn profile.

JAMES SUTTON

(222) 555 5555

Linked in
james.sutton@gmail.com

GLOBAL TECHNICAL SALES EXECUTIVE & KEYNOTE SPEAKER

Team Transformation → **Global Excitement** → **Historic Sales**

☐ Award-winning enterprise and mid-market **sales leader** with a track record of delivering strategic solutions, services, and cloud applications that scale for record growth.

☐ In-demand **keynote speaker** and **technical expert** who ignites enthusiasm among media, customers, and industry analysts at global industry seminars.

☐ **Professional development advocate** recognized for transforming and galvanizing technical teams to unite around a common ambitious goal to achieve peak individual performance.

Fastest-growing Region
Top-producing Teams
100% *President's Club* **Recognition**
Top-ranked Global Leader
Annual Quota Dominance

Key Deliverables

Organizational Restructuring *New Business Unit Builds*	*Customer Experience* *Strategic Solution Selling*	*Global Sales Training & Development* *Media & Analyst Relations*

Cloud § **UCaaS** § **CCaaS** § **CPaaS** § **Mobile** § **VoIP** § **SaaS**

CAREER HISTORY AND IMPACT

VONTAGE — San Francisco, CA

Senior Vice President, Worldwide Sales Engineering (WWSE) — 2018–Present

Tapped by Board of Directors to restore excellence and sense of unified purpose to worldwide sales, network, and channel sales engineering and solutions consulting organization of 200 across 3 continents.

- Quickly transformed international network of Sales Engineers into a cohesive, top-producing team.
- Rebuilt the organization by unifying disparate sales resources across the Americas, Asia, and Europe and establishing a standardized global incentive program. Results included consistent YOY revenue growth of >40% in mid-market and enterprise segments.
- Served as keynote speaker for *Global Vontage Experience Tour* and introduced our award-winning UCaaS and CCaaS single cloud platform.
- Organized and co-hosted a *Global Technology Summit* training program for 1K+ attendees in Boston to update worldwide Sales Engineers (SEs) on the current state of technical competency company-wide and create a plan for skills development.

Vice President, Worldwide Systems Engineering — 2016–2018

Recruited to lead WW Enterprise & Service Provider Systems Engineering organizations, reporting to WW Sales VP.

- Built company's 1st Channel SE organization for the Americas and closed out 2016 with 100% *President's Club* recognition for team members due to 175% year-end quota achievement.
- Orchestrated demos at annual *Mobile World Congress* in Barcelona and *Enterprise Connect Tokyo*. Showcased 1st live software-defined networking (SDN) demo and virtualized session border controller (SBC) demo for HPE's Network Functions Virtualization (NFV) system.
- Drove a 200% sales increase in voice licenses by repositioning Microsoft-certified Vontage session border controllers.
- Presented technical demos at 25 industry events for more than 40K customers and channel partners across the Americas.

3CX   Los Angeles, CA

Vice President, Technical Sales & Engineering—Americas   2014–2016

Promoted to lead technical sales team of 75 SEs and business development managers across the US, Canada, and LatAm.

- Achieved best-in-company NPI (new product introduction) attach rate of 28% on all product sales while exceeding launch target by 33% by mobilizing team leaders around solutions sales for cloud, UC/video, CC, and networking portfolios.
- Ranked among the top 10% of 1K+ global leaders as evaluated by HR's global manager-maker survey, most notably for increasing productivity by 30% through initiatives such as a competitive sales training program.
- Grew sales 30% by restructuring a 70-person Business Consulting Contact Center and US Networking Sales organization by creating a Fortune 10 focus team with the top 12 networking consulting SEs.
- Launched a strategic promotion to drive the legacy installed base to new platforms, generating an incremental $23M.

Director, Technical Operations & Business Development—Americas   2013–2014

Built and led an elite specialist organization responsible for profitable revenue growth in unified communications, contact centers, and networking solutions for the Americas International Theater (Canada, Caribbean, and Latin America).

- Drove strategic growth by recruiting top talent from Microsoft, Cisco, and Juniper to create a Business Development Organization that led monthly business unit reviews for CC, UC, and networking solutions.
- Introduced new product sales strategies to position 70 new products released within 18 months. Achieved 112% of $380M annual quota. Earned recognition for fastest growing region and only area to reach 100% of new product target.
- Served as keynote presenter at various global industry events in San Francisco, Mexico City, Sao Paulo, and Toronto.

VERSATEL NETWORKS   Los Angeles, CA

Systems Engineering Leader   2011–2013

Integrated engineering resources for West Coast region. Aligned 20 SEs for territory and named accounts with a $100M quota.

- Retained customers and partners by delivering roadmap presentation that assured commitment to legacy investments.
- Sparked 125% of quota by landing key partnerships with the city of Tacoma, WA, and the University of CA network.
- Earned the *Top Systems Engineering Manager in North America Award* at the 2011 Global Sales Conference.

National Sales Director, Applications & Software   2007–2011

Quickly promoted to restructure and lead a specialized sales team to grow applications and professional services funnel.

- Led team that landed several key accounts, including Summit Health, Wells Fargo, and Los Angeles County, CA.
- Increased annual call center revenues 54% and UC apps 32%, with highest application attach rate of 35%.
- Served as key spokesperson for media, analysts, and consultants across the Americas for all new solution launches.
- Earned *Achievers Club* 3X, including during severe economic downturn: 2010: 145%, 2009: 135%, 2008: 140%.

Senior Manager, VoIP Sales   2002–2007

Oversaw key accounts, including Allstream, CTS, LATel, and Bell West.

- Positioned top 2 product lines to win Allstream's competitive VoIP $55M 3-year contract.
- Earned *Honors Circle* sales recognition 4X for exceeding sales quotas.
- Achieved *Top Sales* designation within the company for exceeding objectives over 5 straight years.

EDUCATION

MIT | School of Engineering | **MS Electrical Engineering**

UCLA | Henry Samueli School of Engineering | **BS Mechanical Engineering**

To: karismith@xyzinc.com
Subject: President of Global Sales

Dear Ms. Smith:

With a career driving record growth through game-changing sales strategies and robust training and incentive programs, I'm well-positioned to lead XYZ Inc. as your next President of Global Sales.

As the Senior Vice President, Worldwide Sales Engineering at Vonage, I take a two-pronged approach to driving excitement. Internally, I've been committed to the continued development of my award-winning global team of Sales Engineers for one of the fastest growing VoIP companies, and I have the track record to prove my approach to cultivating talent works. The following illustrates my success leading teams and organizations to achieve excellence:

- Transforming Vontage's Sales Engineering organization by unifying disparate teams across the globe, co-hosting a Global Technology Summit training program, and establishing a standard global incentive program.
  Results: Consistent YOY revenue growth of at least 40% in mid-market and enterprise segments.

- Building Vontage's 1st Channel Sales Engineering organization.
  Results: 175% year-end quota achievement and 100% *President's Club* recognition.

- Mobilizing 3CX's team leaders around solution sales for cloud, UC/video, CC, and networking portfolios.
  Results: Achieved best-in-company NPI attach rate of 28% on all product sales. Exceeded launch target by 33%.

- Introducing new product sales strategies and training that positioned 70 new products released within 18 months.
  Results: Earned 112% of $380M annual quota and recognition for fastest growing region and only area to reach 100% of new product target.

The above results were bolstered by my other passion: evangelizing our solutions to partners, analysts, and media around the globe through high-profile sales presentations and new launch demos. Most recently, I served as the keynote speaker at the global *Vonage Experience Tour*, where I introduced our award-winning UCaaS and CCaaS single cloud platform.

I've also delivered technical demos at more than 25 industry events for some 40K customers and channel partners around the world, including at the annual *Mobile World Congress* in Barcelona and *Enterprise Connect Tokyo*, where I showcased our first live SDN demo and virtualized session border controller.

I'm confident that my unique experience driving excitement both internally and externally meets the needs of XYZ Inc., and I would welcome an opportunity to meet in person to further discuss how I can mobilize your Sales Engineering team to achieve dramatic results. I can be reached at (222) 555 5555 to set up an interview.

Sincerely,

James Sutton
(222) 555 5555
james.sutton@gmail.com

James Sutton

Award-winning Global Technical Sales Leader and Keynote Speaker Who Delivers Radical Team Transformation and Record Sales

Vontage
University of California at Los Angeles • Massachusetts Institute of Technology

Greater San Francisco Area • 500+ Connections

About

I'm a Global Technical Sales Leader and Keynote Speaker with experience galvanizing high-performing teams that deliver strategic solutions, services, and cloud applications—including UCaaS, CCaaS, CPaaS, Mobility, and VoIP—that scale for exceptional growth.

Currently, I'm the Senior Vice President of Global Sales Engineering at Vontage, where I built the Global Sales Engineering & Solutions organization by unifying diverse teams across the globe. In that role, I recruited, retained, and promoted high-potential professionals from within to build GSE into an award-winning team that drives record revenue growth in mid-market and enterprise segments.

When I'm not on site building and supporting my teams, I'm on the road evangelizing our products and solutions to large audiences across the globe through keynotes at industry events that include Global Vontage Experience Tour, where we introduced X-Series, an award-winning UCaaS and CCaaS single cloud platform.

I've also presented technical demos at more than 25 industry events for channel partners, media, and industry analysts across the Americas, Europe, and Asia. Most recently, I showcased our first live software-defined networking (SDN) demo and virtualized session border controller (SBC) demo for HPE's Network Functions Virtualization (NFV) system at the annual Mobile World Congress in Barcelona and Enterprise Connect Tokyo.

Prior to Vontage, I served in senior leadership roles at various cutting-edge technology companies, where I was recognized as a top revenue driver and professional development advocate.

AWARDS INCLUDE
► 100% President's Club Recognition by team
► Top Systems Engineering Manager in North America
► Achievers Club 4X
► Honors Circle 3X
► Top Sales designation

SKILLS: Sales Leadership, Change Management, Organizational Efficiency, Keynote Presentations, Unified Communications, Collaboration, Contact Centers, Mobility, Networking, Cloud, Video, Applications, VoIP, IP Telephony, Professional Services, Media & Analyst Relations, Customer Experience, CX, UCaaS, CCaaS, CPaaS, Mobility, VoIP, SaaS, Organizational Restructuring, New Business Unit Builds, Strategic Solution Selling, Global Sales Training & Development, Media & Analyst Relations

Experience

Senior Vice President, Worldwide Sales Engineering (WWSE)
VONTAGE
2018–Present

CHALLENGE:
Restore excellence and sense of unified purpose to worldwide sales, network, and channel sales engineering and solutions consulting organization of 200 across 3 continents.

RESULTS:
► Quickly transformed international network of Sales Engineers into a cohesive, top-producing team by rebuilding the organization and unifying disparate sales resources across the Americas, Asia, and Europe and establishing a standardized global incentive program.
► Drove consistent YOY revenue growth of at least 40% in mid-market and enterprise segments.

KEYNOTES & OTHER PRESENTATIONS:
► Served as keynote speaker for the Global Vontage Experience Tour: Introduced leading UCaaS & CCaaS single cloud platform.
► Organized and co-hosted a Global Technology Summit training program for 1K+ attendees in Boston.

Vice President, WW Systems Engineering
VONTAGE
2016–2018

CHALLENGE:
Lead North American Enterprise & Service Provider Systems Engineering organizations, reporting to WW Sales VP.

RESULTS & RECOGNITION:
► Built company's 1st Channel SE organization for the Americas and closed out 2016 with 100% President's Club recognition for team members due to 175% year-end quota achievement.
► Drove a 200% sales increase in voice licenses by repositioning Microsoft certified session border controllers.

KEYNOTES & OTHER PRESENTATIONS:
► Orchestrated demos at annual Mobile World Congress in Barcelona and Enterprise Connect Tokyo. Showcased 1st live software-defined networking (SDN) demo and virtualized session border controller (SBC) demo for HPE's Network Functions Virtualization (NFV) system.
► Presented technical demos at 25 industry events for more than 40K customers and channel partners across the Americas.

Vice President, Technical Sales & Engineering — Americas
3CX
2014–2016

CHALLENGE:
Assume leadership of and mobilize a technical sales team of 75 SEs and business development managers across the US, Canada, and Latin America around a common goal.

RESULTS & RECOGNITION:

► Achieved best-in-company NPI (new product introduction) attach rate of 28% on all product sales while exceeding launch target by 33% by mobilizing team leaders around solutions sales for cloud, UC/video, CC, and networking portfolios.
► Ranked among the top 10% of 1K+ global leaders as evaluated by HR's global manager-maker organization survey, most notably for increasing productivity by 30% through initiatives such as a competitive sales training program.
► Grew sales 30% by restructuring a 70-person Business Consulting Contact Center and US Networking Sales organization by creating a Fortune 10 focus team with the top 12 networking consulting SEs.
► Launched a strategic promotion to drive the legacy installed base to new platforms, generating an incremental $23M.

Director, Technical Operations & Business Development—Americas
3CX
2013–2014

CHALLENGE:
Build and lead an elite specialist organization responsible for profitable revenue growth in unified communications, contact centers, and networking solutions for the Americas International Theater (Canada, Caribbean, and Latin America).

RESULTS & RECOGNITION:
► Drove strategic growth by recruiting top talent from Microsoft, Cisco, and Juniper to create a Business Development Organization that led monthly business unit reviews for CC, UC, and networking solutions.
► Introduced new product sales strategies to position 70 new products released within 18 months. Achieved 112% of $380M annual quota. Earned recognition for fastest growing region and only area to reach 100% of new product target.

KEYNOTES:
► Served as keynote presenter at various global industry events in San Francisco, Mexico City, Sao Paulo, and Toronto.

Systems Engineering Leader
VERSATEL NETWORKS
2011–2013

CHALLENGE:
Integrate 20 SEs for West Coast region and named accounts with a $100M quota.

RESULTS & RECOGNITION:
► Retained customers and partners by delivering roadmap presentation that reassured them of our commitment to legacy investments.
► Landed key partnerships with the city of Tacoma, WA, and the University of CA network, which sparked 125% of quota.
► Earned the Top Systems Engineering Manager in North America Award at the 2011 Global Sales Conference.

National Sales Director, Applications & Software
VERSATEL NETWORKS
2008–2011

CHALLENGE:
Restructure and lead specialized sales team to grow applications and professional services funnel in unified communications and contact center solutions.

RESULTS & RECOGNITION:
► Led team to land several key accounts, including Summit Health, Wells Fargo, and Los Angeles County, CA.
► Increased annual call center revenues 54% and UC apps 32%, with highest application attach rate of 35%. Earned Achievers Club 3X, including during severe economic downturn: 2010: 145%, 2009: 135%, 2008: 140%.

OUTSIDE ENGAGEMENT:
► Served as key spokesperson for media, analysts, and consultants across the Americas for all new solution launches.

Senior Manager, VoIP Sales
VERSATEL NETWORKS
2002–2007

CHALLENGE:
Maintain key accounts, including CTS, LATel, and Bell West, while prospecting for new customers and landing new contracts.

RESULTS & RECOGNITION:
► Positioned top 2 product lines to win Allstream's competitive VoIP $55M 3-year contract.
► Earned Honors Circle sales recognition 4X for exceeding sales quotas.
► Achieved Top Sales designation within the company for exceeding objectives over 5 straight years.

BACKSTORY: Suzanne Smith (Writer: Darlene M. Dassy)

TARGET ROLE: Marketing Director
CURRENT TITLE: Director of Marketing and Community Outreach (Nonprofit)
INDUSTRY: Corporate or Nonprofit

WRITER'S COMMENTS

Suzanne was looking for career advancement in another organization since she felt she had contributed as much as she could in her role at The Red Cross. At the point we worked together, she was unclear on the companies she wanted to apply to, so we agreed that I would create a master resume that highlighted her experience in a compelling way and leveraged her diversified experience. I advised her on ways to quickly tweak her resume and cover letter for each targeted role for which she was applying.

As her search progressed, Suzanne returned for additional assistance with targeted cover letters and interview follow-up letters. She reported that she had followed my advice and found it a quick and easy process to customize her resume with each submission, thereby boosting the chance of getting a reply and an invitation to interview.

WRITING/DESIGN STRATEGY FOR DOCUMENTS

Resume: Suzanne had diversified experience in different industries, and the goal for her resume was to powerfully highlight her transferrable skills, so she would be viewed as the highly skilled leader that she was (and is). I developed a section called "Key Professional Highlights" on Page 1, allowing me to be creative with a hybrid resume format (combining functional components with the traditional reverse-chronological structure). With this format, her accomplishments are highlighted in a front-and-center section with the keyword terminology attached to the contributions in a clear and concise way for the reader.

Cover Letter: The most eye-catching feature of Suzanne's cover letter is the middle section of four bullet points that highlight specific, measurable achievements. With this structure, she can quickly edit the content so that the bullet points relate to particular items in the job posting. The remainder of the letter offers more general qualifications and needs little if any editing for many different (related) jobs.

Follow-up Letter: Recapping key points from the interview, Suzanne's letter makes a strong case for "why her" to lead the marketing efforts for a new company division. The letter exudes Suzanne's personality and work ethic along with the professional skills she has to offer.

UNIQUE CHALLENGES

Prior to her current role, Suzanne had worked at the same job in the same company for 13 years. The challenge was to choose only the most relevant material from this lengthy stint. I focused on achievements that had measurable outcomes and illustrated her core professional strengths, weeding out items that were interesting but "fuzzy" or less relevant.

OUTCOME

Suzanne landed the position of Regional Director of Marketing, the role described in her follow-up letter.

SUZANNE R. SMITH

Atlanta, GA 30304 • (404) 555-1212 • ssmith44@yahoo.com
www.linkedin.com/in/suesmith

SENIOR MARKETING MANAGEMENT EXECUTIVE

Regional Marketing Manager | Vice President of Marketing | Key Account Executive

Seasoned Marketing Leader offering an impressive record of achievement in high-impact marketing programs delivering results in profit and not-for-profit arenas. Broad experience in all aspects of strategic planning, turnaround management, project management, agency relations, event management, and bottom-line profitability. Track record of consistent contributions to increased production, quality issues, and cost effectiveness.

Persuasive leader, team builder, and negotiator. Key contributor to strategic planning and general management processes.

Core Competencies | Areas of Expertise:

Strategic and Tactical Marketing – Multimedia Advertising – Business Partnership Cultivation – Fundraising
Budgeting and Expense Controls – Staff Development and Motivation – Special Event Management
Relationship Building and Retention – Profit and Cost Analysis – Competitive Positioning

KEY PROFESSIONAL HIGHLIGHTS

Public Relations and Publicity:
- Played key role in driving $300,000 in positive publicity value for company in only 12-month timeframe.
- Guided creation of public relations campaign that generated over $150,000 in publicity and subsequently earned National Award of Excellence in Public Relations.

Strategic Partnerships and Alliances:
- Developed partnership with national firm in support of new business model initiative throughout firm.
- Tripled new business and sparked nonprofit donations by forming strategic alliances with local businesses.

Sales Revenues and Profitability:
- Drove 31% revenue gain in 12 months through special event fundraisers, membership drives, and public awareness campaigns.
- Implemented marketing program from scratch, boosting sales by 10% within 10 months of employment.
- Orchestrated company-wide advertising campaign that increased sales an average of 6% annually.

Fundraising and Advertising:
- Directed key fundraisers involving golf tournaments, dog walks, grand openings, and holiday dinners.
- Credited with bridging the gap between traditional and interactive advertising content platforms.

PROFESSIONAL EXPERIENCE

Director of Marketing & Community Outreach • 2018–Present
THE AMERICAN RED CROSS, Atlanta, GA

Key member of management team involved with public relations, special event planning, fundraising, advertising, marketing, new membership and retention, and educational programs.

- Grew revenue 33% in 2 years ($600,000 to $900,000), enabling expansion of operations and 50% staff increase.
- Reversed 4-year downward spiral of negative media coverage, launching comprehensive media campaign that generated 1,000+ column inches of positive newspaper articles and 7 positive television interviews.
- Drove 17% increase in organizational revenues by developing strong media ties that helped stretch budget by producing much-needed newspaper coverage without the need to purchase advertising space.

Area Director of Marketing • 2005–2018
REAL PROPERTY MANAGEMENT, LLC, Lancaster, PA

Managed event planning, strategic and tactical planning, staff development and motivation, business partnerships, advertising agency management, and communication strategies. Oversaw budgets with combined totals of $850,000 annually. Analyzed sales reports and traffic trends. Accountable for maximizing profitability through development and implementation of marketing plans, communications, advertising, operations, and leadership.

- Consistently surpassed strategically driven revenue generation goals and showed increases, including 38% in gift card sales, 20% in sponsorship sales, and 6% in retail sales.
- Successfully trained and mentored future marketing directors, with one mentee being named Employee of the Year (out of 3,000 employees).
- Drove $300,000 in positive publicity that included a front-page story in *The Lancaster Star* during holiday season—a $40,000 value.
- Played key role in implementing holiday sales event that increased traffic by 80% and sales by 32% in only one evening. Raised more than $35,000 for local charities.
- Created and executed local event marketing plan that ultimately achieved 95% customer service rating (highest ever in company).
- Developed effective corporate marketing plans to facilitate and ensure successful store openings with Saks Fifth Avenue (#2 in sales volume) and The Cheesecake Factory (#1 sales status).

<u>**Previous Related Career Experience:**</u>

Director of Marketing (4 years)
ABC CORPORATION, Columbus, OH

Marketing Director (3 years)
THE MACERICH COMPANY, Falmouth, MA

Marketing Assistant (2 years)
TAUBMAN CENTERS, INC., Buffalo, NY

EDUCATION

Bachelor of Science in Advertising—STATE UNIVERSITY OF NEW YORK, Buffalo, NY

TECHNOLOGY SKILLS

Proficient in Word, Excel, and PowerPoint and JD Edwards Software.

AWARDS & RECOGNITION

Two-Time Winner of Award of Excellence and Award of Merit; Special Recognition Award.

Recipient of Youth Foundation Award for generating largest volume and incremental growth.
(All were received during employment tenure at Real Property Management, LLC)

PROFESSIONAL AFFILIATIONS

Vice President—Advertising Club of Atlanta

Member—Greater Atlanta Chamber of Commerce | International Council of Shopping Centers
Prior Member and Membership Committee Chair—Greater Lancaster Chamber of Commerce

Subject: Senior Vice President of Marketing (#03982-04)

Dear Hiring Manager:

With a career background as Director of Marketing in the not-for-profit, real estate, and retail marketing arenas, I think you'll agree my experience demonstrates the strategic marketing, advertising, and turnaround management skills required to meet your organizational needs. Some accomplishments include:

✓ +31% revenue jump in first 12 months of employment … by initiating special event fundraisers, membership drives, and public relation awareness campaigns.

✓ +10% sales growth in less than a year … through marketing programs implemented from scratch.

✓ +6% average annual sales growth … as a direct result of company-wide advertising campaigns.

✓ Frequent recognition for both personal efforts and company contributions … including a National Award of Excellence, Award of Merit, and Special Recognition Award. Additionally, I was selected as recipient of the Youth Foundation Award.

As proven by these highlights, my key strength is driving business growth through strong expertise in public relations, operations, strategic partnerships, fundraising, profit and cost analysis, and more. I've had a unique exposure to various demographic areas, including tourist and urban markets, high-income households, and small-town marketing. My leadership skills are both strategic and tactical, and I consistently demonstrate what it takes to "get the job done" right!

Standing by to interview at your convenience,

Suzanne R. Smith
(404) 555-1212
ssmith44@yahoo.com
Attachment: Resume

SUZANNE R. SMITH

Atlanta, GA 30304 • (404) 555-1212 • ssmith44@yahoo.com
www.linkedin.com/in/suesmith

SENIOR MARKETING MANAGEMENT EXECUTIVE

Regional Marketing Manager | Vice President of Marketing | Key Account Executive

Dear Joe and Andrea,

Thank you for taking the time to interview me yesterday for the position of Regional Marketing Manager.

Having been given a solid explanation and overview of the job, I am confident of my ability to handle the intricacies of the work, including meeting ABC Corporation's performance standards. As we discussed, I have made it a habit to consistently outperform expectations, and I assure that I will "go the extra mile" to cater to your company's unique marketing needs and ensure top client satisfaction for your key accounts.

What I bring to the table is my diversified marketing background and demonstrated track record of implementing public relations campaigns, strategic partnerships, and fundraising and advertising programs. This type of ground-floor marketing and PR work will be essential in positioning your newly launched division within its community, its industry, and the larger ABC Corporation enterprise.

It is exciting to envision working within the challenging environment at ABC in a position where my strategic marketing, problem solving, and fundraising skills would be highly valued—and where I can make significant contributions to ABC's continued growth and success.

My hope is that you'll consider me the top candidate for this role, and I look forward to hearing back from you soon with your hiring decision. Please feel free to contact me if you have any further questions.

Thank you for your time and consideration.

Suzanne R. Smith

Suzanne R. Smith
(404) 555-1212
ssmith44@yahoo.com

BACKSTORY: Matthew P. Pearson (Writer: Marty Weitzman)

TARGET ROLE: Chief Sales Officer
CURRENT TITLE: VP/Chief Operations Officer
INDUSTRY: Healthcare

WRITER'S COMMENTS

Matthew has had a long and successful career managing healthcare operations to greater financial results, employee engagement, and patient satisfaction. Now, as more and more private equity and venture capital firms have entered the healthcare space, he would like to secure a new position with a PE or VC firm that will provide strong upside potential, including an equity stake.

At the time Matthew retained my services, his resume lacked impact and did not effectively demonstrate his ability to achieve strong top- and bottom-line results, which were clearly the hallmark of his career. The resume was significantly out-of-date in both style and strategy.

Through in-depth interviewing and collaboration, I identified "big picture" accomplishments that became the focus of Matthew's resume, executive bio, and cover letter. Matthew's strength in transforming organizations and building high-performing teams is consistent throughout his career and is affirmed through tight and concise descriptions.

WRITING/DESIGN STRATEGY FOR DOCUMENTS

Resume: Distinctive formatting keeps Matthew's resume quite readable while still being packed with relevant information. Shading below each job title encapsulates job scope, and blue ink is used to make company names quickly identifiable. A heading introduces each bullet point, calling attention to the specific area of achievement.

Cover Letter: A to-the-point letter will capture the immediate attention of venture capital and private equity investors, who are most interested in performance that will translate to their portfolio companies.

Bio: Repeating the headline and mimicking the formatting of his resume, Matthew's executive bio strikes a complementary tone while presenting his career history in a different format. The inset box on the right of the page offers a quick snapshot of Matthew's most notable success stories and areas of expertise.

UNIQUE CHALLENGES

As with many senior executives, the major challenge was presenting a rich and lengthy career in a concise way—without omitting any of the achievements and career details that will capture the attention of his target audience. By focusing on the big picture, we were able to strip extraneous details and keep the attention on what matters most.

OUTCOME

Armed with his new career documents, Matthew executed an email campaign to VC/PE firms as well as a targeted, networking-based search. Within a few weeks, he was in early conversations with several firms.

MATTHEW P. PEARSON

773.123.4567 • mppearson@verizon.net • Chicago, IL 60645 • https://www.linkedin.com/in/matthew-pearson/

SENIOR-LEVEL HEALTHCARE EXECUTIVE | OPERATIONS — BUSINESS DEVELOPMENT — CHANGE MANAGEMENT

Strategic Growth Initiatives | Rapid Business & Profit Expansion | Operational & Culture Transformations

Transformational senior executive with 20+ years of progressive leadership experience in launching, transforming, and navigating complex, multi-site operations to growth and profitability. Certified coach, known for building high-performing teams and leading culture shifts that improve quality, financial results, and clinical outcomes for patient populations.

Career Progression: **Midwest Care Management | MinistryCare | Medi-Data Technologies**
mPayment Technologies | PricewaterhouseCoopers | Accenture

Executive Competencies

▶ Strategic & Business Planning	▶ Executive Project Management	▶ Risk Management/Compliance
▶ Startup & Operations Leadership	▶ Change Management	▶ Contract Negotiations
▶ Operational Streamlining	▶ M&A/Acquisition Due Diligence	▶ New Product Development (NPD)
▶ Efficiency & Quality Improvements	▶ P&L Management	▶ Team Leadership & Development
▶ Business Process Optimization (BPO)	▶ Business Development/Sales	▶ Client Relationship Management

PROFESSIONAL EXPERIENCE

MIDWEST CARE MANAGEMENT (MCM), Chicago, IL | 2014–Present

Full-service healthcare management company that provides technologically advanced services and interventions.

VICE PRESIDENT, CHIEF OPERATIONS OFFICER, 2016–Present • **SENIOR DIRECTOR OF OPERATIONS,** 2014–2016

Direct Reports: 11 | Indirect: 1000+ (Clinical & Non-Clinical) | Division Size: 7 Operations (Population Health Management Programs, Social Determinants of Health, Quality, Contracting, Claims, Data Analytics, Reporting)
Operating Budget: $220M |Report to: Sr. Vice President Population Health / President CMO

Recruited to orchestrate quick turnaround and growth. Overcame profitability and service delivery issues by optimizing MLR and overhauling data warehouse and population health analytics; clinical programs; learning innovation; process engineering; claims and population health operations; contracting; and direct-to-employer contracting and program development.

□ TRANSFORMATION & FINANCIAL RESULTS: **Led organization from $50M loss to breakeven in 2 years** by partnering with CFO on financial strengthening, subsequently **delivering $20M profit** by year 5 after overhauling operations. Led design, implementation, process improvement, and business scalability of ~$2.9B in value based on population health contracts. Resolved union issues to enable staff reductions and changes to job functions.

□ CLINICAL PROGRAMS & QUALITY OUTCOMES: Joined Chief Medical Officer and clinical division chairs in introducing clinical programs to grow CMO Integrated Delivery System of 6,800-provider physicians network, primary care providers, Home Health Agency, Rehabilitation Facility, and 11 hospitals. **Achieved 3-year unconditional NCQA accreditation** for Utilization Management, Complex Case Management, and Credentialing.

□ PATIENT & OPERATIONAL SUCCESSES: **Improved hospital throughput and patient discharge process** by redesigning Health System Central Management Resource Unit. **Championed wider operational and patient successes** as member of key health system committees. Supported IPA board activities and presentations.

MINISTRYCARE, New York, NY | 2012–2014

Non-profit integrated health care delivery system providing services to frail and elderly population through direct care services and 3 individual health plan products (PACE, I/IE SNP, and MLTC); 5 residential centers, 4 PACE Centers, and home health company.

EXECUTIVE DIRECTOR, 2013–2014 • **SENIOR DIRECTOR OPERATIONS,** 2012–2013

Direct Reports: 5 | Indirect: 140+ | Operating Budget: $177M | Reported to: VP, Home & Community Based Services

Promoted quickly to optimize performance of health plan operations and 140-person team serving >3,500 Medicare- and Medicaid-eligible members. Transitioned 3 siloed operations with multi-product, multi-tiered structure into single, unified organization. Championed improvements to processes and workflow tools and methodologies.

□ BUSINESS OPERATIONS CONSOLIDATION: **Cut 5% from OPEX** and **improved MLR 5%** by consolidating business operations for health plan products; improving operational efficiency and regulatory compliance; navigating NPD and data analytics for clinical outcomes; and creating enterprise-wide data repository and key performance indicators.

□ DATAMART DEVELOPMENT & REDEVELOPMENT: Paved the way for wider technological efficiencies by partnering with data architect to develop datamart strategy and self-service reporting methodologies.

(continued on page 2)

MATTHEW P. PEARSON

773.123.4567 • mppearson@verizon.net

Ministrycare continued...

☐ DATA ANALYTICS & REPORTING: **Decreased community pharmacy PMP >$100** with specific pharmacy initiatives; stemmed risk via disease state analysis and risk score enhancement; supported clinical initiatives with predefined business rules; and created financial indicator reports and dashboards for operational corrective actions.

☐ NPD & REGULATORY COMPLIANCE: **Scored superior rating of 92 on Model of Care audit** and **3-year CMS approval** for I/IE SNP product by spearheading clinical, operations, and cross-functional development teams during audit preparations.

MEDI-DATA TECHNOLOGIES, INC., Chicago, IL | 2011–2012
Privately held, private-equity backed, leading nationwide provider of information technology solutions to home healthcare industry.

EXECUTIVE VICE PRESIDENT OF OPERATIONS
Direct Reports: 4 | Indirect: 140+ | Budget Accountability: $40M | Reported to: CEO

Brought on board to position company for growth and expansion. Moved rapidly to reorganize company, build economies of scale, lead business process redesign, cut costs, improve client satisfaction, and install performance KPI reporting dashboard.

☐ REVENUE GROWTH: **Accelerated sales by decreasing implementation time 40%** and **AR backlog 60%;** overhauled department; introduced product-specific implementation playbook and standard methodologies; and instituted staff cross-training program.

☐ CLIENT SATISFACTION: **Raised client retention >30%** and **turned 2 of Medi-Data's largest state customers into profitable accounts** by installing dedicated account management team and executive sponsorship program to build relationships. **Led department to receive 9–9.5 out of 10 customer satisfaction ratings** through training and documentation.

☐ TECHNOLOGY-RELATED IMPROVEMENTS: **Trimmed support-ticket resolution time from 18.73 days to 3** with new ACD phones, ticket tracking system, and interdepartmental SLAs; migrated legacy products to SAS platform via product development; improved messaging for key accounts, joining CTO to create executive dashboard and launch reporting and analytics team.

MPAYMENT TECHNOLOGIES, Alexandria, VA | 2004–2011
Start-up and leader in full-service payment policy management, assisting clients with professional, outpatient facility, and DME claims.

VICE PRESIDENT OF CLIENT SERVICES
Executive Leadership: 6 Internal Client Teams | P&L Management: $20M | Reported to: President

Recruited to grow service revenues and increase client penetration. Improved operations and clinical teams tasked to implement payment policy for 6 commercial, Medicare, and Medicaid accounts processing healthcare claims for professional, outpatient, DME, and Ambulatory Surgery Centers of >$28B per year.

☐ FINANCIAL IMPACT: **Delivered 30% YoY revenue growth** (revenue budget target of >$20M) from existing client base by expanding products, thereby positioning clients to improve MLR by >$40M annually.

☐ FEDERAL RELATIONSHIPS & OPERATIONS MANAGEMENT: **Strengthened relationships** between prime contractor and Center for Medicare & Medicaid and Services (CMS) while managing operations and CMS's regional recovery audit contract.

☐ CLIENT SATISFACTION: **Earned 100% client rating of 9 or higher** (10-point scale) by building team of business partners known for helping clients achieve strategic goals and revenue targets; set team priorities and coached on client management.

— Earlier Successes —

☐ As Senior Manager at **PRICEWATERHOUSECOOPERS, delivered $11M+ in sales** for East Coast Managed Healthcare Practice by shifting strategy, operations, and focus on product development. Managed $1.9M in revenues and up to 25-person project teams.

☐ As Senior Manager at **ACCENTURE,** aggressively expanded payer healthcare practice by leading up to 20-member project teams and fueling eBusiness to **generate >$12M in client fees.**

EDUCATION & PROFESSIONAL DEVELOPMENT

B.A. in International Studies, Major: Economics — Minor: Middle Eastern Studies
George Washington University, Washington, DC

Strategic & Conceptual Selling, Miller Heiman | **Negotiation for Senior Executives Program,** University of Chicago Law School

MATTHEW P. PEARSON

773.123.4567 • mppearson@verizon.net • Chicago, IL 60645 • https://www.linkedin.com/in/matthew-pearson/

SENIOR-LEVEL HEALTHCARE EXECUTIVE | OPERATIONS — BUSINESS DEVELOPMENT — CHANGE MANAGEMENT
Strategic Growth Initiatives | Rapid Business & Profit Expansion | Operational & Culture Transformations

FOR APPROACHING PE/VC FIRMS

Date

Mr./Ms.
Title
Company
Address
City, State, Zip

Dear _____:

If one of your portfolio companies is in need of a C-level leader with verifiable achievements in leveraging operational improvements and sales and solutions strategies to drive business growth and profitability, please consider me a strong candidate. You may be interested in my experience and achievements in propelling revenues and transforming large healthcare operations and cultures while remediating regulatory and quality issues.

A few examples of success include:

- □ As VP/COO at **Midwest Care Management,** I figured prominently in **propelling the organization from a $50M loss to $20M profit** by turning around underperforming operations and partnering with the CFO on wider financial streamlining.

- □ At **MinistryCare,** I consolidated 3 siloed operations to **realize a 5% drop in OPEX** and **5% improvement in MLR.**

- □ Driving revenue growth and expansion at **Medi-Data Technologies,** I guided service delivery and operations teams to **decrease implementation times by 40%, fast-track revenue generation,** earn outstanding client satisfaction scores, and raise the bar in technology support.

- □ Managing $20M P&L as VP of Client Services at **mPayment Technologies,** I mobilized clinical teams to deliver **30% YoY revenue growth.**

Additionally, I have **led start-up operations for a managed care organization** and new division and held strategic positions for 2 major management consulting firms, **PricewaterhouseCoopers** and **Accenture.**

If any of your portfolio companies would like to achieve similar results in improving operations, revenue growth, organizational culture, and services/products, may we discuss? I look forward to connecting with you and thank you for your consideration.

Sincerely,

Matthew P. Pearson

Enclosure

MATTHEW P. PEARSON

SENIOR-LEVEL HEALTHCARE EXECUTIVE | OPERATIONS — BUSINESS DEVELOPMENT — CHANGE MANAGEMENT

Strategic Growth Initiatives | Rapid Business & Profit Expansion | Operational & Culture Transformations

As a transformational leader with 20+ years of success propelling business growth and fueling multimillion-dollar, bottom-line gains for large healthcare organizations, Matthew Pearson is adept at launching, transforming, and navigating complex, multi-site operations and cultures.

A certified coach, Matthew is also credited with building high-performing teams and leading culture shifts in operations that improve not only quality and financial results but also clinical outcomes for patient populations.

In his current role at **MIDWEST CARE MANAGEMENT (MCM)**—a full-service healthcare management company—Matthew leads as VP and Chief Operations Officer. To date, he has **led the organization from a $50M loss to breakeven** in two years and overhauled operations to **deliver $20M in profit by year five.**

Not only that, he oversaw the design, implementation, process improvement, and **business scalability of ~$2.9B in value** based on population health contracts, achieved three-year unconditional NCQA accreditation for three key clinical programs, and improved hospital throughput and patient successes.

Prior to his success at MCM, Matthew served as Executive Director at **MINISTRYCARE,** a not-for-profit integrated healthcare delivery system. Here he turned three siloed operations into a single, unified organization to optimize performance of health plan operations, a strategic initiative that **summarily cut 5% from operating expenses** and **improved MLR 5%.**

In his role as EVP of Operations at **MEDI-DATA TECHNOLOGIES, INC.,** a leading privately held, PE-backed provider of IT solutions to the U.S. home healthcare industry, Matthew is credited with **turning two of Medi-Data's largest state customers into profitable accounts,** raising client retention >30%, and decreasing client implementation times 40%.

While at **MPAYMENT TECHNOLOGIES,** a start-up and leader in full-service payment policy management, Matthew boosted client penetration while improving operations and clinical teams, which resulted in **30% YoY growth in services revenues** for mPayment and **>$40M MLR improvement for clients** per year.

KEY HIGHLIGHTS

▶ **Propelled CMO from a $50M loss to $20M profit** with 180-degree operations turnaround and financial streamlining.

▶ **Realized sharp 5% drop in OPEX and 5% improvement in MLR** by consolidating 3 large, siloed operations.

▶ **Fast-tracked revenue generation, expansion, and implementation times 40%** for PE-backed IT solutions provider.

▶ Managed $20M P&L, mobilizing clinical teams to **deliver 30% YoY revenue growth** for healthcare IT (HIT) start-up.

VALUED EXPERT IN

Strategic & Business Planning
Risk Management / Compliance
Start-Up Operations
Operational Excellence
Performance & Efficiency Improvements
M&A / Acquisition Due Diligence
New Product Development (NPD)
Efficiency & Quality Improvements
Business Development / P&L
Strategic Partnership Building
Regulatory Insight
Payer Relations

Earlier in his career, Matthew also held strategic management consulting positions at **PRICEWATERHOUSECOOPERS** and **ACCENTURE.** He **delivered $11M+ in sales** and managed $1.9M P&L for PwC's East Coast Managed Healthcare Practice and **generated >$12M in client fees** by aggressively expanding Accenture's payer healthcare practice.

Having started his career at **PALMER HEALTHCORP,** Matthew proved instrumental in **fueling $100M in acquisitive growth** as a key member of the start-up leadership team credited with acquiring 40 physician practices, where he developed a practice acquisition model.

An internationally recognized thought leader in the field, Matthew has presented at leading healthcare conferences in England. He holds a Bachelor of Arts degree in international studies from George Washington University. On the personal side, Matthew lives in Chicago and enjoys competitive squash, music, theater, and cooking.

Matthew can be reached at **773.123.4567** or via email at **mppearson@verizon.net**

BACKSTORY: Emma Turner (Writer: Louise Kursmark)

TARGET ROLE: COO or Executive Vice President of Operations
MOST RECENT TITLE: Executive Vice President—Global Operations
INDUSTRY: Sporting Goods Manufacturing/Distribution

WRITER'S COMMENTS

In a 22-year career with XO Sports, Emma had been through many seismic shifts as the company had transitioned from privately held, to PE-owned, to acquisition by a very large public company that made XO Sports one of its divisions. When offered an attractive buyout as a result of the latest ownership change, Emma decided to accept.

Over the decades with XO Sports, Emma's own life circumstances had changed dramatically along with the company. Her children were grown, her spouse was nearing retirement, and she was no longer interested in a hard-charging career that required frequent global travel. Instead, she planned to target mid-sized companies in her local area.

Emma had a great deal of experience in downsizing, cost-cutting, and offshoring, but she did not want those achievements to be the primary focus of her resume. To appeal to her target audience and current interests, I balanced the supply-chain focus with emphasis on her leadership strengths and reputation for getting the job done, no matter the obstacles.

WRITING/DESIGN STRATEGY FOR DOCUMENTS

Resume: Emma's resume begins with a strong introduction that summarizes her personal strengths as well as business successes. Because her roles were progressive and her responsibilities cumulative, the experience section is essentially one long job description for her three most recent roles. Subheadings identify three distinct areas of achievement. Older roles are simply listed, without details. The final section, Board and Professional Affiliations, is brief, but the volunteer experience that is showcased proved to be instrumental in her search.

Bio: Emma's bio recaps her career and provides more depth through a few interesting details, such as her extensive travel. Adding personality is a brief quote, from Emma herself, about discovering her ability to lead and inspire teams.

UNIQUE CHALLENGES

Because Emma was interested only in local opportunities, I did not recommend a recruiter distribution or other wide-ranging search tactics. I encouraged her to activate her impressive local network and see what opportunities might come up.

OUTCOME

Emma's networking activity expanded her contacts in the local business community and also among local nonprofits. Within about six months of leaving XO Sports, she accepted a position as Executive Director of a Portland-area nonprofit focused on developing leadership skills in girls and women. She is using her core abilities and is extremely energized about helping other women succeed in the careers of their choice.

Emma Turner

emma.turner@mail.com | 555-439-9876
www.LinkedIn.com/in/emma-turner

SENIOR EXECUTIVE: GLOBAL SUPPLY CHAIN & OPERATIONS

Supply Chain Optimization | Purchasing, Planning & Logistics | Business Process Improvement

International supply chain leader known for "getting things done"—creating the plan and leading the execution to deliver bottom-line business benefits. Deep expertise in international and domestic supply chain management, project management, and operational leadership with expanding global organizations.

Resourceful problem solver, logical thinker, and cool head in high-pressure situations.

Team builder, relationship builder, and effective communicator internally, externally, and cross-culturally.

Award for Excellence in Team Leadership
"Above and Beyond" Award for Collaboration and Support of the Manufacturing Team

PROFESSIONAL EXPERIENCE

XO SPORTS, Portland, OR   1998–Present
Leading global designer, manufacturer, and marketer of outdoor sporting goods products, with subsidiaries in Japan, Canada, Germany, and Norway. Division of Mastery, Inc., an $8B+ public company.

* **Executive Vice President—Global Operations,** 2018–Present
* **Vice President—Global Operations,** 2012–2018
* **Director of Business Operations,** 2009–2012

Advanced to senior leadership role and repeatedly took on new responsibilities as company grew and evolved from privately held, to VC ownership, through multiple acquisitions, to current status as division of a public company.

Provide strategic and operational leadership to the company's business operations and global supply chain: Purchasing, Sourcing and Planning, Logistics, Customs Compliance, Regulatory Compliance, Customer Service, Distribution, Warranty, IT, Ecommerce, and Human Resources. $5M annual budget; 18 manufacturing and supplier sites in 5 countries; 9 direct and 47 indirect staff.

Executive Leadership

* Member of executive team setting strategic direction for the company.
* Leader of high-performance teams that have been key contributors to XO's financial success.
* Team member/leader for multiple international acquisitions, consolidations, technology implementations, organizational restructurings, and other global initiatives.
* Corporate champion of the Sustainability team, driving steady shift to sustainable products and practices.
* Culturally aware leader and supportive manager/mentor who encourages professional growth and empowers teams and individuals to improve, grow, and excel.

Global Supply Chain Management

* Spearheaded XO's successful transition to offshore manufacturing and global expansion of the supply chain. Travel regularly to supplier sites and manufacturing operations throughout China, Europe, and North America, ensuring the reliability of raw materials and the quality of finished goods.
* Currently serving as Project Champion for strategic initiative to centralize the global purchasing process into Portland headquarters. Projecting $1M annual savings.
* Earned C-TPAT certification for XO Sports (2012) and completed US Customs ISA application (2015).
* Drove improvements in order management that resulted in consistent order fulfillment within 24–48 hours of warehouse arrival.

Emma Turner

emma.turner@mail.com | 555-439-9876

Executive Vice President—Global Operations, XO Sports, Inc. … Continued …

Operations and Technology

- Orchestrated relocation of corporate distribution center to 185,000 sq. ft. operation in Portland. Completed move in less than 120 days—on time and under budget.
- Served as project lead for US ERP implementation including RF technology.
- Implemented Phase 1 of PivotLink BI sales reporting tool.
- Integrated back-office operations of US and European distribution operations.
- Migrated sales order entry from manual, paper-based process to electronic ordering tool.

- **Director of Purchasing & Sourcing,** 2007–2009
- **Director of Purchasing,** 2003–2007
- **Raw Materials Purchaser,** 2001–2003
- **Finished Goods Buyer,** 1998–2001

Prior
Traffic Manager, Skis Dynastar, Colchester, VT • **Import/Export Manager,** Millstone, Inc., New York, NY

EDUCATION

BS, French & Marketing • UNIVERSITY OF VERMONT, Burlington, VT
- Junior Year Abroad: Sorbonne University, Paris, France

Post-Graduate Studies
- COLUMBIA UNIVERSITY, New York, NY
- UNIVERSITY OF PORTLAND, Portland, OR

BOARD AND PROFESSIONAL AFFILIATIONS

Outdoor Industry Women's Coalition (OIWC)
- **Advisory Board of Directors,** 2015–Present
- **Pioneering Women Award,** 2019—Recognizing outstanding commitment to mentoring female colleagues
- **Team Leader** for charity auction, 2016–2019

Special Olympics of Oregon
- **Board of Directors,** 2012–2015

Emma Turner

Emma Turner is Executive Vice President—Global Operations of XO Sports, a leading global designer, manufacturer, and marketer of outdoor sporting goods products.

When she joined XO in 1998 as a Finished Goods Buyer, she never expected her career to take her to China, give her the opportunity to lead business-wide transformations, or elevate her to the company's executive team. She has thrived amid numerous ownership changes as the company transitioned from a small, privately owned, specialty ski company to a diversified sporting goods business that today is a division of Mastery, Inc.

A member of XO's executive team since 2012, Emma advanced steadily through purchasing and supply chain positions to ultimately lead all of the company's global operations. With other senior executives, she has steered the company through challenging economies, multiple ownership structures, and fundamental changes in the global economy and supply chain.

Under her leadership, XO transitioned to offshore manufacturing—an essential step to keep the company competitive. As she expanded the supply chain globally, Emma developed new suppliers and manufacturing sites in China, Vietnam, Philippines, and several Latin American countries … and visited them all, building relationships and ensuring the production and delivery of high-quality materials and finished goods.

Emma has a reputation for "getting things done," including the most challenging operational initiatives—technology implementations, process transformations, and physical relocation. She combines strong planning and analytical skills with clear communication of vision, goals, and tasks to keep everyone engaged and informed.

As a leader, Emma consistently develops high-performing teams united toward a common mission in a culture of collaboration and generosity. "Discovering my strengths as a leader has been one of the most satisfying aspects of my career," she says. "I've learned to empower my people to do their jobs … help them develop new skills … give them the resources and support they need … and step out of the way! The results have been phenomenal, as they have consistently exceeded even very ambitious goals."

Emma's outstanding performance has been recognized with XO's Award for Excellence in Team Leadership and "Above and Beyond" Award. In addition, in 2019 she was awarded the Outdoor Industry Women's Coalition (OIWC) Pioneering Women Award, recognizing an outstanding commitment to mentoring female colleagues.

She is a member of OIWC's Advisory Board of Directors and previously served on the Board of Directors of the Special Olympics of Oregon.

Emma graduated cum laude from the University of Vermont with a bachelor's degree in French and marketing. While in college, she spent her junior year abroad at the Sorbonne University in Paris, France. She has pursued graduate education at Columbia University and the University of Portland and has participated in many executive workshops focusing on the global economy and international trade.

Prior to joining XO, Emma worked in international business in Boston and New York City. She and her husband and two children now take advantage of the many recreational and cultural activities available to Portland-area residents. She is an avid reader and enjoys travel, gardening, hiking, yoga, and skiing—of course using the XO products that she has been instrumental in producing.

emma.turner@mail.com | 555-439-9876

BACKSTORY: Paula T. Rittman (Writer: Jan Melnik)

TARGET ROLE: Chief Sales Officer
CURRENT TITLE: Executive Vice President, Sales
INDUSTRY: Grocery, Supermarket & Retail Food Industry

WRITER'S COMMENTS

With a record of success as EVP with a major grocery chain, Paula was ready to explore a change. In part, she recognized organizational changes that could lessen the likelihood of ascending to CSO.

Paula had made a strategic decision to enter an intensive 2-year MBA program at Stanford in 2014. It was through a fellow student that she was recruited to Fred Meyer upon graduation. She had not structured a job search in nearly 20 years and sought job-search coaching and career documents that would position her as an attractive candidate. To supplement her networking activity with industry contacts, she was interested in a campaign to executive recruiters.

Paula's enthusiasm and high-touch style made it easy to craft authentic, personality-infused documents.

WRITING/DESIGN STRATEGY FOR DOCUMENTS

Resume: I chose a clean resume design, created a focused introduction to lead off each role, and wrote concise, high-impact bullets to keep the focus on her impressive accomplishments and results. It was important to make her recent MBA prominent in her summary and as a segment of her experience (to account for the 2-year gap) as well as including it traditionally under education.

Cover Letter: This letter to a recruiter zeros in on the "pain points" that a hiring company must be feeling—along with solutions that Paula can provide. The letter also provides a few pertinent details regarding compensation, location, and ideal role that will help the recruiter match Paula with the right opportunities.

LinkedIn: After a Headline that succinctly conveys Paula's expertise, I began the About section by high-lighting her blue-chip career history and then calling out the personal/leadership attributes that have contributed to her success. In the Experience section, a storytelling approach engages readers while providing helpful context.

UNIQUE CHALLENGES

The major challenge in writing Paula's career documents was selecting just the right success stories—choosing and highlighting the information that had the most meaning and impact given her current goals. Being strategically selective meant omitting other stories that could be significant for some opportunities.

OUTCOME

Paula commenced her multipronged search with a significant level of confidence. Her new documents prepared her to tell her most relevant stories in greater detail during interviews. Her LinkedIn profile, along with her recruiter campaign, attracted significant attention from search firms, and at press time she was in early discussions for several interesting opportunities.

PAULA T. RITTMAN, MBA

Portland, OR 97221 | 503-296-8496 | paularittman@gmail.com | www.linkedin.com/in/paula-rittman

SENIOR SALES VP | GLOBAL MANAGEMENT EXECUTIVE | GROWTH CATALYST
GROCERY, SUPERMARKET & RETAIL FOOD INDUSTRY

Accomplished Global Senior Sales Professional with passion for leading teams and delivering exceptional results. Flawless record of innovative leadership in growth, profitability, business development, and turnaround across multiple industries.

- **Visionary and strategic leader**—planning and executing numerous transformations, consistently optimizing operations, and delivering successful sales outcomes for top retail grocery, HBA, and household/soft goods brands.
- **25+ years' success** launching operational improvements, leveraging data, and driving proof-of-performance results.
- **Record of delivering extraordinary business growth**—launching start-ups, positioning for rapid-but-sustainable success, and turning around underperforming operations.
- **Outstanding senior sales management career** with such industry leaders as Fred Meyer, AHOLD, Kroger, and Publix—augmented by Stanford MBA.

Global/National Leadership | Strategic Brand Management | Turnaround & Transformation | Supply Chain
Talent/Team Development & Management | Performance & Process Improvement | Product Design & Development

EXPERIENCE & ACHIEVEMENTS

FRED MEYER | Portland, OR ... *$4.9B revenues, 30K employees, NYSE: KR*   **2016–Present**

Executive Vice President of Sales (2019–Present)

Drove profitability, grew market share, and spearheaded strategic kiosk launch across US.

Introduced innovations in strategic selling. Built and manage top-performing sales team comprising 400+ indirect and 10 direct reports supporting all stateside operations.

Key Accomplishments:

➢ Increased overall sales 37% in 2020 and on track to continue double-digit growth in 2021.
➢ Partnered with marketing to enhance features/benefits messages and developed new 3D planogram concept.
➢ Created internal set-up teams in operations, sales, and marketing to standardize processes across units nationwide.
➢ Led integration process between Fred Meyer and 2 acquisitions in late 2019, expediting process by spearheading creation of Advisory Team comprising select sales directors and handpicked field staff.
➢ Established high-visibility seasonal and monthly performance goals and tracking with data analytics through newly launched dashboard (measure and drive performance improvements). Implemented sell-in tools and sales reports.

Senior Director of International Business Development (2016–2019)

Produced average of 50% increase in global business and broadened international brand presence.

Challenged to turn around stagnant global sales; hired by Fred Meyer's president. Brought on board new general managers; reorganized team; instituted cohesive, in-country marketing support; and led multipronged game plan with clear goals and measurements that produced exceptional results.

Key Accomplishments:

➢ Achieved 100% increase in Brazil.
➢ Launched Fred Meyer remote in China (2019) and put in place strategic plan for expansion in LATAM region.
➢ Drove 50% reduction in speed-to-market by creating and implementing tactical strategies.

PAULA T. RITTMAN, MBA   503-296-8496 | paularittman@gmail.com   pg. 2

STANFORD GRADUATE SCHOOL OF BUSINESS | Stanford, CA   2014–2016
Full-time graduate student; successfully completed 2-year residential MBA program.

AHOLD USA, INC. | Quincy, MA ... *$44.1B US revenues, 237K employees, OTC US: ADRNY*   2003–2014
Senior Vice President, Grocery (Giant Food/Food Lion brands; 2011–2014)
Consistently promoted to execute strategic initiatives supporting aggressive growth through acquisition.

Challenged to drive sales in 650+ units nationwide. Hired/managed team of 6 VPs, 8 segment directors, and storewide staff exceeding 750 members.

Key Accomplishments:

➢ Achieved 10%–18% annual increase in sales (2011, 2012, 2013, Q1–Q2/2014).
➢ Drove a 100% increase in sales for Food Lion store brands in the US (2013).
➢ Created innovative business model for redesign/reset of 20+ Food Lion doors that became corporate model.

Vice President, Hannaford (2007–2011)
Generated double-digit increase in business over 4 years during 2008 Recession/period of sharp economic decline.

Managed corporate sales and marketing for the Hannaford brand; annual store sales topped $200M stateside. Recruited, trained, and managed 6 senior account executives. Drove annual marketing spend.

Key Accomplishments:

➢ Spearheaded strategic planning and drove integration of seasonal marketing initiatives.
➢ Instrumental in revamping sales compensation structure for the entire sales team.

Strategic Account Manager, Hannaford Northeast (2003–2007)
Managed national and regional accounts across Northeast territory, providing consultative sales services to match customer needs. Spearheaded market analysis that led to product improvements that drove consistent sales increases. Managed 11 sales reps. Oversaw Boston office operations, directing sales, marketing, and logistics.

Key Accomplishments:

➢ Strategically realigned sales team; result: $45M increase in sales to $320M.
➢ Grew sales YOY 4 consecutive years.

Additional Background includes 10+ years' professional sales leadership/management success with Kroger and Publix.

EDUCATION

MBA — Stanford Graduate School of Business, Stanford, CA (2-yr. residential program)
BBA — Rice University, Houston, TX

AFFILIATIONS

Habitat for Humanities of Portland (volunteer/fundraiser, 2015–Present)
Portland Lions Club (member, 2018–Present)
Portland Public Libraries Commission (appointed, 2019–Present)

Subject: Senior Sales Management Executive and Growth Catalyst

Dear [Recruiter Name]:

With a reputation for **delivering extraordinary business growth and double-digit sales results, consistently exceeding performance expectations, and executing initiatives that transform and optimize operations,** I have brought value to every organization with which I've been associated for more than 20 years. At this juncture in my career, I am confidentially exploring new challenges—whether in my area of proven success with top grocery, supermarket, and retail food brands or in a transferable industry.

Some highlights of my career that help demonstrate the value I can bring to your clients' organizations include:

- **Drove profitability and increased overall sales 37% in 2020 for Fred Meyer; averaged 50% annual growth** from 2016–2019.
- **Achieved 50% reduction in speed-to-market** for Fred Meyer through implementation of tactical strategies.
- **Executed strategies and initiatives that drove exceptional growth for Ahold**—from **achieving 100% increase in sales** for Food Lion store brands to **growing Hannaford sales 16% to $320M** in the Northeast.
- **Consistently built high-performing teams**—demonstrating outstanding skills in talent development with ability to recruit, manage, and retain top performers.
- **Pioneered innovative business models and spearheaded operational transformations**—integrated multiple acquisitions for Fred Meyer, established KPIs and performance goals tracked through data analytics, and planned/launched innovative expansions in China and Latin America.

What are the secrets of my success, and **how can they help your clients' organizations drive sales, improve overall performance, solve problems, position for growth, and achieve aggressive goals?** I can boil it down to a few things: I have built my career with the mindset that no matter what the job, I'm not satisfied unless I know I am doing my best. This extends to my skill in relationship building—with employees, suppliers, and external customers.

I also have a reputation for having a positive "can-do" attitude, exceptional listening abilities (with a high value placed on "group think"), and a talent for motivating others. From developing strategic plans to adopting key metrics that drive performance, I embrace the mantra of "innovate or die" and believe in driving continuous improvements for my sales team.

If you are supporting client searches for an executive sales manager, a candidate with subject matter expertise in grocery/food and retail, and skills that consistently transform organizations to their optimal levels, I believe it would be beneficial for us to talk. I am confident that I can step in and make both immediate and long-term contributions to your clients' organizations. My target compensation level would begin at $375K with performance bonus of 25%–50%; my resume is attached. I look forward to hearing from you soon. I promise you won't be disappointed!

Sincerely,

Paula T. Rittman
503-296-8496
paularittman@gmail.com
www.linkedin.com/in/paula-rittman

Paula T. Rittman

Global Senior Sales Management Executive | Grocery/Retail Expertise | Transformational Leadership Across Multiple Channels | Growth Catalyst

Fred Meyer
Rice University • Stanford University

Portland, OR • 500+ Connections

About

Outstanding senior sales management career with industry leaders Fred Meyer and Ahold. Equally skilled in launching start-ups, positioning for rapid-but-sustainable success, and turning around underperforming operations. Some characteristics that define my brand of management include:

• Team Builder and Motivational Communicator: I coalesce and drive high-performing teams

• Strategic and Visionary Planner: I'm a catalyst for executing complex programs and producing extraordinary growth and results

• Exceptional Listener: I place a very high value on "group think," learning more through listening than speaking

My record reflects a proven ability to develop and lead professional sales and account representatives, maximizing individual potential. With my team, I have a reputation for masterfully executing complex projects with carefully defined objectives, precisely measured expectations, and proof-of-performance results. I am known for instituting visionary and innovative programs.

Committed to the value of developing strategic objectives, I have a skillset that includes leveraging data analytics, instituting Key Performance Indicators, and driving performance.

A highly accessible executive and change agent, I am known for my affinity in cultivating collaborative relationships, communicating effectively with all account stakeholders, and retaining my account relationships—even during periods of challenge and change. From developing strategic plans to adopting sales reports, planograms, and other tools as models within sales organizations, I embrace the mantra of "innovate or die."

Experience

Vice President of Sales
FRED MEYER
2019–Present

I was tapped to bring deep expertise to drive sales growth of 2 newly acquired brands for Fred Meyer. In just over a year, I have spearheaded innovation in strategic selling, produced solid gains, and significantly boosted profitability.

Through 10 direct reports, I lead a team of more than 400 sales professionals supporting all stateside operations.

Strategies I put immediately into place include:

• Implementing high-visibility seasonal and monthly performance goals and tracking with data analytics that measure and drive performance improvements (directly supported a double-digit percentage increase in sales for 2020 and projected for 2021).

• Leading the integration process for the 2 new acquisitions, first creating an advisory team to bring diverse voices and broad expertise into the integration process.

• Implementing sell-in tools and sales reports that have been adopted company-wide.

Results include:

• Increasing sales 37% in 2020.

• Forecasting continued double-digit growth for 2021.

Senior Director of International Business Development
FRED MEYER
2016–2019

I was initially hired by Fred Meyer's president and challenged to turn around and build international sales.

After bringing on board new general managers and pulling together with our existing managers, we turned around performance, delivering the following results:

• Achieved 100% increase in Brazil.

• Launched Fred Meyer remote in China.

• Created a strategic plan for expansion throughout Latin America.

• Realized significant reduction in speed-to-market by creating and implementing sustainable tactical strategies.

To achieve this success, my multipronged game plan included:

• Establishing weekly calls that focused on strategic sales, operations, and product development.

• Instituting top priorities and measurements.

• Putting in place cohesive in-country marketing support.

• Sharing success strategies among stakeholders.

Senior Vice President, Grocery
AHOLD USA, INC.
2011-2014

Promoted into the SVP role, I was challenged to drive sales across more than 650 locations nationwide. My direct reports included 6 Vice Presidents and 8 Segment Directors; indirectly, storewide staff exceeded 750.

My team and I delivered extraordinary results, including:

• Averaging 14% annual sales increase.

• Driving a 100% increase in sales of Food Lion store brands in the US.

• Creating innovative business model for redesign/reset of Food Lion, piloting the plan in 20 stores and establishing a corporate model.

Vice President, Hannaford
AHOLD USA, INC.
2007–2011

I managed corporate sales and marketing for the Hannaford brand. This entailed recruiting, training, and managing 6 senior account executives. I directly managed sales budgets and an overall book of business exceeding $200M.

Other key leadership initiatives included:

• Spearheading the strategic planning process—from seasonal forecasting to multiyear scenario planning.

• Driving integration of Hannaford's seasonal marketing initiatives with the seasonal plans of individual brands.

Strategic Account Manager, Hannaford Northeast
AHOLD USA, INC.
2003–2007

In this role, I managed national and regional accounts across the Northeast. I oversaw the Boston office operations and directly managed 11 sales reps.

Key accomplishments:

• Launched first-ever detailed market analysis for the region, leading to product improvements that drove year-over-year sales growth.

• Delivered $45M sales gain, increasing region revenue to $320M.

BACKSTORY: Marsha L. Standish (Writer: Melanie Denny)

TARGET ROLE: Vice President
CURRENT TITLE: Senior Director of Production
INDUSTRY: Logistics/Production/Manufacturing/Textiles

WRITER'S COMMENTS

Marsha was feeling undervalued and underutilized. She was ready for the jump from Senior Director to VP—and ready for a boost in income to match the greater level of responsibility.

After searching unproductively for several months, she was frustrated that nothing had materialized at the level she was seeking. She approached me about rewriting her career marketing materials to highlight her ability to impact the production process and also emphasize her background in global sourcing.

WRITING/DESIGN STRATEGY FOR DOCUMENTS

Resume: My goal in rewriting and redesigning Marsha's resume was to give her a higher-level look and feel and highlight her ability to impact the bottom line. I created immediate impact by using a bold globe graphic front and center to bring out her international background. I also made sure to use a lot of relevant keywords and strong action verbs.

A businesslike navy blue and gray color scheme signals that she is to be taken seriously as a senior-level production executive. A clean, modern font sends the message that she herself is fresh and modern. Most importantly, I made sure to incorporate numbers throughout to really showcase how she impacted the bottom line and make her value shine through.

Cover Letter: I created a general-purpose application letter for Marsha to respond to posted openings. It highlights her major achievements and explains the reason for her search. With just a few edits she can customize the letter to address specific issues mentioned in the posting.

LinkedIn: Recapping Marsha's career and achievements, her profile is a restatement of her resume with a few notable items. 1) Her headline repeats the strong branding statement from the top of her resume. 2) The About section refers to the personal attributes she brings to the job. 3) The job titles in her Experience section are expanded to include powerful keywords.

UNIQUE CHALLENGES

Although Marsha's most current position held a strong title, the role was below what she was capable of and lower than many positions she had held in the past, so I created a careers highlight section to bring some of the older, yet relevant accomplishments to the forefront.

OUTCOME

Marsha was thrilled with her new documents and reactivated her search with renewed energy and confidence.

MARSHA L. STANDISH

Albany, NY 10705 ■ 510-579-9999 ■ marshastandish@email.com ■ linkedin.com/in/marsha

VP / SENIOR DIRECTOR, PRODUCT DEVELOPMENT
reshaping global sourcing and supply chain systems to guarantee quality, compliance, and on-time delivery

Quality-focused production director consistently recognized for taking initiative to reverse process inefficiencies and reduce costs for global mid-sized to large-scale manufacturing facilities.

Inventory control strategist known for negotiating with overseas vendors (China, India, Turkey, Taiwan) to secure best pricing, guarantee on-time delivery, and boost productivity without comprising compliance, inspection, or supply chain standards.

Global sourcing specialist who guides cross-functional teams in building profitable supplier relationships; known for selecting best-fit factories while streamlining logistical processes to meet company revenue goals.

Inventory Control | Sourcing | Overseas Logistics Management | Vendor Relations | Product Development
Spend Analysis | Cost Reduction | Pricing Negotiation | Raw Materials | Product Research | Trend Forecasting
Global Supply Chain | Quality Control | Process Improvement | Workflow Optimization | Staff Training & Development

Career Highlights

- *Currently steering the production and importation of ~$2.5M product portfolio across 9 categories in collaboration with 20 Chinese factories for leading supplier of promotional products.*
- *Developed first-ever quality and testing manual that improved adherence to US sales restrictions and decreased quality failures 20%–25% across all categories at XY Exchange Company.*
- *Guaranteed 95% on-time delivery for XY Exchange Company's product development department, creating production checkpoints and schedules to seamlessly meet deadline requirements.*

PRODUCTION EXPERIENCE

BBC Corporation; New York, NY   October 2016–Present
Senior Director of Production & Imports

Orchestrate production and importation of ~$2.5M in branded merchandise across 9 categories for leading supplier of promotional products. Supervise team of 12. Ensure expeditious processing of 20–30 purchase orders concurrently ranging from $1K to $250K to 20+ China-based factories. Strengthen and leverage relationships with sourcing team, suppliers, and overseas offices to streamline workload and meet margin requirements.

- Cut operational costs **26%**, collaborating with freight forwarder and brokers to consolidate containers, book vessels, and clear customs upon arrival.
- Prevented delivery delays, reduced quantity shortages **35%**, and minimized quality concerns by partnering with Chinese factories and manufacturing team to proactively resolve raw materials production issues.
- Improved purchasing accuracy **57%** and guaranteed on-time delivery of merchandise, confirming custom orders with factories and tracking production performance against metrics.

National Entertainment Group; New York, NY   February 2014–October 2016
Production Director

Managed production of 30–50 seasonal SKUs across 3 lines of ready-to-wear women's apparel with retail values of $800 to $3K. Consulted with cross-functional teams to guide research, development, and sourcing of raw materials. Reviewed and confirmed invoices for sampling, shipping, and bulk orders.

- Ensured product innovation and value-added pricing while meeting quality goals and **98%** on-time delivery.
- Reversed logistical challenges, improved production time **45%**, and boosted productivity **63%**.

MARSHA L. STANDISH

Albany, NY 10705 ■ 510-579-9999 ■ marshastandish@email.com ■ linkedin.com/in/marsha

XY Exchange Company; New York, NY   **March 2012–October 2013**
Production Director (Apparel and Accessories)

Promoted to support VP in managing design, production, and merchandising of up to 150 seasonal styles of men's woven and leather apparel. Led team of 5 to ensure KPIs were achieved. Developed production communications, confirmed collections, ordered raw materials, finalized costs, and issued purchase orders.

- Slashed missed deadlines **35%**, cut processing time in half, and boosted team efficiency **27%**, restructuring purchasing department and revamping purchase order request guidelines for merchandising team.
- Doubled accuracy of purchase orders to **85%** by restructuring workload distribution for 2,000 POs per season.
- Cut product costs **42%** through negotiating discounts for bulk goods, competitively pricing raw materials, and analyzing cost break sheets based on projected units.
- Maintained compliance by joining forces with globally recognized inspection and fabric testing companies.
- Devised policy and procedures manual to increase productivity and profitability; standards adopted company wide.

XY Exchange Company; New York, NY   **March 2008–March 2012**
Senior Production Manager (Woven & Leather Apparel and Accessories)

Selected to preside over production of men's woven and leather apparel in India, Turkey, Northern China, and Taiwan. Led 4 direct reports while creating systems to streamline merchandising supply processes.

- Met merchant's desired target margin through negotiating cost of raw materials to minimize product costs.

XY Exchange Company; New York, NY   **March 2005–March 2008**
Production Manager (Woven & Leather Apparel and Accessories)

Led the production of all woven apparel produced in India, Turkey, and Taiwan with emphasis on mediating production issues and maximizing efficiencies in delivery and cost. Traveled abroad annually to India to review and approve production of merchandise. Oversaw 1 direct report accountable for managing daily communications with vendors.

**Previously held Production Coordinator position after entering XY Exchange Company organization as Intern.

EDUCATION

State University of New York, College at Oneonta—Oneonta, NY
Bachelor of Science in Apparel and Textiles

Fashion Institute of Technology—New York, NY
Associate of Applied Science in Fashion Merchandising Management

———— Technology Systems ————

MS Office Suite (Word, Excel, PowerPoint, OneNote, and Outlook), Adobe Programs (Illustrator, Photoshop, and Acrobat), QuickBooks, NGC Web PDM, AS 400, ASI Profit Maker, and NetSuite

MARSHA L. STANDISH

Albany, NY 10705 ■ 510-579-9999 ■ marshastandish@email.com ■ linkedin.com/in/marsha

VP / SENIOR DIRECTOR, PRODUCT DEVELOPMENT
reshaping global sourcing and supply chain systems to guarantee quality, compliance, and on-time delivery

Date

Hiring Manager
Title
Company Name

Re: Job Title

Dear [Hiring Manager]:

As a Product Development Director my priority is to drive the production process and maximize profitability while ensuring price, cost, delivery timelines, and quality are at optimal levels.

During my time at XY Exchange Company, I repeatedly adopted new procedures that delivered cost savings, increased productivity, and improved quality controls. As a result, I was promoted 4 times and ultimately advanced into the Director of Production position, where I led a team of 5 in managing design, production, and merchandising of up to 150 seasonal styles of men's woven and leather apparel.

Under my direction, we were able to reduce missed deadlines up to 35%, cut processing time in almost half, enhance team efficiency 27%, and double the accuracy of purchase orders.

[Hiring Manager], at this point in my career, I am looking to leverage my expertise in product development, raw materials sourcing, team leadership, and process improvement to optimize production operations at a forward-thinking firm like [Company Name].

Please feel free to contact me at your earliest convenience as I am interested in learning more about this role and how I can add value to your team. Thank you for your time and consideration. I look forward to hearing from you soon.

Sincerely,

MARSHA L. STANDISH

Marsha L. Standish

VP / Sr Director, Product Development ☆ reshaping global supply chain systems to ensure quality, compliance, and on-time delivery

BBC Corporation
State University of New York • Fashion Institute of Technology

Albany, NY • 500+ Connections

About

I'm a Senior Product Director with expertise in raw materials sourcing, inventory control, team leadership, vendor relations, supply chain management, and process improvement.

With an innate desire to identify and implement innovative new processes to achieve operational efficiency, my focus is to continually optimize pricing, quality, and delivery timelines while upholding the brand aesthetic.

In my current role, I lead the production of up to 9 product lines valued at more than ~$2.5M while coordinating efforts with 20 manufacturing facilities in China, India, Turkey, and Taiwan.

As a passionate leader, I always strive to lead my team by empowering them to perform at optimal levels while coaching and encouraging them to meet production metrics and KPIs.

While I'm well versed in quality compliance regulations for several commodity items, including apparel, accessories, furniture, coolers, appliances, luxury goods, and electronics, I spent a large portion of my career in the production department at global fashion brand, XY Exchange Company.

Some of my notable achievements during my tenure with XY Exchange Company include:

✔ Eliminating 35% of missed deadlines, slashing processing time in half, and improving team efficiency 27% through restructuring of purchasing department.

✔ Raising purchase order accuracy from 43% to 85% after revamping department workload distribution.

✔ Designing first-ever quality and testing manual and decreasing quality failures 20%–25% across all categories.

The key to my success is my ability to develop meaningful business relationships with material suppliers, vendors, internal partners, and my team members, ultimately ensuring revenue and production goals are consistently met.

Let's connect!

▶▶▶ Specialty Areas ◀◀◀

✔ Raw Materials Sourcing Strategies
✔ Production Operations
✔ Product Design
✔ Product Development
✔ Inventory Control Management
✔ Supply Chain Optimization
✔ Cost Reduction Initiatives
✔ Process Improvement
✔ Trend Forecasting
✔ Overseas Sourcing
✔ Vendor Negotiations

Experience

Senior Director, Production & Imports » Inventory Control Management | Overseas Production | Product Development
BBC Corporation
Oct 2016–Present

I currently oversee all aspects of production and importation for a $2.5M product line comprising 9 categories in coordination with 20 Chinese factories. This entails inventory management and process control for up to 30 ongoing orders, each valued at $1K to $250K. I work closely with the sourcing team, raw materials suppliers, and overseas offices to streamline the workload and meet margin requirements.

✔ Reduced operational costs 26%, working alongside freight forwarder and brokers to consolidate containers, book vessels, and clear customs upon arrival.

✔ Prevented delivery delays, cut quantity shortages 35%, and allayed quality concerns by partnering with China-based factories and manufacturing team to proactively resolve raw materials production issues.

✔ Improved purchasing accuracy 57% and guaranteed on-time delivery of merchandise, confirming custom orders with factories, and tracking production performance against metrics.

Production Director » Sourcing Strategies | Raw Materials | Logistics | Quality Control
National Entertainment Group
Feb 2014–Oct 2016

Here, I led production efforts for 30–50 seasonal SKUs across 3 lines of ready-to-wear women's apparel with retail values of $800 to $3K.

✔ Rectified logistical issues, improved production time 45%, and boosted productivity 63% after working closely with regional teams to implement production solutions.

✔ Ensured product innovation, value-added pricing, quality, and 98% on-time delivery by leveraging relationships with raw materials suppliers to meet predefined objectives.

Production Director (Apparel and Accessories) » Merchandising | Process Improvement
XY Exchange Company
Mar 2012–Oct 2013

I advanced into this Director role after successfully fulfilling the position of senior production manager. Here, I supported the VP in managing design, production, and merchandising of up to 150 seasonal styles of men's woven and leather apparel. My team of 5 comprised 2 Assistant Managers and 3 Purchase Order Administrators. We crafted production communications, ordered raw materials, finalized costs, and issued purchase orders for the international division.

✔ Reduced missed deadlines ~35%, cut processing time in almost half, and boosted team efficiency 27% after restructuring purchasing department and revamping purchase order request guidelines.

✔ Formalized policy and procedures manual to increase productivity and profitability; standards adopted company wide.

✔ Doubled accuracy of purchase orders within the first few seasons of hiring a new team member and reallocating workload distribution.

✔ Maintained compliance by joining forces with globally recognized inspection and fabric testing companies to ensure compliance with California Proposition 65 standards.

Senior Production Manager (Woven & Leather Apparel and Accessories) » Production Operations | Quality Control
XY Exchange Company
Mar 2008–Mar 2012

As Senior Manager, I held direct oversight of producing men's woven and leather apparel in India, Turkey, Northern China, and Taiwan. I led 4 direct reports while creating systems to streamline merchandising supply processes.

✔ Met merchant's desired target margin through negotiating cost of raw materials to minimize product costs.

Production Manager
XY Exchange Company
Mar 2005–Mar 2008

Here, I led the production of all woven apparel developed in India, Turkey, and Taiwan with emphasis on mediating production issues and maximizing efficiencies in delivery and cost. I traveled abroad annually to India to review and approve quality of merchandise. I also supervised 1 direct report.

Earlier in my career, I was hired as an Intern at XY Exchange Company. I swiftly ascended through the organization and became a Production Coordinator in 2001, then was promoted into this role 4 years later.

BACKSTORY: Vince Brewster (Writer: Marjorie Sussman)

TARGET ROLE: General Manager
CURRENT TITLE: General Manager
INDUSTRY: Hotels/Hospitality

WRITER'S COMMENTS

Vince Brewster came to me as general manager of a luxury hotel—a role he absolutely loved and one that he had been promoted to just a little over a year before. This was a change—and a welcomed one—from a 15-year career in finance operations roles in the world of casinos. As GM, he took pride in building relationships and cultivating a culture of empowerment and individualism that was already generating positive results from hotel guests.

His immediate goal was a long-overdue update of a 10-year-old resume in order to be ready to act on any new GM opportunities that came his way.

In addition to his record of revitalizing and stabilizing financial operations in a highly regulated industry, I soon discovered that Vince had a passion for service that readily extended into the community. He had been a leader in the face of two natural disasters—a hurricane and a flood—and in one instance established a foundation and raised hundreds of thousands of dollars for distribution to those affected. With every initiative, he acted quickly and efficiently and got superior results.

WRITING/DESIGN STRATEGY FOR DOCUMENTS

Resume: In addition to industry- and accomplishment-specific facts, I incorporated service into the opening summary and interspersed it in the job descriptions just like any other accomplishment. The final section of the resume notes his current board service focused on community action and fundraising.

LinkedIn: My love for creative storytelling took hold. I began the About section with a question, "What makes a hotel unforgettable?" and in the content that followed presented Vince's brand of customer service excellence. In the concluding paragraph, I referred back to the thought I began with by reinventing Vince's own way of explaining who he is and what he stands for.

Bio: The bio gave me the opportunity to write Vince's story in a narrative, presenting financial operations achievements as well as full paragraphs about his community service and the value he placed on the people that make up an organization.

UNIQUE CHALLENGES

My main challenge was summarizing a long and successful career into a succinct and readable 2-page resume…while also including his community service work, because it is so integral to who he is. One technique I used was to present "job scope" details in a single line under the job title, thereby eliminating the need for lengthy paragraphs.

OUTCOME

While Vince is not actively seeking a new job, he is well prepared to respond to opportunities that come his way. And when he's ready for a more active search, he'll need only a quick update before getting started.

VINCE BREWSTER

503-453-1724 | brewster@email.com
www.linkedin.com/in/brewster

SENIOR EXECUTIVE: GENERAL MANAGEMENT, FINANCE, OPERATIONS

HOTELS | HOSPITALITY

Operational and Financial Excellence: Build brand-driven value by evaluating business processes, establishing best practices, upgrading systems, and securing the right talent. **Approachable Leadership:** Cultivate empowered, service-oriented teams in an environment of originality and respect. MBA.

$750M consumer-driven businesses. Multimillion-dollar budgets. 1000+ employees.

- Improved customer service, check-in, and room ratings by roughly 20% in first 6 months. *The Westerly Hotel*
- Introduced a new vision for the financial/operational growth of a $750M organization. *NG&E/Parisienne Hotel*
- Oversaw financial operations, reporting, and compliance for $475M revenue. *BE&C/Grandview Hotel*

PROFESSIONAL EXPERIENCE

THE WESTERLY HOTEL — Portland, OR | 2018–Present

GENERAL MANAGER—THE WESTERLY (2018–Present)
10 direct reports / 120 staff / 300 rooms / 15K SF meeting space / $50M revenue

Promoted within months of hire to GM of the company's flagship hotel (the only AAA Four Diamond hotel in the area) while maintaining oversight of finance operations for all 3 hotels in the hospitality portfolio. Direct reports: Heads of Operations, Finance, Sales & Marketing, HR, Engineering, Food & Beverage, and the Executive Chef.

- **Senior Executive Core Leadership Team:** Partner with senior leaders and ownership to drive strategy and growth, including a **$5M renovation** of the hotel's restaurant, bar, terrace, meeting space, and rooms.
- **Workforce Leadership:** Cultivate a culture of accountability, ownership, and empowerment in a collaborative environment that generates high employee satisfaction scores and best-in-class guest services.
- **Operational Leadership:** Plan and implement initiatives that streamline operations, minimize costs, and inspire productivity to maintain hotel's reputation for high standards, exceptional amenities, and industry dominance.

REGIONAL DIRECTOR OF FINANCE—THE WESTERLY, SANDERS, HILLSIDE HOTELS (2018)
15 direct reports (Controller, Auditor, Staff Accountants) / 240 staff / 500 rooms / $100M revenue

Led overhaul of the finance and accounting operations of 3 properties—the Westerly, Sanders, and Hillside Hotels—to optimize operational efficiencies and oversight of **$100M revenue.** Consulted with individual staff members in a sweeping assessment of processes and procedures to identify and establish opportunities for improvement.

- **In first 6 months:** Recruited new leadership team, established service-based culture, clarified expectations and accountability, and identified KPIs for 10 areas of success that improved by 15–20 percentage points.
- **Sustainable Turnaround:** Began the process of building a legacy to ensure sustainable growth and industry leadership. Spearheaded technology upgrades, best practices, and standard business processes.

PARISIENNE HOTEL—NATIONAL GAMING & ENTERTAINMENT (NG&E) — Lake Tahoe, NV | 2013–2018

VP FINANCE & OPERATIONAL EXCELLENCE (2015–2018) | VP FINANCE & ADMINISTRATION (2013–2015)
10 direct reports / 1500 staff / 1600 rooms / 20 food & beverage outlets / $750M revenue

Brought onboard to breathe new life into underperforming front- and back-of-house finance areas at the 4-star hotel and casino. Promoted to VP Finance & Operational Excellence, broadening authority to include **$750M revenue** and strategic planning at all locations. Represented company to the board, auditors, state police, and community.

VINCE BREWSTER | 503-453-1724 | brewster@email.com

PARISIENNE HOTEL....

- **Operational Turnaround:** Standardized processes and procedures, cleaned up balance sheet and created new reconciliations, ensured timeliness of permits and taxes, and corrected past permit and reporting issues.
- **Financial Improvement:** Improved EBITDA margins every year through labor and business process efficiencies.
- **Performance Excellence:** Scored highest guest satisfaction AND highest employee satisfaction ratings as the company generated record-breaking revenues following enterprise-wide reorganization efforts.
- **Community:** Led recovery efforts for the 2014 Tahoe flood that impacted families of many team members. Created a foundation that raised hundreds of thousands of dollars for tax-friendly distribution to families.
- **Honors:** The Board's Leadership Excellence Award for above-and-beyond success in company and community.

GRANDVIEW HOTEL—BOARDWALK ENTERTAINMENT & CASINO (BE&C)   Atlantic City, NJ | 2005–2013

DIRECTOR OF FINANCE (2012–2013) | FINANCIAL CONTROLLER (2010–2012)

Oversaw all financial operations for $475M+ revenue (reporting, compliance, accounting, audit, cashiering, drop and count teams). Dotted line: property analytics, IT, purchasing, warehouse. Liaison to state police, outside auditors, corporate finance A/P and payroll, shared services, and the City of Atlantic City.

- **Financial Oversight:** Prepared weekly forecasts for **$45M** revenue, expenses, and annual budget/capital spend.
- **Core Leadership Team:** Partnered with CEO and CFO to develop **$5M** pedestrian mall, including negotiations with local authorities and contracts with Gordon Baylor, Grand Cove, and Marino Steakhouse restaurants.
- **Cost Reductions:** Worked with operators and marketers to plan long-term reductions in operating costs for marketing spend, advertising, facilities repair/maintenance contracts, labor, and cost of goods sold.
- **Audits:** Achieved consistently clean SOX audits following overhaul of balance sheets and financial statements.

FINANCIAL ACCOUNTING MANAGER (2008–2010) | REVENUE AUDIT MANAGER (2006–2008)

Transformed struggling finance business unit and recruited new team of audit and accounting supervisors. Drove operational improvements, established SOPs, and retrained auditors, senior accountants, and payroll specialists to firmly position the department's ability to manage **$475M+ revenue.**

- **Precision Accounting:** Oversaw month-end closing, forecasting, budgeting, and capital processes for **$40M** monthly revenue. Dotted-line responsibility for warehouse, purchasing, and receiving operations.
- **Staff Development:** Designed training program that promoted 6 auditors to auditor II level, 3 to positions in other finance/operations departments, 1 to casino accounting supervisor, and 1 to casino manager.
- **Flawless Audits:** Uncovered no significant or material audit findings in 45+ yearly audits by internal auditors, external auditors, and the NJ State Police.

CORPORATE AUDITOR (2005–2006)

Conducted audits that identified **$1.5M cost savings** in cash management, labor efficiency, and fine avoidance.

- **Individual Audit Star Award:** Identification of **$350K** in cost savings opportunities in first quarter.
- **Team Award:** Post-Sandy boardwalk fundraising/recovery and Grandview Hotel restructuring/reopening.

EDUCATION	CURRENT BOARD SERVICE

Columbia University Business School, New York, NY
  MBA Business Administration
	Northwestern Lodging Association:
	  Chair, Community Action Committee

New Paltz State University, New Paltz, NY
  BS Business Management
	American Red Cross Foundation—NW Chapter:
	  Chair, Fundraising Development Committee

Vince Brewster

Senior Executive, General Manager: Hospitality ★ Hotels ★ Food & Beverage ★ Strategy ★ Operations ★ Finance ★ Community Service

The Westerly Hotel
New Paltz State University • Columbia University

Greater Portland Area • 500+ Connections

About

What makes a hotel unforgettable? Exceptional Amenities…Hospitality…Service…Attention to Detail. As GM of a Four Diamond hotel, I strive every day to provide the resources and incentives that inspire our staff members to make every guest's experience exceptional.

WORK CULTURE: As General Manager of the Westerly Hotel (Portland), I'm cultivating a culture of camaraderie that focuses on personalized customer service, and our success is reflected in positive customer reviews, repeat guests, and a growing bottom line. We've identified key areas of success—staff service, guest check-in, anticipation of needs, and more—and results have never been better.

FINANCIAL REBIRTH: Rooted in financial operations in the gaming and casino world, I'm well aware of what drives top- and bottom-line growth in a heavily regulated organization. My reputation for turning around struggling businesses and getting them back on solid ground, along with a passion for service excellence and an empowered workforce, is now focused on the hotel/hospitality industry.

SERVICE: I strongly support programs in the local community and actively engage other businesses to do the same. When Hurricane Sandy struck, I helped recovery efforts in the area and rebuilt the financial operations of a $475M business. When flooding caused heartaches in Lake Tahoe, I raised hundreds of thousands of dollars to help people get back on their feet.

THE CIRCLE OF SUCCESS: As a hospitality professional, I've learned that the rewards of superior, true-to-brand service resonate on many different levels. Not only do they translate directly into competitive advantage and create good will in the community, but they circle back to their source—an empowered workforce—validating their efforts to make every guest's experience an exceptional one.

Experience

General Manager & Director of Financial Operations
The Westerly Hotel
2018–Present

OVERVIEW:
General management of the flagship location of a portfolio of hotels and financial oversight of the entire 3-hotel collection. The Westerly is a AAA Four Diamond Hotel and the benchmark of success in the area.

HIGHLIGHTS:
— Revitalized finance and accounting operations the first year with new talent and business processes, clarification of expectations, and identification of key performance indicators.
— Drive the overall planning and strategy for the hotel collection's long-term growth as member of the core leadership team.
— Cultivate an empowered work culture and provide resources and support that the hotel staff needs to deliver the best possible service to guests.

VP Finance & Operational Excellence
NG&E Parisienne Hotel
2013–2018

OVERVIEW:
Oversight of accounting and finance operations for 4 hotel and casino properties, $750M revenue, and 1500 employees (auditing, FP&A, centralized scheduling, A/P, cage and credit, IT, purchasing/receiving, facilities, security, risk management).

HIGHLIGHTS:
— Turned around financial operations, then broadened authority to include 3 additional properties as a result of an acquisition and organizational restructuring.
— Coordinated regional financial rollups for presentation to C-level leaders and the board.
— Received the CEO's Leadership Award for exceptional performance in reorganizing 4 properties and overseeing record-breaking revenues, while taking the lead in humanitarian efforts in the aftermath of the Tahoe flood.
— Worked with the executive team to establish a foundation that raised hundreds of thousands of tax-friendly dollars for distribution to the families of 100 employees affected by the flood.

Director of Finance | Financial Controller | Accounting Manager | Audit Manager
Boardwalk Entertainment & Casino—Grandview Hotel
2005–2013

OVERVIEW:
Oversight of all finance operations for a $475M business (reporting, compliance, accounting, audit, cashiering, drop and count teams, IT, purchasing, warehouse). Promoted 4 times in 8 years from Internal Auditor to Director of Finance.

HIGHLIGHTS:
— Partnered with the CFO and VP Finance to develop a $5M pedestrian mall, including contracts for key restaurants, while driving cost reductions and operational efficiencies.
— Served as key contributor to rebuilding the Grandview in the aftermath of Hurricane Sandy. Transformed a struggling finance department into a well-structured, process-driven, and credible team of professionals. Recruited new talent and developed an employee appreciation program of performance incentives and training programs that restored morale.

VINCE BREWSTER

HIGH STANDARDS AND PROVEN EXPERTISE in finance and operations are the qualities that Vince Brewster brings to the table.

AS GENERAL MANAGER of the Portland Westerly, he is transforming a vision to reality by hiring the right talent, establishing best-practice processes and procedures, and cultivating a service-based culture that is sure to uphold the hotel's AAA Four Diamond reputation for upscale style, amenities, and service.

FROM THE TIME HIS CAREER BEGAN, when he identified $1M in savings in his first year at the Grandview Hotel (Atlantic City), to present day, Vince has forged a path of transformation and growth for struggling financial operations.

AS AUDIT MANAGER at the Grandview, he revived the finance department with new talent, system upgrades, and morale-building incentives to firmly establish credibility in the aftermath of Hurricane Sandy. He also took a lead role in expediting recovery efforts in the local community.

BREWSTER JOINED THE PARISIENNE HOTEL (Lake Tahoe) in 2013, traveling cross-country to build on his reputation for operational transformation by restructuring front- and back-of-house finance areas at the 4-star hotel and casino. Within 2 years, he was appointed VP Finance & Operational Excellence, and his authority broadened to include additional locations and oversight of $750M P&L.

ONE OF THE HALLMARKS OF VINCE'S BRAND is the value he places in people at every level. He offers training and resources while cultivating a culture of ownership and empowerment that translates into impeccable customer service. This service mindset extends into the community, where he is the first to organize relief efforts for residents coping with situations beyond their control.

SOCIAL RESPONSIBILITY was the driving force in the aftermath of Hurricane Sandy as well as in response to the Tahoe flood of 2014. In Tahoe, he led efforts to help families of 100 employees impacted by the disaster, working with volunteers and vendors to rebuild homes. Brewster worked with core leadership to set up a foundation and raise funds for distribution to those in need.

AT HOME, Vince enjoys time with his family biking and hiking in areas coast to coast. The Pacific Crest Trail is one of their favorites, as well as areas throughout Europe.

BREWSTER EARNED AN MBA in Business Administration from Columbia University. He serves on the boards of the Northwestern Lodging Association as Chair of the Community Action Committee and the American Red Cross Foundation as Chair of the Local Fundraising Committee.

503-453-1724 | brewster@email.com | www.linkedin.com/in/brewster

BACKSTORY: Walter Williams (Writer: Stephen Van Vreede)

TARGET ROLE: CIO or other C-Level Position (CTO, CDO)
CURRENT TITLE: CIO/Digital Transformation Executive
INDUSTRY: Consumer Products (Current) / Banking and Finance (Target)

WRITER'S COMMENTS

Walter has been a disruptive force at companies for most of his career. He's been very successful at driving business transformation through digital solution delivery and product innovation. He was looking for a new external opportunity because his company's appetite for ongoing change had stalled after the successes of his first-year transformation efforts.

To compound the challenge, Walter wanted to transition from a consumer product company to small and regional companies in banking and finance.

My strategy in writing the documents was to showcase Walter's experience and achievements as an entrepreneurially minded technology executive who leads digital disruption programs. I focused his brand or positioning on outcomes most important to the Board and Executive Team at regional financial institutions: namely, scaling the small business for rapid growth, making them competitive in today's digital and mobile economy, and delivering an improved customer experience digitally, all of which became even more important in a COVID-impacted economy.

WRITING/DESIGN STRATEGY FOR DOCUMENTS

Resume: The format, style, and color (with red and blue) of the resume were designed to draw the eye of the reader to the most important messaging to ensure that Walter's brand was evident, even in a review of less than 30 seconds. Bullet points are tightly written so that each accomplishment stands out.

LinkedIn: The About section of Walter's profile tells his career story of leading disruptive change…and consistently delivering business benefits. The results focus is enhanced by details about how he does what he does—his leadership style and the beliefs that drive his actions.

Bio: Walter's bio is a vibrant one-page document that calls attention to his most notable achievements through positioning, color, and large type. A colorful panel at the top provides a career snapshot, and information throughout the bio is segmented to be captured in a quick scan.

UNIQUE CHALLENGES

The primary challenge in creating documents for Walter was keeping his audience in mind. Because he wants to switch industries, it was essential to appeal to executives at his target financial institutions and avoid overemphasizing the industry-specific aspects of his past positions.

OUTCOME

Walter began his search with a great deal of confidence about his value and his message. He has broadened his connections with executives in his target banking/financial industry and is engaged in active outreach and networking.

WALTER WILLIAMS

St. Louis, MO 63107 | wewilliams@gmail.com | 314.929.7811 | www.linkedin.com/in/waltwilliams

TECHNOLOGY & BUSINESS EXECUTIVE | ENTREPRENEURIAL CIO/CTO/CDO

Driving Disruptive Digital Transformation to Create a Competitive Market Advantage to
Scale for Profitable Growth – Optimize Customer Experience – Compete in Digital/Mobile Economy

Revenue Growth ~ New Market Expansion ~ Operations Leadership ~ Digital & Business Strategy ~ E-commerce
Product Development ~ Software Delivery ~ Program Management ~ Budgeting/P&L ~ Capital Planning
Team Building ~ Culture Development ~ Change Management ~ Process Optimization/Automation

Business-focused global technology executive with 22 years of success at start-up and private equity-funded growth firms, IPO track, and public companies across diverse verticals such as apparel, software, consumer packaged goods (CPG), consumer electronics, manufacturing, and professional services.

Entrepreneurial and innovation-minded leader with proven success directing technology transformations focused on disrupting industries, driving enterprise value, and capturing new revenue and market opportunities with a unique vision to promote explosive growth.

Trusted executive and board advisor to help shape business vision, strategic direction, technology roadmap, and capital investments. Shrewd risk taker and tactical change agent who thrives in organizations looking for disruption, challenging the status quo to competitively position firms and fuel innovation and profits.

Digital Disruption & Business Transformation Leadership Showcase

- Powered rapid top- and bottom-line growth by revolutionizing ABC Product's digital capabilities and customer journey by creating "Pet Platform," a first in the pet food manufacturing sector.
- As CIO, navigated Public Apparel Co. from legacy B2B to digital and e-commerce-based B2C model that led to 550% growth and 78% margins in 19 months plus VC/PE investment, M&A, and successful IPO.

PROFESSIONAL EXPERIENCE

ABC PRODUCTS, INC.   2019 – Present
Chief Information Officer | Digital Transformation Executive

Charged with leading digital technology disruption and IT-enabled business transformation strategy to this company entrenched in legacy consumer product manufacturing space. Shaped innovative strategy and technology plan to focus on integrating product sales with target consumer lifestyle choices within the digital world. Led execution of digital product, solution, and brand development efforts to expand into new market opportunities. Oversaw scaling of evolving technology operations for a clear competitive advantage.

- **Created an industry-first "Product Platform" concept, using holistic digital solutions and services that revolutionized customer experience journey** to unite product lovers with award-winning products.
- **Fueled explosive top-line revenue and bottom-line profit growth by enabling massive differentiation** from entrenched competitors through digital capabilities and targeted digital marketing solutions.
- **Accelerated time-to-market and led change management efforts** that integrated sister brands into overall marketing and branding strategy.

PUBLIC APPAREL CO.   2013 – 2019
Chief Information Officer | Information Technology Senior Vice President/VP/Director

Brought in to establish technology group in support of rapid, scalable growth and earned successive promotions up to CIO to steer strategic direction of business, IT organization, and technology framework in alignment with financial and corporate objectives. Directed e-commerce and digital sales P&L as well as governance, IT operations, infrastructure, solution development, and service management with 55 reports and $24M budget. Embedded best practices, methodologies, and internal controls for SOX compliance.

- **Disrupted 57-year-old B2B business model**, creating B2C enterprise with ground-up launch of digital capabilities and e-commerce platform and evolutionary 5-year strategic technology roadmap.
- **Enabled 550% growth in e-commerce revenue in 19 months with 78% margin.**

Private & Confidential   1

Walter Williams

wewilliams@gmail.com | 314.929.7811

- **Played key role in venture capital/private equity plays, M&A integrations, and successful IPO** with restructuring and scaling of technology solutions, IT organization, processes, standards, and deliverables.
- **Supported organization growth at >30% YOY ($800M+ in top-line revenue),** delivering world-class technology services, application development, project management, and solution delivery.
- **Initiated and guided adoption of Cloud-first model as well as robust DR/BCP capabilities** that enabled successful navigation of 2 floods impacting global head office and manufacturing facility.

ADVANCED DIGITAL SOLUTIONS COMPANY   2012 – 2013
Technology Director, Business Enablement

Recruited to transform underperforming division by supporting restructuring and revenue growth initiative. Steered strategic direction of technology and project management office within Digital Application Services segment of parent company. Drove process optimization and efficient project delivery. Managed Agile software design methodology and formulated 6/12/18 month roadmap to fuel revenue growth and efficiencies. Crafted repeatable, reusable code frameworks based on partner platforms. Led 8 direct reports and 125+ resources.

- **Bolstered sales process with MVP product model** proof-of-concept development.
- **Turned around negative EBITDA projects** with Agile adoption and project execution revamp.
- **Accelerated pre-sales intake and new project delivery** by streamlining PMO operations and process.
- **Delivered digital and process automation technologies** to cut admin overheads up to 66%.
- **Forged strategic partnerships for new business opportunities** with Drupal, Ektron, and Microsoft.

PREMIUM NAVIGATION COMPANY   2008 – 2012
Information Technology Manager, Quality Assurance & Product Support

Drove IT / QA strategy and operations for MEP software division, managing 20+ direct reports and $10M budget. Guided training development of IT, QA, and product support staff.

- **Transformed IT from cost center to ROI-driven value creator.** Stimulated growth and cost savings—including 50% headcount reduction, 65% IT platform savings, and 75% annual software licensing savings—through virtualization, Cloud enablement, and negotiation of enterprise licensing agreements.
- **Embedded Agile software release methodology** and piloted project planning/delivery framework.
- **Enhanced customer experience** with operational changes plus new CRM and ERP systems.
- **Led integration of distinct IT / QA functions** following acquisition of XYZ Systems.

**   **   **   **

Early career: Executive Consultant/Managing Partner at LMNOP Co., IT Lead/Specialist at RST Systems, and Principal Consultant at XYZ Life Company.

INVESTOR & BOARD ADVISORY EXPERIENCE

DIGITAL, SAAS, AND AI STARTUP   2018 – Present
Investor | Executive/Board Advisor

Invested in/advising SaaS product firm offering AI-powered content enrichment and discovery solutions.

- **Recommended strategies for digital applications** and simple APIs to make data and content easily consumable despite being housed in disparate silo systems.

EDUCATION & TRAINING

Harvard University—Harvard Business School, Executive Education
Washington & Lee University, Bachelor of Science in Computer Science
Project Management Institute (PMI), Project Management Professional (PMP)

Walter Williams

Technology & Business Executive | Futuristic CIO at ABC Products—Driving Digital Disruption for Scaled Growth/Profits

ABC Products, Inc.
Harvard University • Washington & Lee University

St. Louis, MO Area • 500+ Connections

About

▶ Driving Disruptive Digital Transformation to Create a Competitive Market Advantage
▶ Scaling Companies for Profitable Growth
▶ Enabling Competition in Today's Digital/Mobile Economy
▶ Optimizing the Digital Customer Experience

I believe technology should give companies a competitive advantage in the market and be done in a way that is woven seamlessly in the fabric of business. Over the past 12+ years, this has been my specialty and passion with start-ups, VC/PE-funded firms, M&A acquisitions, and IPO companies in apparel, software, consumer packaged goods, consumer electronics, manufacturing, and professional services.

I engage with Board Directors, CXOs, VC/PE Investors, and Business Unit Executives to create forward-looking strategies and innovative solutions to tackle seemingly impossible challenges.

As an Entrepreneurial Leader and Trusted Advisor, select career accomplishments include:

▶ Revolutionizing the customer experience journey at ABC Products by creating an industry-first "Product Platform"

▶ Disrupting a 57-year-old B2B business at Public Apparel Co. by creating a fully digital B2C enterprise that experienced 550% in e-commerce revenue growth in 19 months while supporting more than 30% in year-over-year enterprise top-line growth

▶ Collaborating in venture capital/private equity plays, M&A integrations, and a successful IPO at Public Apparel Co.

▶ Serving as an Investor and Board Advisor for an SaaS product firm since 2018

Experience

Chief Information Officer (CIO) | Digital Transformation Executive
ABC Products, Inc.
Apr 2019 – Present

I was brought in to ignite a business transformation using disruptive digital technologies. In this executive and C-suite role, I help to shape business strategy, technology planning, digital products, solution roadmaps, technology operating models, customer experience management, and new market opportunities.

Notable Highlights:

▶ Created "Product Platform," a first-in-the-industry concept using digital solutions to revolutionize the customer experience journey.

▶ Delivered digital capabilities and digital marketing solutions that drove aggressive top-line revenue and profit growth.

▶ Led strategic change management initiatives.

Chief Information Officer (CIO) | IT Senior Vice President
Public Apparel Co.
2013 – 2019

Public Apparel Co. was a B2B company that had been in operation for 50+ years when I was hired in an IT Director role. I was tasked with establishing their technology group and helping the business in digital transformation and IT scaling during a period of rapid growth. As I advanced to the SVP and CIO roles, I oversaw IT operations, infrastructure, solution development, service delivery, IT security and controls, SOX compliance, and more.

Notable Highlights:

▶ Created the disruptive digital and e-commerce vision and an accompanying evolutionary 5-year technology roadmap that enabled the company to become a viable B2C enterprise.

▶ Drove the adoption of a Cloud-first model and disaster recovery strategies that enabled the company to survive (and thrive) during a time when 2 major flood events impacted the global headquarters and manufacturing facility.

▶ Enabled 550% e-commerce growth in just 19 months and supported an organization growing at more than 30% annually.

▶ Supported venture capital and private equity (VC/PE) plays, M&A integrations, and the company's successful IPO.

Technology Director, Business Enablement
Advanced Digital Solutions Company
2012 – 2013

I was brought in by the leading technology solution provider to businesses, healthcare, and government across the Midwest to turn around the underperforming Digital Application Services segment. I oversaw the development of short-term and long-term strategies and the restructuring of the organization, including the PMO. I also led new product development (PoC), customer engagement, and pre-sales activities with more than 125 total team resources.

Notable Highlights:

▶ Turned around all negative EBITDA projects.

▶ Delivered digital and process automation technologies.

▶ Increased segment sales and closed key strategic partnerships.

▶ Streamlined business operations with proven methodologies, including the MVP product model for proof of concept, Agile for project execution, and PMO functions for faster pre-sales intake.

IT Manager, Quality Assurance & Product Support
Premium Navigation Company
2008 – 2012

With a team of more than 20 direct reports, I led all facets of IT strategy, QA strategy, and operations for the MEP software division. I managed a $10M budget as well as the training and development of my team.

Notable Highlights:

▶ Transformed IT from a legacy cost center into an ROI-driven value creator for the business.

▶ Enabled a 50% headcount reduction, 65% in IT platform savings, and 75% in software licensing savings.

▶ Led virtualization and Cloud enablement efforts.

▶ Improved the customer experience and software releases using Agile techniques.

▶ Managed the integration of IT and QA functions after Premium acquired RST Systems.

Walter Williams

St. Louis, MO 63107

wewilliams@gmail.com | 314.929.7811 | www.linkedin.com/in/waltwilliams

Technology & Business Executive Biography

2000	2010	2012	2013	2019	Today
**LMNOP	XYZ Life** Co-Founder	Principal Consultant	**Premium Navigation**	**Advanced Digital Solutions**	**Public Apparel Co.**		**ABC Products Inc.**
RST Systems Technology Lead	Specialist	Technology Manager	Technology Director, Business Enablement	CIO	Information Technology Executive		CIO	Digital Transformation Executive

CORE COMPETENCIES

✓ Digital & Business Strategy
✓ E-commerce & Mobile Solutions
✓ Customer Experience Management
✓ Business & IT Goal Alignment
✓ Team Building & Leadership
✓ Tech-Driven Business Transformation

QUALIFICATIONS

Harvard Business School Executive Education

BS in Computer Science

PMP Certification

550% e-commerce growth in just 19 months

Scaled business for >30% YOY top-line growth

Revolutionized product manufacturing space with digital platform concept and CX journey

>50% cut to headcount, IT platform, and software licensing costs

Walter Williams is a **Technology and Business Executive** who has served in Entrepreneurial CIO, CTO, and CDO roles with 22 years of progressive experience driving business improvement and digital transformation in the apparel, software, consumer packaged goods (CPG), consumer electronics, manufacturing, and professional services verticals. This experience includes start-ups, VC/PE-funded growth firms, IPO companies, and publicly traded companies.

Walt earned his reputation as a Trusted Advisor to entrepreneurs, investors, board members, and executives with his ability to shape a business-focused vision for technology that focused on disruptive digital transformation to create enormous business value, especially in the following areas:

Business Value Delivery

✓ Competitive Market Advantage, New Market Expansion, and Opportunity Discovery
✓ Business Scaling for Explosive and Profitable Growth
✓ Customer Experience Optimization
✓ Digital and Mobile Economy Operational Readiness

Walt is an entrepreneur at heart, having launched his first business at the age of 12. Like most entrepreneurs, he has experienced astounding success and epic failures that have helped to shape the leader he is today.

Walt has launched and sold companies; he has been involved in venture capital and private equity plays, M&A integrations, and even a successful IPO. He also is an investor and board advisor for an SaaS product firm offering AI-powered content enrichment and discovery solutions. In each of these cases, his core objective has been using emerging technologies and disruptive digital solutions to position the business for profitable, scalable growth and to prepare them for the digital/mobile economy.

LEADERSHIP HIGHLIGHTS

♦ Drove a strategy to remake Public Apparel Co. into a digital sales and B2C e-commerce juggernaut, replacing a 57-year-old B2B model.

♦ Modernized digital capabilities to fuel explosive top-line revenue, bottom-line profit, and customer experience increases at ABC Products.

♦ Led digital product development and Agile delivery to enable new capabilities and process automation at Advanced Digital Solutions.

BACKSTORY: Ethan Layton (Writer: Wendy S. Enelow)

TARGET ROLE: President, CEO, COO, Managing Director
CURRENT TITLE: Senior Vice President
INDUSTRY: Mortgage Banking, Investment Banking, Fintech

WRITER'S COMMENTS

Ethan is currently secure in his position with the two firms that he works for (Armitage Group and Raymon Holdings), but the thrill of his roles has waned now that he's (1) managed the post-acquisition integration of one firm and (2) delivered the strongest revenue performance in the history of the other company. Now, his role is more status quo, so he's looking for a new challenge.

WRITING/DESIGN STRATEGY FOR DOCUMENTS

Resume: For Ethan, a 3-page resume was the best solution to provide clarity for his most unusual career path. A longer-than-typical summary provides a solid overview of his exceptional qualifications and is packed with relevant keywords. In every role, I explained the context and the relationships—to create clarity and eliminate confusion about his career path—and focused on his outstanding achievements. I did include his early career experience to "connect all of the dots." His first employer is the longest-tenured position he ever held. Later in his career he was hired back by that company on 2 other occasions, and without the early experience, the connection between his various positions would not be as strong.

LinkedIn: I wrote the content of his profile in a narrative, storytelling style that creates an entirely different feel than the resume—despite the fact that the overall information (e.g., scope of responsibility, notable achievements, technological advances) is substantially the same from one document to the other.

Bio: Ethan's bio briefly summarizes the major roles and many achievements of his career, painting a clear and strong picture of a top-performing executive in the volatile banking industry.

UNIQUE CHALLENGES

The two most notable challenges I faced in writing Ethan's career documents were:

1) Avoiding the appearance of job hopping (his original 5-page resume had 12 individual job listings). Once I interviewed him, I understood how "connected" most of his jobs were, and I clearly addressed the interrelationships within each job description.

2) Dealing with the fact that he does not have a college degree. To offset a potential negative impression, rather than omitting the section entirely, as he had done on his original resume, I created an Education section that highlights his major in Business Administration, concentration in Finance, and attendance at a top-tier institution (Georgetown University).

OUTCOME

Within a month or so, Ethan was interviewing for both corporate and venture capital opportunities.

ETHAN R. LAYTON

312-844-9890
Chicago Metro Area

erlayton@gmail.com
LinkedIn Profile

PRESIDENT | CEO | COO | Managing Director

Mortgage Banking, Investment Banking, Fintech
Start-Up, Emerging Growth, Turnaround & Multinational Organizations

Unparalleled career building and leading robust, operationally sound, and financially strong organizations that have consistently outpaced and outperformed the competition. Long tenure of success in galvanizing sales, business development, and operations management teams to deliver peak revenue and profit performance in often challenging economic conditions.

Expert in building relationships with C-suite executives, management teams, board directors, diverse workforces, JV and M&A partners, investors, and financial institutions. Equally talented in capturing and retaining key account relationships valued at hundreds of millions of dollars. Dynamic presentation, communication, negotiation, and decision-making talents.

Deep and rich knowledge of technology solutions: SalesForce, Mortgage Cadence, Fintech Business Applications, Customer Relationship Management (CRM) Systems, Loan Origination Software (LOS), Automated Underwriting & Pipeline Management Systems.

Business Leadership
Strategic Planning & Leadership
Operations Management
Organizational Transformation
Mergers & Acquisitions
Joint Ventures & Partnerships
Corporate Financial Affairs
New Product & Service Innovation
Infrastructure, Process & Policy
High-Performance Team Leadership

**Lending, Finance &
Mortgage Expertise**
Mortgage & Loan Originations
Asset Quality & Loss Mitigation
Portfolio Management
Loan Servicing & Administration
Mortgage Real Estate Services
Regulatory Reporting & Compliance
Secondary Marketing
Portfolio Risk Management

Presenter/Panelist at industry conferences nationwide. **Published Author** in print and online news journals. **Member**—Global Assn. of Banking; Mortgage Bankers Assn. of North America; National Assn. of Mortgage Lenders

PROFESSIONAL EXPERIENCE:

Senior Vice President & Senior Relationship Manager   2018 to Present
ARMITAGE GROUP, INC. & RAYMON HOLDINGS, LLC—Chicago, IL

High-profile executive position with global provider of mortgage insurance and real estate market risk solutions. Led strategy and execution for acquisition, relationship management, and retention of nationwide client base (financial institutions, investors, government entities). Built robust account management organization, negotiated and managed key client relationships, and guided 25-person field sales team.

- **Increased company gross revenue 33%** in first year. **Grew revenue from top 50 clients 28%.**
- **Reduced reliance on top 10 clients 22%** through strategic volume concentration initiative.
- Led roll-out of SalesForce.com throughout the company and investigated emerging fintech solutions.
- Designed protocol for new due diligence product offerings, services, and solutions.

*Initially hired by Raymon Holdings, JV partner of RDQ Funding (previous employer), as **Senior Managing Director** of Consulting & Advisory during their acquisition by Armitage. Orchestrated post-acquisition integration into Armitage and delivered **275% revenue growth in first year.** Promoted to **Chief Revenue Officer.***

ETHAN R. LAYTON ... 312-844-9890 ... erlayton@gmail.com

President & Chief Executive Officer (CEO)   2016 to 2018
RDQ FUNDING, LLC *(JV partner with Raymon Holdings, LLC)*—Atlanta, GA

Retained for 18-month engagement to spearhead start-up of new mortgage origination firm through newly formed JV partnership. Transitioned from business plan through operations development to nationwide market launch and business capture. Set trajectory for early-stage and long-term, sustainable profitability.

- Built business infrastructure, established operational policies for loan origination and fulfillment capabilities, and introduced stringent regulatory compliance and quality standards. Recruited top talent.
- Defined portfolio of new mortgage products and services to capture immediate market share.
- Crafted and launched business development and branding initiatives to push market entry throughout US.
- Leveraged technology, including emerging tech solutions, to support operational scalability.

Co-Chief Executive Officer (Co-CEO)   2013 to 2016
KINGSTON LENDING MANAGEMENT *(Portfolio of Excel Capital, LLC)*—Atlanta, GA

Recruited to wholesale mortgage banking firm to lead merger/acquisition and integration of Davis Residential into Kingston's business portfolio. **Appointed CEO of Davis** and orchestrated complete transformation of the organization. Defined future years' financial and personnel performance to reach aggressive goals.

- **Restored Davis to profitability.** Transitioned product focus from distressed assets to mortgage origination, facilitated organic growth of wholesale account executive team, and introduced sound fiscal, compliance, and risk management policies. **Put Davis on path for accelerated market capture.**
- Led final integration of LoanTech Partners, an emerging fintech solution, to gain competitive advantage.
- Completed 18-month assignment with Kingston as **Co-CEO of wholesale mortgage banking firm,** building-out/strengthening mortgage pipeline and eliminating origination fulfillment backlogs.

President & Chief Administrative Officer (CAO)   2011 to 2013
MIAMI/DADE MORTGAGE CORPORATION—Miami, FL

Recruited by Chairman of the Board of 35-year-old mortgage banking company to restore financially non-viable company back to peak performance and profitability. Held full autonomy for strategic planning, operations leadership, talent management, and P&L. Far surpassed all operating goals and financial metrics.

- **Achieved profitability within 60 days** following turnaround and revitalization. Delivered **most profitable quarter** in the history of the firm. **Improved gross gain-on-sale by 60 BPS.**
- **Reduced operating costs 33% and eliminated unproductive staff.**
- Restructured executive team, reinvigorated sales force and operating management, introduced sound business and leadership practices, and positioned company to recapture competitive market lead.

Managing Partner & Executive Consultant   2008 to 2011
FINANCE SOLUTIONS ADVISORS, LLC—West Palm Beach, FL

In response to financial markets collapse, founded management consulting firm specializing in financial services industry. Delivered expertise in corporate planning, operations, risk, regulatory affairs/compliance, litigation, JV formation, VC investment, equipment leasing, finance/accounting, and process/performance improvement.

- Transitioned firm from concept through start-up and business-building to achieve **profitability in first year with $6M revenue.** Built talented team of 15 financial services experts to service clientele.
- Negotiated and closed key accounts with global market presence: **AIG, American Express, Bank of America, Lehman Brothers, PNC, SunTrust, Wells Fargo,** and many others.
- Retained as **Subject Matter Expert** on engagements involving complex transactions and negotiations.

President & Chief Executive Officer (CEO)   2003 to 2008
FIRST WASHINGTON BANK *(Lehman Brothers Company)*—Miami, FL

The most-senior executive of one of the largest, most profitable nonprime mortgage banking firms in the US. Led organization during a period of accelerated growth from 600 to 2800+ employees. Directed EVP-level team managing wholesale organic growth, retail expansion, learning and development, new product and service development and pricing, risk management, quality, and technology. **Delivered unprecedented results.**

- **Grew quality loan origination to $35B+ annually** during period of increased market consolidation.
- **Lowered cost-to-produce nearly 40 BPS** in one year.
- Enhanced risk management and delivered **100% clear record with no predatory lending practices.**
- Achieved strong peer group survey results: **#1 number of units originated, #2 origination volume.**

Provided calm and decisive leadership during the 2007–08 financial markets crisis. Successfully managed major corporate transformation and massive reduction in workforce to provide stability for future recovery and growth.

Executive Vice President & Chief Operating Officer (COO)   1998 to 2003
FIRST WASHINGTON BANK *(American Financial Company)*—Washington, DC

Recruited back to First Washington (under new ownership) to provide expert leadership for mortgage banking organization. Restructured operations, introduced emerging technologies, controlled regulatory and credit risk, mitigated losses, and managed accounting/finance functions. **Led 250-person team at HQ.**

- Built investment-grade loan portfolio of $22B. Exceeded YOY expectations by average 38% annually.
- Contributed to improvements across all performance metrics: **gains in sales, fees, and interest income; reductions in loan loss reserves, cost to produce, and interest expense.**
- **Lowered early payment default ratios to lowest in industry** with fiscal responsibility campaign.

Executive Vice President & Chief Operating Officer (COO)   1997 to 1998
GREENSTREET CAPITAL, INC.—Vienna, VA

At the request of VC group, accepted 2-year executive assignment with multiple leadership roles:

- Guided strategic and operational start-up of new mortgage company and new leasing company.
- Provided executive oversight for firm's financial services **portfolio valued at hundreds of millions of dollars:** Danbury Mortgage, Eastern States Capital Leasing, Danbury Bank, Layton Development.

Executive Vice President—Quality Control   1996 to 1997
CRYSTAL FINANCIAL SERVICES GROUP—Fairfax, VA

Established Crystal's first QC division to provide structure and standardization for portfolio of banks and mortgage origination/servicing companies. **Built from start-up to 100+ employees. IPO experience.**

- **Executed successful rescission of Cease and Desist Order** by completing OTS directives.
- **Orchestrated numerous multimillion-dollar portfolio acquisitions** to accelerate growth.

Regional President / Senior Vice President—Loan Administration   1986 to 1996
FIRST WASHINGTON BANK *(acquired by Dean Witter in 1994)*—Miami, FL / Washington, DC

Fast-track promotion through increasingly responsible investor reporting and loan administration positions. As SVP, **grew loan portfolio to $25B.** As Regional President, led successful integration of 4 loan servicing portfolios into a single operation as part of First Washington's aggressive acquisition and market roll-up plan.

EDUCATION: **Business Administration Major / Finance Concentration**—Georgetown University

Ethan Layton

President | CEO | COO | Managing Director—Building Robust Mortgage Banking, Investment Banking & Fintech Organizations

Armitage Group, Inc. / Raymon Holdings LLC
Georgetown University

Greater Chicago Area • 500+ Connections

About

I've been fortunate to have the very best of careers ... in positions that have challenged me and solidified my leadership skills ... within an industry that has changed, evolved, contracted, expanded, and otherwise reinvented itself.

As the President, CEO, COO, and Managing Director of numerous financial services and mortgage companies, I have repeatedly demonstrated my talents in:

▶ Building strong and sustainable organizations with monthly origination growth valued from $800M to $3.5B+.
▶ Identifying emerging business opportunities, launching new ventures, and building long-term account relationships with major players in the industry.
▶ Participating on the executive teams that successfully executed 20+ mergers, acquisitions, joint ventures, and IPOs.
▶ Orchestrating rapid turnarounds and business transformations to restore profitability to organizations hard-hit in the volatile mortgage industry.
▶ Introducing leading-edge fintech solutions across core business functions.

My sphere of influence has been vast—from the Boardroom to C-suite offices and from operating management teams to every employee within my organizations. In turn, I've positioned myself as the person that everyone wants to work for and with. Who wouldn't want to be on the winning team?

I consider my greatest value to be my success in building relationships—within the organizations I've led, with my customers, and with our business partners. I'm confident, trustworthy, and determined. I'm a savvy negotiator who understands that all parties need to win at the table, and I'm able to make that happen.

Perhaps most relevant to the industry, I thrive in challenging, fast-paced organizations where it's critical to provide strategic direction, make sound decisions, manage with a cool and calm leadership style, and move businesses forward. These talents, combined with my professional qualifications, are at the very foundation of all that my teams and I have achieved.

Contact me at 312-844-9890 or at erlayton@gmail.com.

Experience

Senior Vice President (SVP) & Senior Relationship Manager
Armitage Group, Inc. & Raymon Holdings, LLC
2018–Present

I was initially recruited as Senior Managing Director of Consulting & Advisory Services by Raymon Holdings (a JV partner of my previous employer, RDQ Funding) during their acquisition by the Armitage Group. First, I led a seamless post-acquisition integration, then launched a massive business development initiative. Following that success, I was promoted to Raymon's Chief Revenue Officer and, again, delivered phenomenal results.

► Grew revenues 275% in first year, far exceeding the outlined performance goals.

After my success at Raymon, I transitioned into the dual roles of SVP and Senior Relationship Manager with Armitage, a global provider of mortgage insurance and real estate market risk solutions. In this—my current—position, I orchestrate sales, new business development, and client relationship management/retention, while guiding a 20-person field sales force. Again, I've delivered top-flight financial and operational performance.

► Grew total company gross revenues 33% within the first year through expertise in building client relationships, understanding client needs, and consistently delivering to expectations.

► Restructured key account base through an innovative volume concentration effort to extend market reach, limit potential loss liabilities, and protect company revenue streams. Increased sales revenues from the top 50 clients by 22% while reducing reliance on the top 10 clients by 22%.

► Championed the implementation of emerging fintech and other technology solutions to enhance productivity, streamline reporting, and protect the company's intellectual capital. Led the successful roll-out of SalesForce.com throughout the organization.

President & Chief Executive Officer (CEO)
RDQ Funding, LLC
2016–2018

I was recruited as the President and CEO of a newly formed joint venture between RDQ Funding and Raymon Holdings, LLC. This mortgage origination firm was established to take advantage of emerging market opportunities and position itself as an alternative financing/hard money lender of choice.

In 18 months, I led the venture from concept and business planning through the entire process of operations development, technology selection and implementation, staffing, nationwide market launch, and loan origination and administration. Held full strategic planning, operating leadership, and P&L responsibility.

► Built fully operational new company, established organizational infrastructure, introduced best practices for all business functions, and staffed with top talent. Positioned RDQ for long-term growth and financial stability.

► Spearheaded innovative branding and business development initiatives to penetrate the highly competitive loan market, capture key accounts, and orchestrate nationwide market penetration. Established an immediate foothold and demonstrated ability to outperform well-established competitors.

► Leveraging my 20+ years of experience in the lending industry and my knowledge of competitive offerings, established new mortgage products and services for instant market capture and long-term market recognition.

► Introduced stringent regulatory compliance and reporting procedures, a series of risk management and loss mitigation controls, and quality control standards governing the entire organization.

► Identified current and long-term technology needs to achieve/maintain operational scalability, sourced emerging fintech solutions, and facilitated tech implementations, training, and support.

2013–2016
Co-Chief Executive Officer (Co-CEO)
Kingston Lending Management

I was brought into this wholesale mortgage banking firm to assume operating leadership during the acquisition and integration of Kingston's newest asset—Davis Residential, a company plagued by a host of operational and financial challenges. When I assumed responsibility, the company was on the brink of bankruptcy and needed immediate action to sustain its existence.

Most significantly, I helped to change the investment strategy of the company, shifting from a distressed asset portfolio into mortgage origination, transitioning the company into a much more profitable marketplace.

► Restored Davis to profitability within the first year and set the stage for future growth, market expansion, and product/service innovation.

► Galvanized the wholesale field sales team, introduced new performance incentives, and put company on the path for double-digit growth over the coming years.

► Took over a failed technology project, redefined business needs, and then led the final implementation of an emerging fintech solution (LoanTech Partners).

► As Co-CEO of Kingston, I worked in partnership with the other CEO and C-suite team to eliminate mortgage origination backlogs and accelerate growth of the mortgage pipeline. We were able to solidify the company's operations and ensure its sustainable growth and profitability.

2011–2013
President & Chief Administrative Officer (CAO)
Miami-Dade Mortgage Corporation

I was initially approached at my management consulting firm (see next job) by the Chairman of the Board of this 35-year-old mortgage banking company that was in the midst of a severe financial crisis. The Chairman offered me the opportunity to come aboard for a 1-year contract as President and CEO, working with him to reengineer the entire business and return it to its earlier years of strong performance and profitability.

► Restored the company to profitability within 2 months and subsequently delivered the most profitable Q1 in the history of the organization.

► Reduced operating expenses by 33% through wise planning and decision making while restructuring core business practices and processes.

► Improved gross gain-on-sale by 60 BPS.

► Rightsized the management team, streamlined the management hierarchy, and cut staffing costs 25%. Concurrent with this reduction in workforce, I was able to markedly improve employee morale.

2008–2011
Managing Partner & Executive Consultant
Finance Solution Advisors, LLC

Following the financial markets collapse in 2007-08, and in response to the numerous requests I was receiving for business leadership to help companies solve their specific needs, I established this management consulting firm—formed the LLC, launched marketing and outreach programs, established business processes and standards, developed contracts, recruited 15 top-tier consultants, and managed high-profile engagements.

► Built the company from concept through start-up and business development to full-scale operations with business engagements with companies throughout the US. Established a notable clientele, including AIG, AmEx, Bank of America, Lehman Brothers, PNC Bank, SunTrust Mortgage, Wells Fargo, and others.

2003–2008
President & Chief Executive Officer (CEO)
First Washington Bank

I was promoted to the #1 executive position at one of the largest and most profitable nonprime mortgage banking companies in the US. I directed the company (10 EVPs) during a period of explosive growth from 600 employees to 2800+ with an average of 38% YOY profitability.

► Provided strong and decisive leadership to further the company's market dominance. Grew quality loan origination to $35B+ annually within just 3 years. Lowered cost-to-produce by nearly 40 BPS in just one year.

► Restructured risk and credit management functions and achieved/maintained a 100% clear record with no class-action lawsuits for predatory lending practices—a remarkable achievement in a volatile industry.

► Consistently ranked as one of the best leaders in the organization through multiple peer review surveys. This included ranking #1 in number of units originated, #2 in origination volume, and #4 in total revenue BPS.

1998–2003
Executive Vice President & Chief Operating Officer (COO)
First Washington Bank

Recruited by a previous colleague to return to First Washington following its acquisition by American Financial, I directed all mortgage operations, regulatory affairs, credit/risk management, loss mitigation, and accounting/corporate finance. I led 8 direct management reports and a team of 250 at corporate headquarters.

► Built investment-grade portfolio valued at $22B in just 4 years. Introduced an innovative fiscal responsibility campaign that lowered early payment default ratios to less than 1%, the lowest in the industry nationwide.

► Spearheaded the selection and implementation of emerging technology solutions, including a CRM system, loan origination software (LOS), and several underwriting and loan pipeline management systems.

1997–1998
Executive Vice President & Chief Operating Officer (COO)
Greenstreet Capital, Inc

► Retained by venture capital (VC) group to build new portfolio of 4 independent companies that grew to hundreds of millions of dollars in value. Appointed COO of all 4 ventures.

1996–1997
Executive Vice President—Quality Control
Crystal Financial Services Group

► Built Crystal's first-ever quality control organization following the savings and loan crisis in the US. Executed all OTS directives and put Crystal back on the path of operational success and profitability.

► Won rescission of Cease and Desist Order by executing all requisite Office of Thrift Supervision (OTS) directives. This was the single most instrumental effort that put Crystal back on the path of operational success and profitability.

ETHAN R . LAYTON

PRESIDENT | CEO | COO | Managing Director
Mortgage Banking, Investment Banking, Fintech

Ethan Layton is best known for his expertise in building and leading top-performing organizations. Whether challenged to launch a start-up venture, orchestrate a complex turnaround, or lead a multinational organization through accelerated growth, he has consistently delivered strong results despite the complexity and volatility of the mortgage and investment banking industries.

In his current role as a member of the executive enterprise team of Armitage Group, Inc., and its wholly owned subsidiary, Raymon Holdings, Ethan delivered unprecedented, double-digit revenue growth. Prior to that, he led the start-up of RDQ Funding, another of Raymon's JV projects, taking this start-up mortgage origination firm from business plan to nationwide market launch with an innovative portfolio of product and services offerings, setting the trajectory of long-term, sustainable growth.

Ethan's success in business turnaround is best exemplified by his tenure with Kingston Lending Management, where he was tasked with the aggressive turnaround of their latest acquisition—Davis Residential. As Co-CEO, he led a massive transformation of this company, transitioned its product focus from distressed assets to mortgage origination, and restored it to profitability in less than one year.

Much of Ethan's early career was with First Washington Bank and its parent companies—Lehman Brothers, American Financial, and Dean Witter. During his more than 20-year executive tenure, he built a new $25B loan portfolio when the company was in its early stages of growth, then moved on to lead a 250-employee nationwide organization, delivering strong gains in sales, fees, and interest income while reducing loan loss reserves, cost to produce, and interest expense. Most notably, he slashed early payment default ratios to the lowest in the industry.

In his last position with First Washington, he served as President and CEO of one of the largest and most profitable nonprime mortgage banking firms in the nation. During his tenure, he led the team that grew loan origination to $35B annually and delivered a 100% clear record with no predatory lending practice class-action lawsuits or regulatory fines/violations.

Following the financial markets collapse in 2007–08, Ethan consulted with major players in the industry—AIG, American Express, Bank of America, Lehman Brothers, SunTrust, Wells Fargo, and others—providing executive leadership and subject matter expertise on a host of engagements involving complex transactions and negotiations.

Throughout his career, Ethan has structured, negotiated, and directed 20+ mergers, acquisitions, and joint ventures and helped to guide a successful IPO. Further, he's introduced emerging fintech solutions.

Based on his deep and rich industry experience, Ethan has been chosen to lead numerous presentations at industry conferences and symposia nationwide, and he has authored publications for both print and online news journals. He is an active member of the Global Association of Banking, Mortgage Bankers Association of North America, and National Association of Mortgage Lenders.

Ethan resides in the Chicago metro area with his wife of 25 years and their 3 adult children. His personal passions include golf, cooking, and deep sea fishing.

Chicago Metro Area • 312-844-9890 • LinkedIn Profile • erlayton@gmail.com

BACKSTORY: Connie Sutherland (Writer: Jan Melnik)

TARGET ROLE: GM/Plant Manager/Director
CURRENT TITLE: Director/Head of Manufacturing
INDUSTRY: Pharmaceutical/Biotech Industry

WRITER'S COMMENTS

From her earliest experiences in Chemical Engineering, then rapid acquisition of her Master's degree in Global Management of Technology, Connie had a specific game plan to advance quickly in the field of pharma. Over the past 15+ years, she has done exactly that, advancing three times with her first employer, Inter-Pharma (including a choice role in Singapore) and then recruited to Domnall Biopharmaceuticals, where she has successfully managed operations both stateside and abroad.

She is ready for the next move—ideally staying in biotech/pharma and either running major manufacturing operations for a multi-site manufacturer or assuming the GM role for a global company.

WRITING/DESIGN STRATEGY FOR DOCUMENTS

Resume: In creating a design that prominently displayed numerous quantifiable accomplishments and results, I started with a visually strong profile that emphasizes Connie's three areas of differentiation: Management Skillset, Technical Expertise, and Global Mindset. This is supported with short, quantified achievements and value statements for each of her more recent roles.

Cover Letter: The letter created for Connie provides a look at many of the skills that support her success as an executive in biotech/pharma manufacturing. In addition to tapping her network and pursuing direct contact with hiring managers, she expects to apply to appropriate posted openings. Her letter is formatted for her to upload, along with her resume; when sending by email, she will simply omit the letterhead.

LinkedIn: Connie's Headline presents her same differentiators, plus her strong educational background stands out in this profile section. Telling her story in the About section boils down some of her most notable areas of success. Strategic details illuminate each of her primary accomplishments throughout the Experience section.

UNIQUE CHALLENGES

Understated and reserved, Connie tends to be less than expansive in telling her story. Pushing her with "so then what happened," "so what was the consequence?" and "what was the result?" questions helped to pull out the key details to create a strong representation of her capabilities.

OUTCOME

Connie has just begun a methodical networking program (with coaching) to fully explore her many industry connections and contacts. She is not dissatisfied in her present role—just ready for the next jump—and, therefore, will take her time in identifying the right opportunities.

Connie Sutherland

919-999-1234 | conniesutherland@gmail.com
Raleigh, NC 27605 | LinkedIn.com/in/connie-sutherland

GENERAL MANAGER | PLANT MANAGER | DIRECTOR
Pharmaceutical/Biotech Manufacturing & Engineering

Unparalleled record of success improving business and optimizing manufacturing processes; driving individual performance gains; championing and executing turnarounds; and leading cross-functional teams.

Management Skillset	Technical Expertise	Global Mindset
•cGMPs/Best Business Practices •Green Belt Training •Lean Six Sigma—DMAIIC, DMADVC	•MS, Global Management of Technology •BS, Chemical Engineering	•Bilingual English/Spanish •Conversational fluency in French •Lived/worked in 4 countries

Professional Experience

DOMNALL BIOPHARMACEUTICALS | Raleigh, NC, and Dublin, Ireland (2012–Present)

Director/Head of Manufacturing (2019–Present)

Promoted to spearhead direction and site-based projects for manufacturing plant for 3 commercially approved products. Manage 140+ staff and cost center budget of $25M. Establish site priorities and strategy to meet production schedule, improve productivity, ensure cGMP compliance, and optimize operational metrics and business systems.

- **Synthesized and aligned operations** across 4 plants while leadership team consolidated from 8 to 6 directors.
- **Slashed cycle time** from 125+ days to just 75 days. Improved control of product release timeframes.
- **Simultaneously instituted focus on human performance** and key EHS measures as well as positive reporting culture—driving OSHA accident-free days to record of 340+ days without a workday case.
- **Leveraged plant's "yes we can!" attitude**—identifying process improvements while securing employee buy-in.

Director, Cross-Plant Operations (2017–2019)

Elevated to Director leading 3rd-shift operations comprising 9 managers and ~200 employees across 4 manufacturing plants. Devised and implemented site goals, aligned with Site and Technical Operations leadership strategy.

- **Drove strategic change management initiatives,** garnering senior management support for development and execution of Human Performance program (trained nearly 1K employees overall) and site Visual Management system and Governance model.
- **Recalibrated organizational design,** driving optimal alignment of operations across 4 manufacturing sites; incorporated findings from current vs. future-state evaluations to deliver greatest team value to respective sites.
- **Identified and instituted performance turnaround goals,** eliminated non-value-add/low-value-add work effort, and ensured group cohesion that effectively bridged multiple cultural and language barriers.

Associate Director, Bioreactor Operations (2013–2017)

Promoted to direct a team of 6 supervisors and 45 employees across 3 shifts in Cell Culture Operations. Created department strategies aligned with plant objectives, including department KPIs and budgetary goals.

- **Conformed operations and documentation to cGMP standards and SOPs.** Instituted process for batch records maintenance, reflecting current manufacturing methods and conformity with product licenses.
- **Ensured compliance commitments were completed on time;** provided appropriately documented evidence.

Operations Manager, Dublin, Ireland (2012–2013)

Brought on board to turn around and optimize Domnall's Dublin-based facility. Led a team of 3 supervisors/30 employees across 2 shift operations.

- **Achieved performance turnaround in <1 year.** Resolved issues of consistency in manufacturing, improved production speed and efficiency, and instilled culture of teamwork.
- **Developed emerging leaders** through mentoring, clear communication, and leadership by example.

Connie Sutherland | Page 2 | 919-999-1234

INTER-PHARMA COMPANY | Durham, NC, and Singapore (2004–2012)

Senior Reliability Engineer (2011–2012)

Supported 3 facilities manufacturing $5.2B in annual EMEA-, FDA-, and DEA-approved products. Developed, documented, and implemented site maintenance strategies; supported Reliability Centered Maintenance (RCM) activities, including QRM, FMECA/FMEA, CRA, and PMO. Split living/working time between Singapore and Durham.

- **Assembled and co-chaired cross-functional team** conducting broad FMECA/FMEA analyses for both short- and long-term preventative maintenance. Result: Reduced labor, material, and inventory cost by 35%, increased employee engagement and equipment availability, and eliminated non-value/reactionary maintenance tasks.

- **Transitioned from reactionary maintenance methods to proactive strategies** and predictive techniques— including thermography and vibration analysis.

- **Performed regular RCM analyses** on production equipment in Durham facility. Analyzed equipment failure rate data to establish proper maintenance schedules. Fluent in Maximo and SAP-PM plant management software.

Project Portfolio Manager (2009–2011)

Facilitated portfolio management processes/procedures for projects within business unit. Identified areas for improvement and worked closely with management to execute projects and meet site targets.

- **Developed and instituted Project Prioritization tool** to evaluate cost, quality, EHS, and optimal headcount. Eliminated 40+ projects over 2 years; increased effectiveness and efficiency.

- **Proactively managed project schedule** for Downstream Purification operations; prioritized projects as necessary, evaluated cost/ROI, and guaranteed timely completion of activities to meet project site goals.

- **Requested by VP Global Manufacturing to lead cross-functional team** to resolve critical raw material supply issue. Worked with vendor to guarantee consistent delivery of raw materials and avoid future deficits.

Manufacturing Supervisor (2006–2009)
Manufacturing Associate (2004–2006) | **Recipient, Inter-Pharma Leadership Award** (2005)

Education

NEW YORK UNIVERSITY | New York, NY
Master of Science, Global Management of Technology (2004)
Through joint program with University of Lyon, lived/studied 9 months in France.

DUKE UNIVERSITY | Durham, NC
Bachelor of Science in Chemical Engineering (2002)
3-year starter, women's varsity basketball.

Community & Other Pursuits

ATHLETE...Recreational basketball and soccer leagues, Raleigh-Durham
COACH..."Empowering Girls" team sports leagues, Raleigh-Durham (2013–Present)
BOARD MEMBER...Boys and Girls Clubs of Raleigh (2018–Present)

Connie Sutherland

919-999-1234 | conniesutherland@gmail.com
Raleigh, NC 27605 | LinkedIn.com/in/connie-sutherland

GENERAL MANAGER | PLANT MANAGER | DIRECTOR
Pharmaceutical/Biotech Manufacturing & Engineering

| Management Skillset | Technical Expertise | Global Mindset |

Dear Hiring Manager:

I am very interested in being considered as a candidate for the Director of Manufacturing position for which you are currently recruiting. I'm confident you will see a strong alignment between my background—spanning more than 15 years in manufacturing/plant operations and management within the pharmaceutical/biotech industry—and the characteristics you are seeking in the qualified candidate.

Briefly, I bring the following skills and experience to this opportunity:

- A proven track record of turning around underperforming operations and optimizing existing operations with focus on implementing and conforming to cGMP standards and SOPs augmented by expert servant leadership strengths.

- A reputation for enhancing productivity, improving quality and efficiency, and cutting costs—while improving product release timeframes and exceeding overall performance expectations.

- A history of identifying and cultivating top performers—and promoting key organizational talent.

- Specific and highly transferable technical expertise and biotech/pharmaceutical knowledge, along with demonstrated skill in not only coming up to speed very rapidly, but making a measurable, impactful difference throughout an organization.

- A global mindset through experience directing manufacturing sites in Singapore and Ireland—and the ability to meld different cultures and styles into a unified and focused team.

- Master of Science degree in Global Management of Technology (New York University) and Bachelor of Science in Chemical Engineering (Duke).

I would value the opportunity to discuss your hiring objectives for this position and my ability to bring the right knowledge and expertise. I am confident of the value-add role I can play with Primo Biopharmaceuticals and represent the right fit on your senior leadership team. Thank you for your consideration.

Sincerely,

Connie Sutherland

Connie Sutherland

Manufacturing/Engineering Executive, Pharmaceutical/Biotech | Management Skillset, Technical Expertise, Global Mindset

Domnall Biopharmaceuticals
New York University • Duke University

Raleigh-Durham Area • 500+ Connections

About

Accomplished Senior Manufacturing Management Executive. Talented Operations Leader. Proven record of turnaround expertise. Demonstrated global experience. Expert servant leadership strengths.

These are among my defining skills that define a brand of leadership that spans 15 years of executive management experience in the biotech and pharma industries.

Key areas where my visionary leadership has led to success include:

== A reputation for enhancing productivity, improving quality and efficiency, and cutting costs—while improving product release timeframes and exceeding overall performance expectations.

== Turning around and optimizing Dublin manufacturing site for Domnall—exceeding all defined performance parameters and instilling sustainable manufacturing practices and a culture of teamwork.

== Delivering global optimization of facilities manufacturing across 3 sites for $5.2B Inter-Pharma.

Spanning every role I have held has been a dogged pursuit of performance excellence—creating opportunities for pathways to success for my direct and indirect reports, instilling a shared culture of accountability, and maintaining absolute focus on operations and conformance to cGMP standards and SOPs.

I'm keen to further cross-industry relationships and collaborations—let's see where we can help one another!

===================================

Master of Science degree, Global Management of Technology. Conversational fluency in Spanish; early language skills in French. Green Belt training, best business practice and cGMPs; Operational Excellence, Lean Six Sigma (DMAIIC and DMADVV).

Technical expertise includes Chromatography, Chemical Viral Inactivation, Virus Removal Filtration, Purification, Ultrafiltration, Equipment Maintenance, Lab Equipment; proficiency with Trackwise, Documentum, eDoc, LIMS, SAP, MAXIMO.

Experience

DOMNALL BIOPHARMACEUTICALS
Raleigh, NC and Dublin, Ireland
Director/Head of Manufacturing
Aug. 2019–Present

I was handpicked to head up all manufacturing for 3 commercially approved products. My team comprised 6 directors and indirect reports exceeding 140. Overall P&L responsibility: $25M.

At the time of my promotion, changes across all plant operations were generating noticeable results. Our teams were motivated, performance improvement measures had cut cycle times from 125 to 75 days, and new EHS measures were creating an even safer work environment (we're at 340+ days without a workday incident).

This year's goal emphasizes synthesis as we've aligned operations across 4 plants. Our organization is becoming more customer-centric as we collaborate regularly with key stakeholders within our strategic accounts.

Additionally, one of my personal goals has been driving a culture of "yes we can!" across every facet of our operations. Combined with new process improvements, tactics that ensure/improve cGMP compliance, and system enhancements that optimize operational metrics, we are on track for production and performance excellence over the next 12-18 months.

DOMNALL BIOPHARMACEUTICALS
Director, Cross Plant Operations
2017–2019

Key in this role was assuming leadership for our underperforming 3rd-shift operations (9 managers and ~200 employees strong across 4 manufacturing plants).

Highlights include...
- Developing and implementing change management strategies—gaining both staff and executive management support.
- Rolling out training program featuring site Visual Management system and Governance model—and getting everyone on board in <6 months (950+ employees).
- Instituting organization-wide alignment, driven by findings from current vs. future-state evaluations—positioning our teams for optimal success.

DOMNALL BIOPHARMACEUTICALS
Associate Director, Bioreactor Operations
2013–2017

With my promotion to the AD role, I directed a team of 6 supervisors/45 employees across 3 shifts in Cell Culture Operations. Central among my achievements were standardized approaches to align all of our plant operations—instituting KPIs, fiscal accountability, and performance dashboards across the organization.

DOMNALL BIOPHARMACEUTICALS
Operations Manager, Dublin
2012–2013

I was recruited to join Domnall and relocate to Dublin to turn around a 2-shift operation in one of the company's Dublin facilities. My organization comprised 3 supervisors and 30 employees. The goal was to accomplish this effort and attain production goals/profitability in 3 to 4 years, then be brought stateside for my next challenge. I delivered success in less than a year by identifying top performers, creating a development plan into higher levels of management, and building a business case that cemented our production practices.

INTER-PHARMA COMPANY
Durham, NC and Singapore
Senior Reliability Engineer
2011–2012

In this role, I provided executive engineering leadership to 3 facilities that manufactured more than $5B in annual EMEA-, FDA-, and DEA-approved products. Key contributions:

• My team developed, documented, and implemented site maintenance strategies for all 3 plants. This included QRM, FMECA/FMEA, CRA, and PMO activities following a strategic acquisition in Q42011.
• I identified a critical need and assembled/co-chaired a cross-functional team to conduct broad FMECA/FMEA analyses for both short- and long-term preventative maintenance. Through this effort, we were able to reduce labor, material, and inventory cost by 35%. Additional benefits included increasing employee engagement and equipment availability as well as eliminating non-value/reactionary maintenance tasks.
• I oversaw the transition of our largest site from reactionary maintenance methods to proactive strategies and predictive techniques—including thermography and vibration analysis.
• Tech fluency included Maximo and SAP-PM plant management software.

EARLIER ROLES WITH INTER-PHARMA INCLUDED:
• Project Portfolio Manager (2009–2011)
• Manufacturing Supervisor (2006–2009)
• Manufacturing Associate (2004–2006)

BACKSTORY: Noah Zeiss (Writer: Louise Kursmark)

TARGET ROLE: CEO or CFO
CURRENT TITLE: CEO
INDUSTRY: Technology and Technology-Related

WRITER'S COMMENTS

Noah describes himself as a "builder." He loves finding opportunities for growth and leading the charge, whether that means a change in direction, an overhaul of existing operations, or another somewhat radical shift in the way things have been done.

His most recent role was as CEO (previously CFO) of a company that he had guided to steady growth. After five years, at the request of the Board, he had launched a fundraising and roadshow process that resulted in an offer to buy the company at a very attractive premium to investors. Noah's tenure ended and he was looking for a new opportunity.

During his roadshow activity, he had become acquainted with a private equity investor who told Noah he would be "perfect" for a leadership role with one of their portfolio companies. Typically, the directive is to move in, move fast, get results, and move on to the next portfolio company. Noah found the idea quite attractive and decided to actively pursue this type of opportunity. He knew that he needed to network his way in to other PE and VC firms where he could get on the radar, start a dialogue, and be top-of-mind as opportunities arose for either a CFO or a CEO.

WRITING/DESIGN STRATEGY FOR DOCUMENTS

Resume: To get the message across repeatedly and consistently—that Noah was at heart a growth builder—I used relevant language in the introduction, highlighted results in bold type in the experience section, and used an up-arrow graphic to encapsulate major results for his most recent positions.

LinkedIn: The words "build" and "grow" appear frequently in Noah's profile, starting with the headline and continuing through the About section. In the Experience section, I used headlines to announce each "Opportunity" and related "Results"—again to reinforce the themes of action and outcomes.

UNIQUE CHALLENGES

Because of Noah's dual focus (CEO or CFO), it was important to equally emphasize his finance-related capabilities as well as his executive leadership skills. I made sure that his prior titles (all finance-related) were prominently featured in bold/all caps, so that a quick skim of the resume reveals his pedigree.

OUTCOME

Noah has been able to connect with several VC/PE investors through networking and referrals. He continues to build these relationships and is hopeful that they will lead to the kind of opportunity he is seeking.

Noah Zeiss

San Francisco Bay Area | 415-555-3456
noahzeiss@mail.com | LinkedIn.com/in/noah-zeiss

CEO/CFO/EXECUTIVE LEADER FOR GROWTH-ORIENTED GLOBAL TECHNOLOGY COMPANIES

Senior executive with a 15-year record of unlocking potential, creating and executing growth strategies in rapidly changing arenas, and delivering positive outcomes for shareholders.

- **Criterion:** Drove double-digit growth and sale of business to #1 competitor at a 50% premium to market cap.
- **Grainger:** Set up key financial structures and cross-cultural teams for $1.5B spin-out/JV.
- **Mastery:** Directed and scaled F&A for Emerging Markets throughout massive regional expansion.

Strategy & Planning | P&L Management | M&A Transaction & Integration | Debt & Equity Financing
Board & Shareholder Relations | Public Company Finance | Risk Mitigation | Asset & Resource Management
Global & Cross-Cultural Operations | Team Building & Partnering | Joint Ventures & Corporate Global Expansions

PROFESSIONAL EXPERIENCE

CRITERION TECHNOLOGIES (NASDAQ:CRIT) | 2016–2021
Leading developer/producer of advanced energy storage products ($20M+ annual revenue).

CEO/CFO   **San Mateo, CA**

Recruited as CFO to new executive team charged with scaling the business and accelerating growth. After 10 months, requested by Board to assume CEO role. Navigated through extreme financial and market challenges, created a phased long-term strategy, drove rigorous business planning and execution processes to grow the business, and guided the company to a successful M&A exit.

- **Grew revenue 17% CAGR**—maintaining gross margins—while industry leader declined 7%.
- **Raised $9M debt and equity** from existing shareholders via private-placement and a rights-offering. Unwound prior equity investment that exposed the business to unacceptable risks.
- **Recaptured technology leadership** by launching 2 new performance-leading products.
- **Boosted capacity 30%** and improved manufacturing operations with minimal investment.
- **Spearheaded a major fundraising roadshow** with investment bank support that ultimately formed the basis of successful M&A strategy and exit for shareholders.
  - Negotiated term sheets with 3 separate potential M&A partners.
  - Led and completed sale of operating entities to the industry leader in exchange for shares.
  - Provided shareholders with a 50% premium to public market capitalization along with a large equity stake and board representation in combined entity with significant synergies.

GRAINGER TECHNOLOGIES | 2012–2016
Flash-memory JV between XYZ and Mastery Microelectronics; $1.5B annual revenue, 6000 employees.

FINANCE DIRECTOR — Sales and Marketing Group   **San Jose, CA | 2014–2016**

Drove all financial functions for the Sales & Marketing group—revenue reporting and controls, forecasting, channel profitability initiatives, budgeting ($60M), sales commissions, and spending controls.

- **Delivered $20M first-year margin improvement** by designing and implementing a new "ship and debit" global distribution pricing process. Gained executive approval, then managed complex 9-month project that included new data system implementation and global process restructuring.
- **Enhanced executive visibility and decision making** by developing innovative and easy-to-use tools: a revenue forecast reconciliation tool and consigned inventory cost/benefit model.

FINANCE DIRECTOR — Wireless and Data Business Units   **Hong Kong | 2012–2014**

Built P&L frameworks for 2 of 3 business units of the new JV, supporting GMs accountable for $1.5B annual revenue. Created internal P&L models, financial processes, and controls, resulting in robust platforms for reporting, margin analysis, inventory management, budgeting, and product line rationalization.

- **Defined organizational structure** and deliverables, then combined existing players with strategic hires to build strong team able to deal with complex challenges in a startup environment.

FINANCE DIRECTOR — Wireless and Data Business Units — continued

- **Reconciled diverse cultures and conflicting processes** into a singular BU support model.

- **Provided rationale to exit unprofitable lines of business and mitigate millions of dollars in losses,** delivering solid financial analysis and recommendations to executive team.

- **Led a cross-functional team that delivered $60M+** in Wireless product margin improvement.

MASTERY MICROELECTRONICS (NASDAQ:MSTR) | **2003–2012**
A leading global semiconductor company, headquartered in Germany; $25B annual revenue, 50,000 employees.

FINANCE DIRECTOR — Emerging Markets Region — Ho Chi Minh City, Vietnam | 2007–2012

Promoted to lead Finance and Administration (F&A) in fast-emerging region that surged from $400M to $1B annual sales during tenure. Built and scaled Finance processes, controls, and compliance frameworks. As the company's most senior support function executive in the region, exercised considerable business influence while building a lasting organization to support and safeguard significant investment in a challenging emerging market environment.

- **Supported R&D investment that grew sharply from negligible to $50M, 1000+ engineers.** Collaborated with global business units on strategy and financials to support investment decisions, then scaled operational infrastructure accordingly. Supported 3 M&A deals, creation of a shared-service center, and completion of a complex land/building purchase in Vietnam.

Rapid Growth to $50M

- **Created the first holistic budget for the region** and an ROI-based resource allocation model.

- **Transformed a small local-accounting organization into a savvy multidisciplinary business engagement team** that delivered $1M+ cash savings during a period of accelerated growth.

FINANCE MANAGER — Strategic Planning, Mobile Products Group — Berlin, Germany | 2004–2007

Delivered strategic financial support for $1.5B mobile computing business unit. Provided financial analysis and recommendations to support microprocessor roadmap decisions and Bluetooth commercialization/enablement plans.

- **Selected to 4-member team to create complete business plan** for emerging Bluetooth peripherals business that was successfully incubated inside Mastery and spun off as an independent company.

- **Avoided $100M+ in potential losses** by presenting detailed analysis that valued a potential acquisition at $30M—not the $200M rated by investment bankers—and led to decision not to purchase the company.

SENIOR FINANCE ANALYST — Worldwide Sales and Marketing — Berlin, Germany | 2003–2004

Managed $300M revenue reserve for distributor inventory. Implemented distributor reporting and third-party inventory audits. Directed revenue recognition training. Reduced cross-region pricing arbitrage.

PRIOR PROFESSIONAL EXPERIENCE

SMALL BUSINESS CONSULTANT — European Consulting Corp. — Berlin, Germany | 2002–2003
AUDITOR/SENIOR AUDITOR — Grant Thornton LLP — Boston, MA | 1998–2002
FINANCE ASSOCIATE — Smith & Rogers, Inc. — Cambridge, MA | 1996–1998

EDUCATION

MBA | Questrom School of Business, BOSTON UNIVERSITY, Boston, MA — 2002
BSBA | College of Business, NORTHEASTERN UNIVERSITY, Boston, MA — 1996

Noah Zeiss

CEO/CFO: Build, Scale, and Grow Technology Companies | Unlock Potential | Create Shareholder Value

Criterion Technologies
Boston University • Northeastern University

San Francisco Bay Area • 500+ Connections

About

WHAT I DO BEST: At heart, I'm a builder. I get excited about opportunities to jump-start growth or create from the ground up—develop and execute the strategy, build the operating infrastructure, and lead/inspire a team to new heights.

WHERE I DO IT: Start-up, growing, and established technology-centric companies. I've been CEO, CFO, and Finance Director for public companies from $20M annual revenue (Criterion Technologies) to $1B+ (Grainger Technologies, Emerging Markets region of Mastery Microelectronics).

MY CAREER HIGHLIGHTS REEL:
► Leading Criterion through an industry downturn to double-digit annual growth and acquisition.

► Building and directing a finance organization at a Mastery Microelectronics startup JV, melding 2 very diverse cultures into a performance-driven and smoothly functioning team.

► Moving to Vietnam as the senior functional executive for Mastery's emerging markets region and learning to maneuver in several different—all highly complex—arenas at a time of explosive growth.

► Working with a small team to create a business plan for Mastery's Bluetooth peripherals.

► Getting my first taste of business-building in the developing world as a volunteer consultant in Berlin.

KEY TAKEAWAYS:
► Integrity matters. Colleagues, partners, and customers will believe you (and allow you to lead them) if you are honest, direct, and trustworthy.

► Persistence pays.

► Problem-solving is a muscle that is strengthened by challenge and adversity.

► Versatility and agility allow you to succeed in companies large (with many resources) and small (with limited resources and support structures).

► Passion for the mission is essential to success and job satisfaction—mine and my team's.

WHAT'S NEXT: Winding up the acquisition/integration of Criterion into Anteron Technologies, I'm interested in a new opportunity to build and grow a business in the US and/or internationally.

Experience

CFO / CEO
Criterion Technologies
2016–2021

OPPORTUNITY: Accelerate growth of a $20M developer/producer of advanced energy storage products.

Hired as CFO, within 10 months I was asked to assume the role of interim CEO and became permanent CEO shortly thereafter, with full financial/P&L responsibility for the publicly traded company.

I began by defining a strategy for growth, then secured additional financing, directed R&D toward strategic new products, and accelerated manufacturing operations to bring them quickly to market.

As a key component of the turnaround, I built strong relationships with the Board and effectively communicated strategy and results to the investor community.

RESULTS:
▶ I built Board confidence in my vision, created and executed a long-term growth strategy, and carefully analyzed new opportunities to steer resources to the right markets—and avoid overly risky segments.

▶ Through strategic R&D investments, we made technology, product, portfolio, and manufacturing operations significantly more attractive to investors and M&A prospects.

▶ Working with the Director of Finance, I raised more than $7M in equity and debt financing.

▶ We realized 17% compound annual growth rate while maintaining steady margin.

▶ As the company stabilized and grew, I sought out potential M&A partners, performed due diligence, negotiated the deal, and executed sale of the company's operating entities to our #1 competitor (Anteron Industries).

▶ The outcome for shareholders was very positive: a high premium to public market cap as well as an equity position and board representation in the combined entity.

Finance Director
Grainger Technologies
2012–2016

OPPORTUNITY: Launch and help lead a Mastery Microelectronics flash memory startup/joint venture.

Originally hired as Finance Director for the Wireless and Data business units (2 of the 3 BUs of the JV, $1.5B annual revenue) based in Hong Kong, I built a solid operational foundation and a strong, capable team.

In 2014, as acquisition negotiations were underway, I was asked to take on the Finance Director role for the Sales and Marketing Group at corporate HQ.

When the acquisition closed in 2015, I played a key role in integrating Grainger into the acquiring company, XYZ Technologies.

RESULTS:
▶ Bringing together the different cultures, diverse nationalities, and often conflicting processes of the 2 venture partners, I created a top-notch Finance/Admin team.

▶ My analysis and recommendations to the executive team steered business decisions toward promising opportunities and away from unprofitable lines of business.

► We improved the margin of the Wireless product line by $60M.

► I designed a global distribution pricing process that delivered $20M margin improvement in the first year. Post-acquisition, I implemented this process into XYZ's entire $2B distribution channel. Projected margin improvement was $30M annually.

Finance Director—Emerging Markets Region
Mastery Microelectronics
2007–2012

OPPORTUNITY: Take on diverse business challenges and gain invaluable experience within one of the world's leading technology corporations.

I advanced from Senior Finance Analyst (2003–2004) to Finance/Strategic Planning Manager for the Mobile Products Group (2004–2007). There I helped avoid $100M in potential losses by recommending against a proposed acquisition (and against investment bankers' recommendation and valuation). I also was part of a 4-person team that created a business plan for Bluetooth technology.

In 2007, I jumped at the chance to move to Ho Chi Minh City as senior functional executive for Mastery's Emerging Markets Region. It was a wild ride as we grew quickly from $400M to more than $1B revenue and more than 1000 R&D engineers.

RESULTS:
► I built a finance organization that was regarded as a major asset in managing and growing Mastery's investment in a volatile region.

► By instituting tight financial controls, we delivered $1M+ savings, created the region's first formal budgets, and developed an ROI-based resource allocation model.

► As the business expanded, I set up new entities in several countries, supported multiple M&A deals, and provided operational infrastructure for the acquired entities.

BACKSTORY: Ricardo Perez (Writer: Jan Melnik)

TARGET ROLE: Senior Vice President/Executive Vice President
CURRENT TITLE: Director
INDUSTRY: Facilities Management

WRITER'S COMMENTS

Ricardo had established a strong name for himself in the facilities management field—bringing value in senior leadership roles to a number of key players in the industry. In his current role for more than four years, and having achieved every performance milestone, he is anxious to move on and up to a new organization where he can have an even greater impact on organizational results and team leadership. He has a solid "go get 'em" mantra and is unstoppable in his ethical pursuit of exceptional performance.

WRITING/DESIGN STRATEGY FOR DOCUMENTS

Resume: A straightforward design with clear goals outlined—supported by verifiable accomplishments—dictated the look of Ricardo's executive resume. Numbers were easy to extract and present for this high achiever.

Cover Letter: I took a classic approach in writing Ricardo's cover letter, providing key examples and the story of his advancement.

LinkedIn: For Ricardo's Headline, we mirrored key elements of his value proposition that also populate his resume profile. Turnaround expertise, exceptional leadership, and one of his several high-energy mantras are reflected. (From "going above and beyond" and "go get 'em" to "whatever it takes," Ricardo definitely talks the talk *and* walks the walk, despite the heavy cliches!)

UNIQUE CHALLENGES

The client we all love: If anything, Ricardo's unbridled enthusiasm for his work, his passion for making a difference, and his love of turning around underperforming team members and organizations needed to be appropriately tempered with supporting details telling the real story. He was fully on board with this recommendation.

OUTCOME

At a state of readiness, Ricardo is selectively communicating with networked contacts and recruiters who've reached out to him in the past for his expertise in facilities management. I'm confident he'll quickly transition to a new, great role.

RICARDO PÉREZ

Houston, TX 77004 | 281-345-6789
ricardo-perez@gmail.com | LinkedIn.com/in/ricardo-perez

FACILITIES MANAGEMENT: SENIOR-DIRECTOR/VP LEVEL
TURNAROUND EXPERT | BUSINESS OPTIMIZER | DYNAMIC CHANGE CATALYST

Results-driven Vice President/Senior-level Facilities Director with deep industry experience. Exceptional staff management and development practices—from recruitment and onboarding to coaching and promoting.

Excel in facing turnaround challenges and aggressive business optimization goals. Strong interpersonal and communication skills—interact effectively across all organizational tiers. Consistently bring keen attention to detail and outstanding organizational skills to all client projects.

▶ Reputation for expert leadership and team-building skills—fair and articulate with clear goals and performance expectations. Recognized optimistic leadership style, inspiring organizations with great motivational skills.

▶ Trajectory of consistent advancement within facilities industry spanning >20 years.

▶ Track record as a change catalyst—advancing continuous improvement initiatives, influencing others, and quickly adapting to new opportunities and challenges.

Facilities & Real Estate Account Management | Business Development/Sales
Complex Project Management & Execution | Construction/Renovation/Repair | CPM Certification

PROFESSIONAL EXPERIENCE

XCEL MANAGEMENT, INC. | Houston, TX   **Aug. 2015 to Present**
Privately held, superior quality facilities management company with nationwide accounts and annual revenues >$125M.
Executive Director, General Maintenance and Construction

Manage complex territory comprising company's premier clients across Western U.S. (including $22M FedEx account, Citibank, and Staples)—**with oversight of all maintenance activities for >2,800 discrete client sites.**

Recruited, hired, manage, and coach team of 9 direct reports; align talent with business needs to optimize performance and job satisfaction. Facility management reflects self-performed and vendor-managed services in more than 20 trades.

▶ Conceived and implemented innovative Preventative Maintenance Checklist Program—used with virtually all clients, whether on weekly, biweekly, or monthly schedule—for proactive on-site management to efficiently manage each location. Process has proven instrumental in successful business development/sales cycle.

▶ Average 97% customer retention, inking multiyear contract renewals—credited to exceptional service delivery.

▶ Built and manage 400+ relationships with qualified vendors nationwide to deliver professional client services.

▶ Solidified relationship with demanding regional manager at company's largest strategic account, earning confidence in XCel's ability to execute and deliver.

▶ Brought value of industrial psychology background to HR practices and training of Community Service Manager (staff turnover policies, quality standards, project-specific systems orientations, etc.).

▶ Key contributor to business development—from processing RFIs and collaborating with Project Manager on new job bids to interfacing with general contractors, property owners, and owners' consultants. Ensure timely submission of all project closeout documents in accordance with contracts.

RICARDO PÉREZ

281-345-6789 | ricardo-perez@gmail.com

CONSOLIDATED SERVICES, INC.	Houston, TX	Aug. 2009 to Aug. 2015

Facilities management firm with retail-mall specialty.
Director, Vendor Management

Hired into newly created role managing vendor relationships as member of senior leadership organization. Developed team of nearly 40 vendor managers overseeing vendor compliance for respective clients.

▶ Established and managed highly qualified vendor network of subcontractors across the United States (all trades, from HVAC and plumbing to electrical).

▶ Instituted time- and cost-efficiency measures—including clustering of appointments (new concept at time)—to serve multiple clients in shared sites.

▶ Spearheaded biannual review meetings with executive leadership of largest contractors; planned and implemented strategies for improving client services, delivering greater value, and driving enhanced efficiencies.

▶ Through SWOT analysis, implemented process for consistently evaluating competition, market conditions, and trends.

ACME CORPORATION	Houston, TX	July 1997–July 2009

Well-established convenience store chain dominating Texas landscape.
Senior Facilities Manager *(2003–July 2009)*

With promotion from Sales Manager to Senior Facilities Manager, assumed strategic management and leadership of 600 retail properties across Texas.

▶ Achieved highest possible net operating income as compared with other regions nationwide through implementation of strategic cost control and revenue improvement programs.

▶ Directed proactive measures to provide for optimal functioning of all facilities; ensured superior customer satisfaction through strong field presence.

▶ Partnered collaboratively with cross-functional teams to leverage business opportunities and address challenges.

▶ **Sales Manager** (2000–2003; 400 stores) | **Field Manager** (1997–2000; 8 corporate franchise stores).

EDUCATION

UNIVERSITY OF HOUSTON | Houston, TX
Master of Arts degree, Industrial & Organizational Psychology (Major: Negotiations and Conflict Management)

TEXAS SOUTHERN UNIVERSITY | Houston, TX
Bachelor of Arts degree, Psychology

Subject: Senior Vice President

Dear Hiring Manager (or Executive Recruiter):

Why should I be Global Dynamics next Senior Vice President? A quick look at my brand of operations management, strategic business development philosophy, and commitment to sales excellence plus visionary leadership precisely aligns with the values expressed in Global Dynamics mission statement.

In a snapshot, I rapidly ascended to Executive Director of General Maintenance & Construction with XCel Management, where I have oversight for the company's highest profile/strategic accounts and a record of achievements building top-performing teams and optimizing performance.

I was recruited to XCel from my role heading up Vendor Management at Consolidated Services, where my track record reflects strategic wins across the facilities management landscape through SWOT analysis, program implementation, and vendor network development. I built my initial career rapidly in Sales from Field Manager and Sales Manager to Senior Facilities Manager with Acme—driving strategy and growth across 600 Texas locations.

Examples of what I've been able to deliver:

- ▶ Contributed significantly to business development, pipeline-building, and successful incremental sales because of results achieved through an innovative Preventative Maintenance Checklist program I developed and instituted (cost-saving, proactive on-site management of multiple locations)—*XCel.*

- ▶ Developed and executed highly productive and efficient client management protocols featuring clustered appointments, new to the industry and a complete game-changer—*Consolidated Services.*

- ▶ Implemented comprehensive cost-control and revenue-improvement programs that delivered the company's highest net operating income in my region, comprising 525 locations—*Acme.*

- ▶ Simply put, I have a record of consistently delivering both top- and bottom-line value to an organization and am willing to do *whatever it takes* to drive performance improvements, sales results, and satisfied customers.

Augmenting my experience in the facilities management field for more than 20 years, I hold a Master's degree in industrial and organizational psychology and a Bachelor's degree in psychology. I am able to travel without hindrance and able to work very successfully remotely from my base location in Houston.

I'm confident of my ability to deliver exceptional value to Global Dynamics as your next Senior Vice President and would welcome the opportunity to explore possible fit. I'll reach out with a call next week.

Sincerely,

Ricardo Pérez
281-345-6789 | ricardo-perez@gmail.com | LinkedIn.com/in/ricardo-perez

Ricardo Perez

Director/VP Facilities | General Maintenance | Construction Management | Delivering Superior Results and ROI: "Going above and beyond."

XCel Management
University of Houston • Texas Southern University

Houston, TX • 500+ Connections

About

Results-driven Executive-level Facilities Director/VP—with proven turnaround expertise.

►Track record of generating exceptional profitability while cultivating and retaining valued vendor and client relationships—a trajectory of advancement within the facilities industry spanning 20+ years.
►Superb staff management and development—from recruitment and onboarding to coaching and promoting.

Simply put, I lead by example and have a record of consistently delivering both top- and bottom-line value to an organization. I am willing to do *whatever it takes* to drive performance improvements, produce outstanding sales results, and retain satisfied customers.

My vendors, customers, and team all recognize these values reflect my brand of executive leadership. A few examples of what I've been able to deliver:

► Contributed significantly to business development, pipeline-building, and incremental sales because of an innovative Preventative Maintenance Program I instituted to deliver cost-saving, proactive on-site management of multiple locations—XCel Management (Executive Director, Maintenance & Construction).
► Introduced highly productive and efficient client management protocols featuring clustered appointments, new to the industry and a complete game-changer—Consolidated Services (Director, Vendor Management).
► Implemented cost-control and revenue-improvement programs that delivered the highest possible net operating income for 600 locations—Acme (Senior Facilities Manager).

Augmenting my facilities management experience, I hold a Master's degree in industrial and organizational psychology and a Bachelor's degree in psychology.

There's nothing I love more than taking on a challenge—such as the need for a turnaround or a set of steep performance goals—and delivering extraordinary results.

My signature strengths:
► Change Catalyst: Identifying what needs to be done and doing "whatever it takes" to make that happen.
► Business Optimizer: Driving continuous improvement via both radical changes and gradual adjustments.
► Outstanding Communicator: Building consensus, gaining support at all levels of the organization, inspiring top performance in my team, creating long-lasting client and vendor relationships.

Let's connect on LinkedIn!

Experience

XCEL MANAGEMENT
Executive Director, General Maintenance and Construction
Aug. 2017 to Present

As Executive Director of General Maintenance & Construction, I manage all accounts in the entire Western U.S.—comprising many of the company's most complex and premier clients. My team of 9 direct reports oversees all maintenance activities for >2,800 discrete store locations.

Select accomplishments include:
► Conceiving and implementing an innovative Preventative Maintenance Program that drives the most efficient on-site management of every location and has proven highly instrumental in closing front-end sales.
► Bringing the value of my industrial psychology background to HR. As a result, we have set new policies to reduce staff turnover, implemented new quality standards, created project-specific systems orientations, and devised processes and systems that improve morale, increase effectiveness, and drive positive behaviors.
► Ensuring exceptional service delivery—a hallmark that has been key to consistently retaining our strategic accounts and successfully closing multiyear contract renewals.

Top initiatives include:
► Recruiting, hiring, managing, and coaching my team—aligning talent with business needs to optimize performance and job satisfaction.
► Developing and managing 400+ relationships with qualified vendors nationwide, representing >20 trades, to deliver professional client services.
► Managing high-profile, escalated outages and problems throughout the territory (80% of service calls are handled professionally through automated system and dispatch).
► Enhancing business development outcomes—from processing RFIs and collaborating with Project Manager on new job bids to interfacing with general contractors, property owners, and owners' consultants.

CONSOLIDATED SERVICES, INC.
Director, Vendor Management
2009–2015

I was recruited into a newly created role on the senior leadership team and challenged to develop and expand vendor relationships throughout the US to support strategic accounts nationwide. Our business focused on tenants of retail malls, and we had a strong presence with numerous mall-based chains.

Key successes included:
► Developing a team of almost 40 vendor managers overseeing vendor compliance for our clients.
► Establishing and managing a highly qualified vendor network of subcontractors across the US.
► Launching critical time- and cost-efficiency programs including a concept I developed (innovative at the time) that clustered appointments to serve multiple clients in shared sites.
► Spearheading biannual review meetings with executive leadership of our largest contractors.
► Executing SWOT analyses and implementing a consistent process for evaluating competition, market conditions, and trends—keeping us at the head of the pack.

ACME CORPORATION
Senior Facilities Manager
1997–2009

Beginning my career with Acme in Houston, I was quickly elevated to Field Manager (overseeing operations at 8 corporate franchise stores), then to Sales Manager (directing sales and marketing across a 400-store Texas territory), then to Senior Facilities Manager (overseeing 600 retail properties across Texas). I consistently delivered the highest possible net operating income as compared with other regions throughout the US.

BACKSTORY: Kristofer Nagy (Writer: Louise Kursmark)

TARGET ROLE: General Manager or VP of Sales
CURRENT TITLE: Director of US Sales
INDUSTRY: Software and Technology

WRITER'S COMMENTS

Kristofer has been a top sales performer throughout his career, primarily with entrepreneurial and early-stage software companies. Often he was the primary revenue generator, and when he had a team, invariably he was a "player/coach," responsible for both revenue generation and sales team leadership. He doesn't mind the dual role, but he wants to focus more on setting business strategy, building and leading the team, and running the business … less on managing accounts and closing sales.

WRITING/DESIGN STRATEGY FOR DOCUMENTS

Resume: I wanted Kris's resume to convey energy and excitement, qualities that would be attractive to busy recruiters and tech executives. The highlight color (not visible in this black-and-white book) is an upbeat orange, the graphic and the "Milestones" at the top command attention, and the ample white space between every piece of text makes it easy to quickly grasp his career story and his value.

Cover Letter: Written in response to a posted opening, this letter creates instant rapport by identifying specific challenges the company is very likely facing—then points out how Kris has delivered strong results when facing similar challenges.

LinkedIn: The About section introduces Kris's sales philosophy, touches on his early military background, and describes his successes both in sales and in business and team leadership. In the Experience section, I outlined the challenge of each job and then highlighted quick and impressive results.

Bio: In the bio, I created a framework around Kris's military service—a character-defining experience that continues to shape how he approaches his work today.

UNIQUE CHALLENGES

To help Kris achieve his current career goal, it was important to focus his career marketing documents on both his sales successes and his executive leadership skills—even when he was serving as the primary sales person, as was the case for his two most recent roles.

OUTCOME

Kristofer's story is an excellent example of how our Four-Week Accelerated Job Search Plan provides structure and momentum to what can seem an overwhelming process. Kris tapped into his network, responded to posted openings, sent out a recruiter campaign, and prepared for interviews. About six weeks into his search, he applied to a posted opening for General Manager of a software company in his immediate neighborhood—and he was hired for that job a few weeks later.

Kristofer Nagy

kristofer.nagy@gmail.com ▪ 555-876-1234 ▪ LinkedIn/com/in/krisnagy

Senior Sales Executive: Software/Technology

- **Growth catalyst** for technology sales—15-year history of opening doors to new business opportunities in areas never before penetrated.

- **Business strategist** who devises meticulous processes, structures, and checkpoints in sales planning for complex products.

- **Sales team champion,** developing top performers supported by proven sales methodology that identifies, qualifies, and delivers.

B2B Consultative Sales

Strategic Business Development

Enterprise SaaS Market

Fortune 500 Accounts

Milestones

- Added $3.5M new revenue to a $20M company in first 9 months post-acquisition.

- Nearly doubled software revenue ($4M to $7.6M) through partnerships/sales to Fortune 500 accounts.

- Created $10M life sciences business of a $25M entrepreneurial enterprise software firm.

- Spearheaded strategy that propelled startup sales from $500K to $6M.

Experience and Accomplishments

STREETER SYSTEMS, INC.   San Jose, CA, 2015–Present
Privately owned international software, hosting, and systems development solutions provider to online content publishers; $20M annual sales. Streeter acquired the eSolutions division of MicronSystems in 2019.

Director of US Sales—eSolutions, 2019–Present

Promoted to invigorate stagnant sales for newly acquired brand of print management solutions. Guide, mentor, and develop team of 7 sales professionals deployed nationwide. Personally manage key accounts.

- Crafted aggressive strategy to drive new business development in untapped markets. Created plans, set competitive milestones, provided tools and resources, and rewarded performance.

- Delivered $3.5M in new business in first 9 months post-acquisition—without any formal marketing programs, new product development, or lead-generation services.

- Singlehandedly shored up existing client base during transition and negotiated $4.8M in contract extensions.

Major Account Manager—eCommerce & Entitlements Management, 2015–2019

Recruited to drive sales of desktop, software license, and digital publisher enterprise solutions. On-boarded new clients and initiated strategic partnerships as the company grew through multiple acquisitions.

- Grew sales by double digits annually for 4 straight years, increasing segment revenue from $4M to $7.6M.

- Carved local-level strategic partnership with Microsoft that quickly expanded nationally. Leveraged partnership to build new business through joint sales efforts and best practices seminars aimed at customers and the local user community.

- Negotiated and closed company's first US digital publisher's deal of nearly $2M with Roxy Media, and inked $millions additional contracts with Genzyme, Bose, EMC, Hasbro, Boston Scientific, New Balance, and more.

PRO-PRINT TECHNOLOGY, INC.   San Francisco, CA, 2012–2015
$25M entrepreneurial enterprise software company specializing in web-enabled industrial label-printing applications.

VP of Sales & Business Development—Life Sciences Group

Conceived, developed, and executed aggressive growth strategy for life sciences division. Created new business model, operational structure, and multi-channel marketing and distribution strategy to capitalize on highly regulated space of pharmaceutical/medical device and aerospace/defense industries. Trained, coached, and supervised pre-sales, sales, support, and implementation teams. Managed 7 direct reports.

- Generated $10M in new sales and grew bottom-line profitability 20% over 2 years.

- Created channel partner program that drove 40% of total sales.

- Inked first enterprise contract ($1.7M) with Medi-Scientific. Added Stryker and Medtronic for additional $4M.

LOCATION SOFTWARE, INC.   San Jose, CA, 2010–2012
Second-stage VC-funded RFID software and hardware manufacturer, providing real-time locations data from tagged objects to the healthcare, manufacturing, and distribution markets. Estimated annual sales: $50M.

Director of Sales

Trained, coached, and guided team of 5 Account Managers in C-suite selling skills while personally managing a portfolio of strategic accounts representing $2M annual revenue.

- Led team in elevating sales 14% YOY.

- Designed new sales pipeline tracking process that improved accuracy 50% and reduced costs $800K.

- Created $500K partnership with GE Medical Systems and cemented $15M opportunity with leading international shipping enterprise.

INDUSTRIAL SYSTEMS, INC.   Chicago, IL, 2006–2009
$20M privately held startup software and services provider to a wide spectrum of industries and government.

Director of Sales, Business Development & Marketing

Led, trained, and mentored regional account management team in developing customer-focused, cross-functional sales approach with professional services and support to increase average sale 20%.

- Instrumental in igniting overall revenue from $500K to $6M.

- Singlehandedly sold $2.1M automobile-tracing solution to US Customs.

PRIOR

- **National Sales Manager,** Fallon Technologies, Inc.: Catapulted sales from $900K to $12M in 1 year.

- **Divisional Sales Manager,** Gourmet Partners: Reenergized sales and market share of mature product in a highly competitive market. Played a key role in integrating sales functions following acquisition by Pillsbury.

Education ■ Military ■ Community

MBA, UNIVERSITY OF CALIFORNIA, Berkeley, CA
BA in Marketing, NORTHWESTERN UNIVERSITY, Evanston, IL
US Air Force, 8 years
Board of Directors, Family Resource Center, Oakland, CA, since 2018

Kristofer Nagy

kristofer.nagy@gmail.com ■ 555-876-1234 ■ LinkedIn/com/in/krisnagy

Techno-Solutions, Inc.

Re: Vice President National Sales

Global competition, cost containment, and changing market conditions are critical issues in today's marketplace. I can help your organization meet these tough challenges—this is what I have been doing for more than 15 years. With roots in consumer goods followed by continued success in software and technology services, my ability to plan and execute transformative sales strategies and business plans through market analytics, resource optimization, team leadership, and goal focus has made me the "go-to" expert for steep challenges companies are facing.

Some very brief highlights of my career are:

- As VP of Business Development for a young software firm, I identified a specialized niche market, structured an entirely new division, and boosted revenue to $10M and bottom-line profit 20%.
- As Director of US Sales for a $20M software, hosting, and systems development firm, I singlehandedly delivered $3.5M in new business in 9 months—while concurrently leading the national sales team.
- As Major Account Manager of a $200M software solutions provider, I resurrected revenue growth by building a local-level strategic partnership with Microsoft that expanded to include additional sales categories due to its quick success.

Throughout my career, I've provided business peripheral vision using trend-spotting, intuition, and new methodologies; continually revisited the value proposition of a business and adapted to fluctuating conditions; and swiftly corrected course to remain a winner.

In summary, I'm a versatile leader who enjoys tackling challenging situations and developing strategic solutions that deliver solid, sustainable gains. Your currently advertised VP National Sales opportunity is an ideal fit for my expertise, and I look forward to speaking with you at your earliest convenience.

Sincerely,

Kristofer Nagy

Attachment: Resume

Kristofer Nagy

Sales Executive, Software/Technology: Finding untapped markets, rejuvenating brands, building high-performing teams

Streeter Systems, Inc.
University of California at Berkeley • Northwestern University

San Francisco Bay Area • 500+ Connections

About

I bring a unique perspective to technology sales. I firmly believe that people are not "sold" anything, and I base my sales approach on providing clients what they cannot live without.

Once I understand my clients' essential needs, I deliver every step of the way. My expertise lies in meticulously creating processes, structures, and checkpoints—backed by in-depth understanding of markets and technologies—to drive strategy and execution for sales of complex products. I have a track record of building relationships that open doors to new opportunities.

As a former fighter pilot in the US Air Force, I know firsthand the importance of leadership and the value of teamwork. In business, I bring together internal capabilities for a team approach in landing new opportunities. The results, consistently, have been revenue and profit growth … including these highlights:

▶ Streeter Systems: Recently we acquired a new brand of print management solutions, and I led the sales ramp-up that produced more than $3M in new sales in 9 months … after several years of stagnation for the product line.

Previously, I carved out a strategic partnership with Microsoft to build new business through joint sales and best practices seminars.

▶ Pro-Print Technology: I saw an opportunity, then planned, structured, launched, and led a new division that, in 2 years, grew to 40% of total revenue.

▶ Location Software: The account managers under my leadership were accustomed to transaction selling at the end-user level. I transitioned them to C-suite sales experts, elevating our solution to a strategic product and growing sales by double digits year-over-year.

▶ Industrial Systems, Inc.: As Director of Sales, Business Development, and Marketing for 3 years, I played a key role in igniting overall revenue from $500K to $6M.

Bottom line: I build the team, provide the leadership, and instill the approach of finding and meeting what our customers truly need. The results benefit everyone involved.

Experience

Director of US Sales—eSolutions
Streeter Systems, Inc.
2019–Present

When Streeter acquired the eSolutions division of MicronSystems, I was promoted to revitalize sales for a product line that had stagnated for several years.

The challenge was compounded by the fact that we had no additional resources available to help build a pipeline—no marketing programs, no new product development, and no lead-generation services.

I brought together my national team (7 sales professionals) and laid out the challenge. We needed a sales "blitz" to prove the value of the acquisition and reestablish eSolutions' position in the market. I coached them on consultative sales, and together we defined the key value proposition of our product.

In 9 months …
▶ My team and I generated more than $3.5M in new business.
▶ I personally connected with existing clients, establishing a new relationship and sharing our commitment to the product. As a result, we inked nearly $5M in contract extensions and gained keen insights into what was needed to make our solution even more valuable.
▶ We firmly reestablished eSolutions in the print solutions market and set the stage for growth through product advancements and continued business development.

Major Accounts Manager—eCommerce and Entitlements Management
Streeter Systems, Inc.
2015–2019

When I was recruited to Streeter Systems, it was an exciting time. We were in an active acquisition phase and rapidly bringing on new clients both through acquisition and through organic sales.

I quickly identified a strategy for sustainable growth: partnering with the providers of major software products that worked in tandem with our solutions, together educating our users in product use and best practices.

In 4 years …
▶ We nearly doubled revenues of the ecommerce segment, averaging 18% growth annually.
▶ I launched Microsoft partnerships at the local level and quickly expanded nationally.
▶ I then targeted the digital publishing industry, closed the company's first deal, and went on to secure additional contracts worth millions of dollars in annual revenue.

VP of Sales & Business Development / Life Sciences Group
Pro-Print Technology, Inc.
2012–2015

Shortly after joining Pro-Print, I recognized an opportunity to develop an entirely new business segment— the highly regulated pharmaceutical/medical device industry—for our industrial label-printing applications.

I persuaded senior management to let me run with it.

Within 3 years …

▶ I created the business plan and then developed the operational structure, marketing strategy, and distribution process for the new "life sciences" division.
▶ I trained a new 7-person sales team and carefully integrated the new division into the company's existing pre-sales and support processes.
▶ I partnered with other company divisions to integrate our sales process into their channels.
▶ We generated $10M in sales while boosting profits 20%.

Director of Sales
Location Software, Inc.
2010–2012

In this role, I recognized the limitations of the existing sales approach and worked to transform my team from "order takers" to consultative sales professionals selling at the C-level. I provided training, mentoring, and ongoing support to build a top-notch sales team.

In 2 years …
▶ My team and I increased overall sales 14%.
▶ I personally delivered $2M in contract sales.
▶ We created a lucrative partnership with GE Medical Systems.
▶ The new sales pipeline tracking process that I created improved accuracy 50% while cutting costs by $800K company-wide.

VP of Sales, Business Development & Marketing
Industrial Systems, Inc.
2006–2009

In my first sales management role, I had the opportunity to train and mentor my team of regional account managers in customer-focused, consultative sales.

In 3 years …
▶ We increased the size of our average sale by 20%.
▶ My team and I were instrumental in increasing total company revenue from $500K to $6M.

Previously, I advanced through sales roles with Gourmet Partners, prior to its acquisition by Pillsbury, and as National Sales Manager for Fallon Technologies, I increased sales from $900K to $12M in 1 year.

Kristofer Nagy

Senior Sales Executive: Software/Technology

Kristofer Nagy brings a unique perspective to his 15-year sales career in the technology market.

His view is shaped by additional years in the consumer products industry and as an Air Force fighter pilot, where he learned firsthand the value of teamwork. From experience as an individual sales contributor, sales team leader, and senior business strategist, he views the sales mindset as universal, regardless of industry—with market knowledge, client insight, and teamwork at the top of the list of success factors.

Throughout his career, Kris has become convinced that people are not *sold* anything—rather they *buy* products and services they are convinced will benefit them and their companies. He has built his reputation on market knowledge, detailed planning, and meticulous execution.

His ability to sell is evidenced by his most recent experience with Streeter Systems. When Streeter bought MicronSystems' enterprise software solution, the brand had lost its prominence, competition had caught up, and clients were not motivated to buy. Kris and his team generated more than $8M in revenue within nine months of the acquisition, both shoring up the existing client base and generating substantial new business.

Kris's business acumen is demonstrated by his conception, planning, and startup of a promising new division for Pro-Print Technology, a manufacturer of industrial label-printing software. Through research and market analytics, Kris identified a highly regulated market sector that spent tremendous amounts of money on labeling to ensure product safety and avoid hefty fines, yet had no enterprise-level solution to control errors. He immediately set out to devise a plan to penetrate the market and soon executed the very first sale that launched the business. The division's revenue grew to $10M of the $25M company.

With a reputation for relationship building and team leadership, Kris adapts his style to respond to constantly changing organizational, financial, and economic conditions. His strength lies in his ability to create change and growth and to execute strategic programs in the complex, competitive software/technology arena.

Kris's academic credentials include a Master of Business Administration from UC Berkeley and a bachelor's degree in marketing from Northwestern University.

A strong advocate of community involvement, Kris is on the Board of Directors of the Family Resource Center in Oakland, CA. Additional community action includes campaigning for fair, affordable housing and recruiting bone marrow donors.

While Kris's military service occurred a few decades ago, the lessons he learned—of leadership, commitment, teamwork, and meticulous preparation—remain at the core of his professional life today. He goes to bat for his teammates and brings a fighting spirit to every challenge.

kristofer.nagy@gmail.com ■ 555-876-1234 ■ LinkedIn/com/in/krisnagy

BACKSTORY: Jacqueline Miles (Writer: Marie Zimenoff)

TARGET ROLE: Senior Executive—President, CEO, Vice President
CURRENT TITLE: President, International Operations
INDUSTRY: Enterprise Technology/Data Storage

WRITER'S COMMENTS

Jacqueline had spent the bulk of her career with one company, AVNET—after first launching a pioneering data-storage business, leading it for 9 years, and then negotiating its acquisition by AVNET. At AVNET she had risen steadily based on her reputation as a problem solver—someone who could jump into the most difficult challenge, disrupt where necessary, and get results that were both quick and sustainable.

Because of her contributions to the company and her perception of her value there, she was blindsided when she was downsized in what was termed a "reduction in force" (RIF) and a flattening of executive layers in the company. Her naturally positive nature helped her to adjust, and she launched a search for a similar leadership role in the enterprise technology industry, where she had so much expertise and an impressive track record.

WRITING/DESIGN STRATEGY FOR DOCUMENTS

Resume: Jacqueline's unique strength—in addition to her many accomplishments—was her success in both startup and Fortune 100 leadership roles. I made sure to highlight this combination in her resume and to emphasize her ability to solve problems and quickly generate growth. Everything in the resume is designed for easy reading, with succinct copy, ample white space, and effective use of bold type to introduce each bullet and highlight different areas of oversight and accomplishment.

Because the transitions between her jobs at AVNET were not always sharply defined (in several cases one role bled into another), I combined roles/descriptions when it made sense to do so. In other cases, it was important to tell the career advancement story, so those jobs stand on their own.

Cover Letter: Targeting VC/PE firms, Jacqueline's letter gets quickly to the point and calls out precisely the kinds of experience and achievements that will interest her audience seeking an executive who can come into a portfolio company, turn things around, accelerate growth, and position the business for sale or sustainable success.

LinkedIn: Jacqueline's headline calls out her brand as a disruptive growth driver. The About and Experience sections use a natural storytelling style to describe the arc of her career, specific challenges, and impressive results.

UNIQUE CHALLENGES

Although not an element in creating her documents, Jacqueline's reaction to being downsized—and how she explained it—played a critical role in her job-search preparation. I helped her craft a message that was brief, non-defensive, and confident and quickly moved the conversation on to "what I can do for you."

OUTCOME

Jacqueline felt confident and fully prepared as she launched her job search.

Jacqueline Miles

Fort Collins, CO 80526 | 970.252.8413
jacquelinemiles@outlook.com | linkedin.com/in/jacquelinemiles

Senior Executive—Business Development, Sales Leadership & Digital Transformation
Combine Fortune 100 Leadership Experience + Entrepreneurial Creativity to Grow Profitable Businesses

Tech startup founder turned Fortune 100 executive who leads through disruption and pivots organizations, seeking creative and impactful solutions to business challenges. Foster environments where teams flourish and bring discipline to operations to transform ideas into reality.

Create and grow businesses by finding the opportunity in any marketplace—irrespective of the business environment—understanding market drivers and gaps, aligning to customer values, turning strategy into action, measuring what matters, and using feedback to take corrective actions and refine strategy.

Transformed losers into winners—setting the trajectory for a $100M business to grow to $1.8B in 9 years.

Led disruption with calculated risk—shifting startup focus to distribution business that grew to $60M in 11 years.

Turned technology into business results—leading a $6M technology integration project that saved $3.4M annually.

Areas of Expertise
Global Strategy Formation | Tactical Execution | Key Partnership Development
Financial Planning & Forecasting | Mergers & Acquisitions | CXO Relationship & Engagement
Operational Optimization | Business Transformation | Channel Operations | Digital Marketing Leadership

Professional Experience

AVNET, Longmont, CO 2008–2021

President, International Operations (2020–2021)

Scope: Ongoing operations and expansion in Brazil, Australia/New Zealand, and APAC; global alliance for largest supplier and customer relationships; global account team for system integrators

Business Turnaround & Growth: Brought in to deliver on the promise of a budding business in Australia/New Zealand and APAC and reset previously profitable business in Brazil by infusing operations with discipline.

- Created fastest-growing, most-profitable region and positioned company for deeper market penetration.

Strategic Partnerships: Spurred growth despite restrictions preventing mergers and acquisitions by negotiating master distribution agreement for Asia region.

- Grew revenue and created profitability that offset operating-margin challenges compared to other suppliers.

Senior Vice President, Global Marketing and Business Development, ECS (2018–2020)

Scope: Global marketing; ongoing operations and expansion of ECS APAC business; supplier acquisition; global customer account management; $1B global cloud business

Digital Transformation: Recruited to lead global marketing and align US and European operations, collaborating with Global President on strategy and changing interaction between suppliers and internal marketing team.

- Launched programs that generated funds used to create promotional videos and execute digital brand development initiatives, disrupting marketing operation status quo and interaction with suppliers.

Global Leadership: Brought consistency across regions for 8 of the largest suppliers and 19 system integrators, creating global agreements with system integrators and filling in service gaps.

- Grew revenue **6%–7%** YOY and increased margins faster than other customer cohorts companywide.

Jacqueline Miles

AVNET, CONT.

President—Americas (2015–2018)
Vice President, Americas Sales and Business Development (2013–2015)

Scope: $9.8B enterprise across US, Canada, and Brazil; 1200+ employees

M&A Leadership: Managed acquisition and integration of immixGroup, a **$1.2B** distributor focused on US public sector, accelerating growth by increasing capabilities and providing differentiation.

- Transformed struggling public sector segment into fastest-growing segment in the company.

Business Development: Handpicked team to lead business development initiative and competitive recruitment drive.

- Delivered **$1.1B** in net new customers over 9 months with minimal margin dilution.

Process Innovation: Created private-label leasing business, forging bank relationships and managing pricing, quoting, and sales within model unique to the industry that limited exposure to risk.

- Increased margins **50%** on an additional **$200M** in annual revenue.

Account Management: Elevated performance of 100 largest customer accounts by introducing sales metrics and standardizing field sales processes, methodologies, and management with Salesforce.com.

- Grew revenue **12%** and outpaced revenue growth of accounts across company.

Digital Transformation: Co-led $6M project to create and deploy digitally enabled order processing tools still in use today across multiple markets.

- Saved **$3.4M** annually while improving time to market and customer experience.

Vice President, Storage Lines (2008–2013)

Scope: 300+ sales, technical, and marketing staff

Business Turnaround: Tapped to rescue floundering business. Created supplier-dedicated teams to align field sales, internal sales, and sales operations with supplier imperatives.

- Set foundation for **$100M** business to grow to **$1.8B** in 9 years with **65%+** market share.

SKYNEXX, Toronto, Canada   1997–2008

CEO & Founder

Scope: Sales operations, business development, and business strategy for data-storage distribution; 40 employees

Business Launch: Pioneered value-added distribution in region, shifting as marketplace moved to fiber channel and connecting partners and clients to launch unique business model.

- Grew sales to **$60M** and gained **94%** market share by creating virtually exclusive distribution arrangement for channel sales.
- Named to CRN's "Top 25 News Makers" in 2007 and negotiated 2008 acquisition by AVNET.

Education

MBA, Finance—University of Illinois School of Business, Chicago, Illinois

BA, Economics—University of Colorado, Boulder, Colorado

Subject: Disruptive, Growth-focused Executive—Startup to Fortune 100—Technology/Distribution Industries

When companies face tough situations, they need leaders who can transform teams and operations to meet these challenges head on. As companies position themselves for growth, they need leaders who can disrupt markets with innovation and discipline.

I am one of these leaders.

As we're all busy, here's a brief outline of my primary qualifications for you to match to your search assignments:

> I've always had a knack for seeing opportunities and pivoting teams to turn the idea into profits. At AVNET, this has led to some of their most profitable acquisitions—most recently the identification, courtship, and integration of a $1.5B acquisition that transformed a struggling public-sector business into the company's fastest-growing segment.

> Early in my career I launched and grew a technology distribution startup from the ground up to $60M with 94% market share. I learned quickly that leadership to drive business growth is all about relationships. This served me well in my first role at AVNET, where my team closed $1.1B in net new customers in 9 months.

> Multiple times at AVNET I've been tapped to shepherd wandering divisions into a cohesive team. It's been a bonus when these open the doors for international travel and business opportunities, such as creating the most profitable region (Australia/New Zealand) companywide and aligning marketing operations across the US and Europe.

Currently, I am exploring executive leadership positions that would leverage my international strategy, business growth, sales leadership, and digital transformation strengths. I'm accustomed to total compensation around $600,000 and would prefer to target companies in Colorado, Texas, or Georgia, with up to 50% travel for the right position.

If you have a client who is seeking a leader in business growth, turnarounds, digital transformation, and strategic partnerships in the technology or distribution industries, I look forward to exploring how I can leverage my background to achieve their business goals.

Thank you for your consideration. I look forward to speaking with you.

Sincerely,

Jacqueline Miles
>>>>>>>>>
970.252.8413
jacquelinemiles@outlook.com | linkedin.com/in/jacquelinemiles

Jacqueline Miles

Senior Executive | Identify Market Opportunity, Lead Innovation to Differentiate, and Infuse Discipline to Spur Growth

AVNET
University of Colorado • University of Illinois

Fort Collins, CO • 500+ Connections

About

That moment—when we see the writing on the wall and realize it's time for a shift—the decisions we make in that moment define us.

My first shift came in 1997—leaving a job without a plan when I could see there wasn't a future there.
I sought out an industry built on growth: data storage.
>> With a partner and $150,000 of our own money, SKYNEXX launched.

We meandered through the fledgling market trying to figure out where to scale and saw our big chance coming—the shift to fiber channel.
>> We created an omnichannel go-to-market model no one has replicated, while attaining double the margins of anyone in the market.

When AVNET acquired SKYNEXX, I pivoted again to stay and restore a $100M division.
>> I handpicked a team that grew it to $1.8B by 2015.

As I progressed through Americas and Global executive roles at AVNET, I refocused teams, took risks to spur innovation, and led technology integration. Leading change became one of my top strengths.

Overcoming "that's the way we've always done it" requires going beyond communicating vision to paint a picture that makes change worth the discomfort.
>> I've reveled in reviving underperforming teams that no longer believe they can win.

Launching a startup taught me to seek out and execute strategies that capitalize on resources, even if they require a bit of risk.
>> I championed one of AVNET's most beneficial acquisitions, negotiating to form AVNET Capital Solutions.

Growing businesses requires technical agility. I've repeatedly led digital transformation to generate tangible business benefit.
>> I co-led a $6M automation project that paid for itself within 2 years and brought an entrenched marketing team into the digital era.

If you want to realize the vision of growth for your organization, we should talk.

Experience

AVNET
President, International Operations | Senior Vice President, Global Marketing & Business Development
2018–2021

As my President (Americas) role came to an end, the C-suite asked me to take on a global challenge in a functional leadership role.

AVNET's US and European operations had been operating in silos and needed to come together on a new vision to catch up with the digital transformation in marketing.

>> I reworked the way marketing interacted with suppliers, designing specific programs that fulfilled AVNET's digital marketing aspirations while meeting supplier requirements.

While taking on this marketing transformation, I also oversaw the 8 largest global suppliers and 19 global system integrators. These partners wanted consistency across the regions, and we delivered.

>> In the process, we grew revenue 6%–7% YOY and grew margins faster than other customer cohorts through a land-and-expand strategy, creating global agreements with the system integrators and filling in service gaps.

My success in these roles opened the door for another pivot to the President, International role.

AVNET's business was ripe with opportunity—under distress in Brazil following an ERP conversion and on the cusp of becoming the fastest-growing, highest-margin business in Australia/New Zealand and APAC.

>> We achieved region-leading profitability as I provided executive sponsorship for key supplier relationships, infused operations with discipline, and led a global account team focused on system integrators and a global alliance of our largest supplier and customer relationships.

>> I negotiated a master distribution agreement for the Asia region that grew the bottom line and offset other operating margin challenges.

AVNET
President—Americas | Vice President, Americas Sales & Business Development
2013–2018

As I advanced at AVNET, I moved into the VP role and took on the challenge of revitalizing performance of the 100 largest customer accounts. I started by integrating Salesforce.com, creating specific goals by customer, and measuring activity and customer retention.

>> The team bought into the changes; they couldn't argue with the results: revenue grew 75% in these accounts—outpacing the rest of the company.

The next project was a $6M revamp of a manual order-entry process that was eroding productivity and top-line growth. We automated order entry, enabled customers to self-enter data, and provided pricing algorithm data to ISRs for quicker, more profitable quotes.

>> The project paid for itself in <2 years, saving $3.4M annually and improving time to market and customer satisfaction.

As the business grew, I sought other areas to maximize and identified the public sector segment as the next target. I identified, courted, and managed the acquisition of immixGroup, a $1.2B distributor focused on the public sector, to build our capabilities.

>> This division quickly became the fastest-growing segment in the company.

I listened to the market and identified customers' need for a financing partner. We had buying power and needed a creative solution with minimal risk exposure. A credit manager and I devised and conceived AVNET Capital, and I negotiated relationships with banks to provide leases they would fund.

>> This solution—still unique in the industry—increased margins 50% on an additional $200M a year in revenue.

With a business transition on the horizon, leadership asked me to launch a recruitment drive to proactively fill the revenue gap. I handpicked the team and set the strategy.

>> We delivered $1B+ in net new customers over 9 months with minimal margin dilution.

AVNET
Vice President, Storage Lines
2018–2015

Within a few months of joining AVNET with the acquisition of SKYNEXX, the leadership team asked me to step in and win back a key supplier, knowing I wasn't a stranger to disrupting process.

I broke down the complex processes, wove them back together, and handpicked a team with the understanding and desire to execute. They became the company's first supplier-dedicated teams of field sales, ISRs, and sales operations who better aligned with supplier imperatives.

>> After setting that $100M business on its course to eventually reach $1.8B by 2015, I was entrusted with all storage vendors and led a team of 300+ across sales, technical, and marketing.

SKYNEXX
CEO & Founder
1997–2008

Starting out in an emerging market like data storage provided plenty of opportunities to lead strategic business shifts, and I realized that my passion for growing businesses was also a strength.

We pioneered value-added distribution in the region with a unique model where we sold to end users without transacting with them. I created a virtually exclusive distribution arrangement for channel sales.

>> We grew sales to $60M, gained 94% market share, and produced double the margins of other distributors. Our success earned us recognition on CRN's "Top 25 News Makers" in 2007 and caught the attention of AVNET for acquisition in 2008.

BACKSTORY: Raj Kumar (Writer: Louise Kursmark)

TARGET ROLE: General Manager/Managing Director/President
CURRENT TITLE: General Manager
INDUSTRY: Grocery, Supermarket & Retail Food Industry

WRITER'S COMMENTS

I had worked with Raj throughout several career transitions as he progressed from sales leadership to general management roles in locations around the world. Most of his career was with Danone, the multinational food products company, and with each promotion he gained a wider scope of responsibility and delivered exceptional results.

Three years ago he left Danone, moving to Abbott Nutrition to take on a steep challenge: the turnaround of its business in the Middle East. Achieving the turnaround required him to reorganize the entire business and reenergize the team. Again he was successful—but he knew that increased regulations affecting his primary product line (infant formula) were a threat to further growth.

Raj's major assets were his undisputed record of success and his ability to thrive in diverse cultures and regions. As noted on his resume, he has "lived and worked in 8 countries."

WRITING/DESIGN STRATEGY FOR DOCUMENTS

Resume: Because Raj had such stellar and consistent results, I chose to include three tables in his resume to spotlight impressive numbers in his three most recent positions. In the introduction, a section titled "Value Offered" calls out four roles in which he has excelled: Growth Catalyst, Turnaround Architect, Business Strategist, Respected Leader. The overall design of the resume is distinctive while remaining somewhat conservative, as is appropriate for his target audience of primarily European companies.

Cover Letter: Written to accompany a recruiter campaign, Raj's letter gets right to the point, highlighting the very different circumstances in which he has achieved consistently strong results. The letter then summarizes his global background, broad skill set, and reason for seeking a new opportunity.

UNIQUE CHALLENGES

Raj's resume could easily have been three pages, as he had significant successes in every role. But by truncating the details of his five earliest positions, I was able to create a highly readable two-page document that clearly conveyed his value and expertise.

OUTCOME

Through his recruiter outreach, Raj learned of an opportunity in the growing field of natural nutrition products. He assumed the role of Managing Director for three different divisions of a trend-setting company.

RAJ KUMAR

+ 971 3456 7890 | raj.kumar@mail.com | LinkedIn.com/in/raj-kumar

GENERAL MANAGEMENT EXECUTIVE: ASIA | EUROPE | MIDDLE EAST

Catalyst for strategic transformation and sustainable top- and bottom-line growth.

VALUE OFFERED

- **Growth Driver:** Delivered strong revenue and EBIT growth in both saturated and developing markets.

- **Turnaround Artist:** Transformed stagnant operations to vibrant, growing businesses with highly energized teams.

- **Business Strategist:** Tackled diverse challenges for some of the world's leading companies, steering major change initiatives from strategic plan through flawless execution.

- **Respected Leader:** Demonstrated full range of executive management competencies and notable talent for inspiring teams to reach ambitious goals.

Fluent in English and French. Lived and worked in 8 countries. Cambridge MBA and INSEAD AMP (2018).

PROFESSIONAL EXPERIENCE

ABBOTT LABORATORIES | ABBOTT NUTRITION
A global leader in infant and child nutrition (major brand: Similac); US$3B annual revenue.

General Manager: Abbott Nutrition Middle East (Dubai)	2018–Present
*€70M P&L	150 direct management/administrative staff	700-subcontractor field team*	

Turned around and regrew a declining business in a very competitive environment. Assumed GM responsibility for business that needed a deep-dive reorganization and shift of direction to regain growth. Identified opportunities and inspired new passion and commitment within struggling organization.

- Returned sales and profit to strong growth after 5 years of decline:

	2018	2019	2020
Volume Growth	+7.5%	+11%	+14.6%
EBIT Growth	+4.9%	+10.6%	+22.1%

- Grew market share by 200 basis points to become #2 in premium formula category (previously #5).
- Developed a clear vision and simple, executable strategies.
  - Streamlined portfolio to focus on super-premium category and high-margin products.
  - Implemented SAP and improved sales processes and tools, allowing flawless execution of initiatives.
  - Achieved strong visibility in the top 1000 stores and 250 hospitals.
- Launched a full range of initiatives to attract, retain, and develop talent. Replaced 70% of managers, adopted "Best Place to Work" program, and relocated head office to new, inspiring environment.
- Reestablished strong relationships with distributors, customers, and authorities. Implemented regular top-to-top with key accounts.

DANONE
World leader in all 4 business divisions: Dairy and Plant-based Products; Early Life Nutrition; Medical Nutrition; Waters.

General Manager: Danone Lebanon	2016–2018
*€103M P&L	170 management/administrative staff*	

Achieved/surpassed all performance goals in a challenging multicultural region and volatile environment. Challenged to drive growth for business that was already the dominant market leader. Restructured operations and inspired new passion and commitment within complacent organization.

Raj Kumar +971 3456 7890 | raj.kumar@mail.com

General Manager: Danone Lebanon, continued

- Delivered immediate sales and profit growth, surpassing targets each year:

	2016	2017	2018 (Proj.)
Volume Growth	+22%	+10.2%	+10.0%
EBIT	17.5%	18.5%	18.8%

- Met aggressive goal of improving EBIT by 100 basis points in 2017 by waging a vigorous war on waste.
- Delivered additional €4M via an innovative micro-distribution concept and other new routes to market.
- Collaborated with the Ministry of Education to put in place a "Healthy Kids" project that heightened Danone's social responsibility in the market and reinforced strong networking with key influencers.
- Represented the company on strategic and regulatory issues with local authorities, media, and partners.

General Manager: Danone Indonesia   2014–2016
€37M P&L | 60 management/administrative staff, both local nationals and ex-pats | Unionized labor force

Revitalized, restructured, and transformed business to deliver best EBIT results in its history. Promoted to GM of established business with little opportunity for organic growth. Transformed operations and downsized organization by 30% to develop a leaner structure focused on generating demand.

- Delivered both revenue and profit growth every year:

	2014	2015	2016 (Proj.)
Sales Growth	+7.5%	+8.5%	+9.0%
EBIT	16.6%	18.0%	18.5%

- Openly communicated new goals, plans, and expectations, creating a new culture of teamwork and results. Weeded out underperformers and strengthened the team through strategic new hires.
- Streamlined SKUs 40%. Renegotiated distributor contracts from fixed % to cost-plus, KPI-based model.
- Developed strategic plan and solid program to meet Danone corporate goal of positive social impact.
- Delivered 50M AUD savings as part of 6-person team of Internal Consultants chosen to drive a cost-reduction initiative across Danone Australia in spring 2015.

Prior Roles with Danone—Europe and Asia

Sales Director, Danone Vietnam, 2011–2014: Amid fast-growing competition, achieved double-digit sales growth every year and increased profits more than 100 basis points in 2013.

Special Assignments, 2010–2011: Prior to assuming leadership role in expanding Asian market, took on several short-term positions to broaden exposure to finance, sales, and Pan-Asian business operations.

Business Development Manager, Danone Eastern Europe, 2008–2010: In 2 years, built business from €0 to €10M, captured 40% market share, and reached breakeven profitability.

Key Account Manager, Trade Marketing Manager, Danone Germany, 2005–2008.

Trade Marketing Manager, Sales Area Manager, Danone United Kingdom, 2001–2005.

EDUCATION

- **INSEAD Advanced Management Program (AMP),** Fontainebleau, France—2018
- **MBA,** University of Cambridge, Judge Business School, Cambridge UK—2001

Subject: General Management Candidate—Global Experience—Abbott Nutrition, Danone Experience

In management roles with Abbott Nutrition and Danone in Asia, Europe, and the Middle East, I have demonstrated the ability to achieve swift results under very different circumstances:

- **Turnaround and Revitalization:** Inheriting a declining business and a defeated team, I led Abbott Nutrition Middle East to 22% EBIT growth in 2020 by reinspiring the team, restructuring the organization, and refocusing on strategic targets.

- **Established Business:** Already owning the market for Danone in Lebanon, I developed comprehensive business strategies that delivered both top- and bottom-line growth above 10% per year.

- **Fast Growth:** Leading a sales organization in Vietnam, I restructured to better serve our rapidly expanding customers, the supermarkets and hypermarkets that control the lion's share of retail. We achieved 15% year-over-year sales growth and 100-point profit growth.

- **New Markets:** In 2 European countries where our product was not viewed as a necessity, I built the business from the ground up to €10 million (and 40% market share) in just 2 years.

My experience is truly global. Currently General Manager for Abbott Nutrition in the Middle East, I previously served with Danone as GM in Lebanon and Indonesia, Sales Director in Vietnam, and special team member for a major cost-cutting overhaul in Australia, after beginning my career with posts in the UK, Germany, and Eastern Europe. I am fluent in both English and French.

Offering well-balanced executive skills, I have particular strengths in sales, marketing, brand management, and business development. I approach steep challenges from both an analytical and a creative viewpoint, combining data-driven strategies with the willingness to turn things upside down (if need be) to get results.

The current and expected regulatory environment for infant nutrition products will impact our future growth, and I am eager for a new opportunity where I can continue to deliver strategic and rapid results. If one of your clients seeks an executive with my background, I would welcome the opportunity to speak with you. Thank you.

Raj Kumar
****
+ 971 3456 7890 | raj.kumar@mail.com | LinkedIn.com/in/raj-kumar

BACKSTORY: Michelle Dowd (Writer: Jan Melnik)

TARGET ROLE: President or Chief Medical Officer
CURRENT TITLE: Orthopedic Surgeon/Practice Lead
INDUSTRY: Healthcare/Hospital Administration

WRITER'S COMMENTS

Michelle reached out to me for assistance in positioning for a top hospital leadership role—President or Chief Medical Officer. She was also interested in simultaneously leading orthopedic surgery.

Over the course of her career, she had amassed significant experience and prestigious experiences while delivering exceptional value both in the private healthcare sector as well as throughout her distinguished career in the United States Air Force. At the time of her retirement from the USAF, she'd completed 23 years of service as a decorated Medical Officer with significant achievements in organizational transformation and medical leadership. She earned half a dozen honors, including gold stars and a bronze star.

WRITING/DESIGN STRATEGY FOR DOCUMENTS

Resume: To create the appropriate space for Michelle's newest role and provide the key details of her prior private-sector healthcare leadership successes, it was necessary to substantially truncate her valuable military background. This required a few rounds of "red pen" edits to ensure her unique story portrayed the right value proposition.

One-page Executive Resume: Michelle's one-page document came together seamlessly once the lengthy CV was tightly edited. At a very quick glance, readers are able to discern her outstanding record of achievement as an orthopedic surgeon, a progressive healthcare executive, and a recognized medical officer with the U.S. Air Force.

LinkedIn: Michelle's LinkedIn About section wove together readily—balancing her executive healthcare background across military and private sector experiences.

Bio: A one-page bio highlights Michelle's core strengths and transferable capabilities. Brief stories—quantified—bring to life her brand of making a difference and provide proof-of-performance to her next employer.

UNIQUE CHALLENGES

Michelle had a 6-page CV when she sought my help. While there were numerous key stories to be told, synthesizing great details and accomplishments into a concise, 2-page document (augmented by a 1-page executive resume, bio, and LinkedIn) was the top objective.

OUTCOME

As her documents reflect, Michelle was successful in rather quickly being identified for several top hospital leadership roles—ultimately selecting the CMO post with Pasadena Medical Center where she will also direct the Orthopedic Surgery department. Typical of a highly motivated and professional client, she asked me to immediately update her documents to share her story with her large audience of followers.

Michelle Dowd, MD, MBA

Greater Los Angeles, CA | 213-555-5543 | michelle.dowd@gmail.com | www.linkedin.com/in/michelle-dowd-md

Senior Healthcare Executive & Chief Medical Officer
Strategic, Innovative Leader

Senior Medical Executive with exceptional breadth and depth of experience—respected career as Orthopedic Surgeon and Chief Medical Officer complemented by military medical career, rising to the rank of Major General, USAF.

- ❖ **Accomplished Orthopedic Surgeon**—Leading doctor in field of minimally invasive robotic technique: Established an exceptional program ranked #1 in volume in Western Region and #14 in United States.
- ❖ **Avid Proponent of Advances in Medicine and Healthcare**—Champion of numerous initiatives and innovative solutions that consistently improve quality of care and patient outcomes.
- ❖ **Lead Clinical Physician**—Skilled educator tapping state-of-the-art innovations in healthcare and evidence-based practices to provide general surgical residents with outstanding surgical training at nationally ranked hospital.
- ❖ **Resourceful, Results-Focused Visionary**—Advocate of lifelong learning: MD complemented by Stanford MBA.

Savvy and Dedicated Healthcare Executive Committed to Optimizing Organizational Performance, Delivering Leading-Edge Care, and Generating Exceptional, Cost-Effective Results

Clinical/Executive Experience

PASADENA MEDICAL CENTER | Pasadena, CA	Jan. 2021–Present
Chief Medical Officer & Director of Orthopedic Surgery	

Recruited into newly created position to co-lead 750-bed urban healthcare system, in dyad relationship with Senior Vice President. Initiatives will include formulating parameters for assessing hospital system mergers, aligning policies among physician practices/hospitals, and optimizing performance and quality outcomes.

Select Objectives

- ❖ Transition from fee-for-service model to overall quality emphasis, influence new healthcare policies, modernize practices, and further cement PMC's reputation as provider of exceptional community healthcare.
- ❖ Build an outstanding and cohesive physician organization.

SCRIPPS MERCY HOSPITAL | San Diego, CA	2017–2021
Orthopedic Surgeon/Practice Lead	

Recruited as **Lead Physician** for 8-physician surgical specialty staff providing orthopedic services across multidisciplinary delivery-of-care model. Provided strategic vision, standardized quality healthcare practices, and introduced measures to reduce/contain healthcare delivery costs through evidence-based, supporting data.

- ❖ Developed quality assurance and data-driven performance improvement metrics as well as introduced robust performance appraisal process.
- ❖ Initiated protocols leveraging analytics to better define quality/desired outcomes within orthopedic practice.
- ❖ Contributed to professional development among staff of allied health practitioners (7 Physician Assistants and 2 Nurse Practitioners) through CME-funded initiative.
- ❖ Named 1 of **Top Doctors, San Diego,** by peers (3-year award recipient).

HIGH DESERT REGIONAL HEALTH SYSTEM | Lancaster, CA   **2012–2017**
Chief, Department of Orthopedic Surgery | Surgeon, Lancaster Orthopedic Surgical Associates

Serving as **Chief of the Department of Surgery** (3 years), brought extensive leadership to growing organization (125+ physicians) in the High Desert Regional Health System, comprising 300+ care locations throughout the region.

- ❖ Instrumental in providing leadership and bringing value throughout 3 mergers. Instituted centralized credentialing system, ensuring consistency of practice standards across common operating system.

- ❖ In highly collaborative role as **Chief of the Department of Surgery,** established code of behavior and professional ethics, raising accountability and performance standards.

- ❖ Expertly performed 375+ orthopedic surgical procedures annually.

- ❖ Held multiple leadership roles within the health system and an affiliated medical education program:
    - — **Surgical Preceptor/Clinical Assistant Professor** (University of California, Los Angeles). Developed/implemented orthopedic surgery educational curriculum for general surgery residents.
    - — **Co-Chair, Medical Staff Development Committee** (High Desert Regional Health System).
    - — **Practice Head** (Lancaster Orthopedic Surgical Associates).

UNITED STATES AIR FORCE   **1989–2012**
Major General/Medical Officer

Retired in 2012 from 23-year military career as a decorated **Medical Officer** in the United States Air Force. Career spanned roles that included **Medical Officer of the Air Force** and practicing **Physician/Orthopedic Surgeon.**

- ❖ Promoted to **Commanding Officer,** 6th Medical Group. Directed 350+ U.S. Air Force personnel delivering medical care/healthcare services across multiple venues. Challenged to turn around organization; transformed perception and enhanced overall performance.

- ❖ Named **Major General of the Medical Corps**, recognizing exceptional leadership and performance.

- ❖ **Member, Military/Private Sector Clinical Advisory Council.** Named to Council in 2010 to provide clinical expertise and represent the Air Force's interests in developing Electronic Health Records (EHR) for the overall military health system. Program launched across all military branches in 2014.

- ❖ **Recipient of United States Military Honors:**
    - — Meritorious Service Medal—2 Gold Stars
    - — Air Force Commendation Medal—1 Gold Star
    - — National Defense Service Medal—1 Bronze Star
    - — Global War on Terrorism Service Medal
    - — U.S. Public Health Service Unit Commendation

Education | Certifications | Affiliations

Master of Business Administration | STANFORD UNIVERSITY SCHOOL OF BUSINESS | Stanford, CA   2018
- ❖ **Runner-Up,** Biotechnology Case Competition (March 2018) … Stanford team was 1 of 10 top business schools nationwide participating in competition examining new biotechnology.
- ❖ Selected as 1 of 18 MBA students out of 850+ candidates to discuss business principles and meet with executives at Y Combinator in Mountain View, CA.

Doctor of Medicine | UNIVERSITY OF CALIFORNIA SCHOOL OF MEDICINE | Davis, CA   1984
- ❖ Internship and General Surgery Residency, Keck Hospital, Los Angeles, CA (1989)
- ❖ Orthopedic Surgery Residency, Keck Hospital (1992)

Bachelor of Science, Biology (Magna Cum Laude) | **UNIVERSITY OF SOUTHERN CALIFORNIA | Los Angeles, CA**   1980

Certifications: American Board of Surgery | American Board of Orthopedic Surgery

Affiliations: Society of Orthopedic Surgeons | California Surgical Association | American College of Surgeons

Michelle Dowd, MD, MBA

Greater Los Angeles, CA | 213-555-5543 | michelle.dowd@gmail.com | www.linkedin.com/in/michelle-dowd-md

Senior Healthcare Executive & Chief Medical Officer
Strategic, Innovative Leader

Senior Medical Executive with exceptional breadth and depth of experience—respected career as Orthopedic Surgeon and Chief Medical Officer complemented by military medical career, rising to the rank of Major General, USAF.

❖ **Accomplished Orthopedic Surgeon**—Leading doctor in field of minimally invasive robotic technique: Established an exceptional program ranked #1 in volume in Western Region and #14 in United States.
❖ **Avid Proponent of Advances in Medicine and Healthcare**—Champion of numerous initiatives and innovative solutions that consistently improve quality of care and patient outcomes.
❖ **Lead Clinical Physician**—Skilled educator tapping state-of-the-art innovations in healthcare and evidence-based practices to provide general surgical residents with outstanding surgical training at nationally ranked hospital.

Savvy and Dedicated Healthcare Executive Committed to Optimizing Organizational Performance,
Delivering Leading-Edge Care, and Generating Exceptional, Cost-Effective Results

Education and Certification

MD, UCLA School of Medicine, 1984 | **MBA, Stanford University,** 2018
American Board of Surgery (Cert., 2020); **American Board of Orthopedic Surgery** (Cert., 2022)

Select Clinical/Executive Experience

**PASADENA MEDICAL CENTER	Pasadena, CA**	Jan. 2021–Present
Chief Medical Officer & Director of Orthopedic Surgery	

❖ Recruited into newly created position to co-lead 750-bed urban healthcare system, in dyad relationship with SVP.
❖ Strategic leader for initiatives that will include formulating parameters for assessing hospital system mergers, aligning policies among physician practices/hospitals, and optimizing performance and quality outcomes.

**SCRIPPS MERCY HOSPITAL	San Diego, CA**	2017–2021
Orthopedic Surgeon/Practice Lead	

❖ Recruited as **Lead Physician** for 8-physician surgical specialty staff providing orthopedic services across multidisciplinary delivery-of-care model. Provided strategic vision, standardized quality healthcare practices, and introduced measures to reduce/contain healthcare delivery costs through evidence-based, supporting data.
❖ Initiated protocols leveraging analytics to better define quality/desired outcomes within orthopedic practice.

**HIGH DESERT REGIONAL HEALTH SYSTEM	Lancaster, CA**	2012–2017
Chief, Department of Orthopedic Surgery	Surgeon, Lancaster Orthopedic Surgical Associates	

❖ As **Chief of the Department of Surgery,** led 125+ physicians within large healthcare system. **Surgical Preceptor/Clinical Assistant Professor** (University of California, Los Angeles).
❖ Instrumental in providing leadership throughout 3 mergers. Instituted centralized credentialing system.

UNITED STATES AIR FORCE	1989–2012
Major General/Medical Officer	

❖ Completed 23-year military career as a decorated **Medical Officer** and practicing **Physician/Orthopedic Surgeon.**
❖ **Member, Military/Private Sector Clinical Advisory Council.** Represented the Air Force's interests in developing Electronic Health Records for the military. Program launched across all military branches in 2014.

Michelle Dowd, MD

Strategic and Innovative Senior Healthcare Executive — Leading Organizational Excellence While Delivering Proven Value

Pasadena Medical Center
Stanford University | University of California School of Medicine | University of Southern California

Greater Los Angeles Area • 500+ Connections

About

* Accomplished Senior Healthcare Medical Executive and Chief Medical Officer
* Orthopedic Surgeon with active practice, 25+ years
* Major General/Medical Officer, United States Air Force, retired in 2012 after 23 years of service

These are just some of the hats I wear/have worn during my career as a surgeon and healthcare executive. Currently the Chief Medical Officer and Director of Orthopedic Surgery at Pasadena Medical Center, I also continue to practice medicine (orthopedic surgery).

Complementing my medical knowledge as a physician was my thirst to augment management experience—both military and healthcare—with the depth of business management knowledge that would come from a rigorous MBA program. Thus, after retiring from the Air Force, while continuing to practice clinical medicine full time, I enrolled in the evening program at Stanford University School of Business and completed my MBA in 2018.

As a Chief Medical Officer, Orthopedic Surgeon, Lead Physician, and Skilled Educator, I have indeed worn many hats while earning a track record of achievement:

* Known as an expert in the field of minimally invasive robotic surgical techniques, I established an exceptional program that ranked #1 in volume in the Western Region and #14 in the United States.

* Working with general surgical residents at UCLA, I tapped state-of-the-art innovations in healthcare and evidence-based practices to provide them with outstanding orthopedic surgical training at the nationally ranked healthcare facility.

* As avid proponent of advances in medicine and healthcare, I have a record that reflects numerous initiatives and innovative solutions that consistently improve quality of care and patient outcomes.

==

Savvy, Dedicated, and Visionary Healthcare Executive Committed to:
* Optimizing Organizational Performance
* Delivering Leading-Edge Care
* Generating Exceptional, Cost-Effective Results

Experience

Chief Medical Officer & Director of Orthopedic Surgery
Pasadena Medical Center
Jan. 2021–Present

I was recruited into a newly created position, working with the Senior Vice President to co-lead the 750-bed urban health system.

As a strategic leader for the organization, I am focusing my initial efforts on programs that include formulating parameters for assessing hospital system mergers, aligning policies among physician practices and hospitals, and optimizing performance and quality outcomes. Specific priorities include:

* Transitioning from a fee-for-service model to an overall quality emphasis, influencing new healthcare policies, modernizing practices, and further cementing Pasadena's reputation as a provider of exceptional community healthcare.
* Building an outstanding, cohesive physician organization.
* In conjunction with my leadership role, I divide my time between administration and my practice as a clinical orthopedic surgeon.

Orthopedic Surgeon/Practice Lead
Scripps Mercy Hospital
2017–2021

I was recruited by Scripps Mercy as Lead Physician for the 8-physician surgical specialty staff providing orthopedic services across a multidisciplinary delivery-of-care model.

* My primary contribution was to provide strategic vision, institute standardization of quality healthcare practices, and implement measures to reduce and contain healthcare delivery costs, promulgating evidence-based, supporting data.
* To support these initiatives, I developed quality assurance and data-driven performance improvement metrics and introduced a robust performance appraisal process.
* Other contributions include initiating protocols that leveraged analytics to better define quality and desired outcomes within the surgical practice.
* I furthered professional development among the staff of allied health practitioners (including 7 Physician Assistants and 2 Nurse Practitioners) by requiring use of available CME funding.
* During this timeframe, I was a multi-year recipient of "Top Doctors, San Diego" (awarded by my peers).

Chief, Department of Orthopedic Surgery
High Desert Regional Health System
2012–2017

As the Chief of the Department of Surgery, I brought extensive leadership to a rapidly growing organization (125+ physicians) across a network of more than 300 care locations. Key contributions include:

* In a time of rapid change and growth via 3 mergers, I was instrumental in providing leadership to capture value and promote smooth integration. Under my leadership, we centralized the credentialing system and created consistent practice standards across a common operating system.
* In a highly collaborative role as Chief of the Department of Surgery, I established a code of behavior and professional ethics, raising both accountability and performance standards.
* As a surgeon, I performed more than 375 orthopedic surgical procedures each year.
* In an ancillary role, I served as Surgical Preceptor/Clinical Assistant Professor at the UCLA Medical School.

In that capacity, I developed and implemented an orthopedic surgery educational curriculum for general surgery residents.
* I was appointed Co-Chair of the Medical Staff Development Committee of the High Desert Regional Health System.

Major General / Medical Officer
United States Air Force
1989–2012

My 23-year career with the Air Force spanned progressive roles that included Medical Officer of the Air Force and practicing Physician/Orthopedic Surgeon.

* When I was promoted to Commanding Officer of the 6th Medical Group, I was challenged to turn around the organization. We successfully transformed the perception of the entire organization and enhanced overall performance.

* In 2009, I was named Major General of the Medical Corps, recognizing exceptional leadership and performance.

* I was appointed to serve as a member of the Military/Private Sector Clinical Advisory Council in 2010. My role with the council was to represent the Air Force's interests in developing electronic health records (EHR) for the overall military health system. The program we developed was launched across all military branches in 2014.

United States Military Honors:
* Meritorious Service Medal – 2 Gold Stars
* Air Force Commendation Medal – 1 Gold Star
* National Defense Service Medal – 1 Bronze Star
* Global War on Terrorism Service Medal
* U.S. Public Health Service Unit Commendation

*Strategic and Innovative
Senior Healthcare Executive*

213-555-5543
michelle.dowd@gmail.com
www.linkedin.com/in/michelle-dowd-md

Competencies

❖ Organizational turnaround and performance optimization

❖ Patient care and quality controls

❖ Strategic vision and initiatives

❖ Evidence-based practices

❖ Revenue-driving and cost-management strategies

❖ Physician and practice relations

❖ Team collaboration

❖ Principled leadership

Education

Doctor of Medicine
University of California School of Medicine

Master of Business Administration
Stanford University

Bachelor of Science, Biology
University of Southern California

Michelle Dowd, MD, MBA

Senior Healthcare Executive

Michelle Dowd is an accomplished and strategic healthcare professional and the Chief Medical Officer as well as Director of Orthopedic Surgery at Pasadena Medical Center in Pasadena, California. A recognized expert in orthopedic surgery in private practice for more than 20 years, she previously completed a decorated medical career in the United States Air Force, where she advanced to Major General and Medical Officer.

With a flawless record of developing and championing strategies that propel organizations to achieve exceptional results, Michelle focuses on quality healthcare improvements, business and performance optimization, and initiatives that ensure premier community healthcare services.

Michelle's track record reflects consistency in turning around underperforming organizations and positioning already successful teams for even greater results. A catalyst for instituting evidence-based practices and metrics that transform performance, Michelle has earned a reputation for leading teams to develop and implement innovative solutions that consistently improve quality of care and patient outcomes.

Her reputation as a leading doctor in the field of minimally invasive robotic techniques in orthopedic surgery is well known: She established an exceptional program that is ranked #1 in volume in the Western Region and #14 in the U.S. An advocate for lifelong learning, in addition to the recent completion of her MBA, Michelle was a Surgical Preceptor and Clinical Assistant Professor at UCLA for 5 years. In that role, she created and implemented an orthopedic surgery educational curriculum for general surgery residents.

Complementing her training, Michelle is dually certified by the American Board of Surgery and the American Board of Orthopedic Surgery. Named multiple years by her peers to San Diego's list of Top Doctors, Michelle is actively involved in the Society of Orthopedic Surgeons, the American College of Surgeons, and the California Surgical Association.

MODERNIZE
Your Executive Job Search
Get Noticed ... Get Hired

This book covers the territory of executive job search with proven, practical guidance gleaned from our work with senior-level clients. Still, we couldn't include every client anecdote or lesson-learned, every bit of insider knowledge that our clients have shared with us. So we've created an add-on—a series of 6 podcasts in which we talk about careers and share even more advice and time-tested recommendations.

In engaging, informative conversations, we walk you through exactly what steps to take to get started, build momentum, and make tangible progress in your search for a new executive opportunity.

Each episode focuses on a specific area of executive job search and features wide-ranging conversation, advice, practical tips and tools, and roadblock-removing solutions to help you gain mastery in managing your career—today and in every career transition you will face throughout your lifetime of work.

We conclude each half-hour session with an exercise that will cement the learning and put ideas and strategies into practical execution.

Listen during your commute…while working out…when making dinner…whenever you have a few minutes to invest in expanding your expertise in the crucial topic of career self-management. The sessions are lively, fast-paced, and filled with useful knowledge that we've gained from our decades of working with executives in career transition.

You can zero in on the topic that's most pressing or take advantage of all 6 programs. Sessions cover:

#1: Your Resume & Career Docs Are Set—What's Next?

#2: Messaging & Outreach

#3: Networking

#4: Recruiters & Posted Openings

#5: Interviewing & Negotiating

#6: Troubleshooting: Roadblocks & Hidden Opportunities

Email us to learn more: jan@janmelnik.com or louise@louisekursmark.com.